Cultural Frontiers
in Ancient East Asia

THE RHIND LECTURES
1965-6

Cultural Frontiers
in Ancient East Asia

WILLIAM WATSON

at the University Press
EDINBURGH

*

© William Watson 1971
EDINBURGH UNIVERSITY PRESS
22 George Square, Edinburgh
ISBN 0 85224 203 4
North America
Aldine Publishing Company
529 South Wabash Avenue, Chicago
Library of Congress
Catalog Card Number 70-159591
Printed in Great Britain by
T. and A. Constable Ltd., Edinburgh

Preface

The matter of this book is little altered from the form in which it was
delivered in November 1965 as the Rhind Lectures for 1965/6. It then went
under the more specific if cumbersome title of *Structure and movement in the
neolithic and bronze-age culture of East Asia*. The reference and annotation
which have now been added should increase the documentary value of the
book irrespective of the theses which motivate the various chapters. The
treatment which is intended is historical and selective, and the reader who
wishes for a more conventional and systematic account of the fruits of
recent archaeological excavation must look elsewhere. Cultural frontiers, in
the sense meant here, mark the limits to which one can trace the existence
and influence of the individual components of material and artistic culture
which are united in any society. These limits may lie beyond the sphere of
the society itself and may differ markedly in their respective geographic
extensions. Applied to the archaeological record a structural principle of
this kind presents a given community as included in a web of various
cultural fields, these conforming to numerous, fluctuating and possibly
widely discrepant boundaries. The study of the variation and discrepancy
of these boundaries can throw a valuable historical light on cultural development, especially perhaps in East Asia. In the first two and the last two
chapters of this book geographical factors are given a prominent place. The
central chapter, on technology, is less obviously concerned with outward
relations, but the singular individuality of the two technical traditions it
describes, in metallurgy and architecture, mark off ancient China within
tight-drawn frontiers of its own, and so these themes may be thought
justified in the context of the book.

In addition to my great debt to Chinese and Japanese authorities it will
be seen that I am beholden at many points also to the work of Soviet
Russian scholars engaged in Siberian archaeology. Of the latter the most
inspiring on the Inner-Asian relations of the Chinese bronze age is S. V.
Kiselev.

To the Society of Antiquaries of Scotland my thanks go for the invitation to lecture and for the encouragement to proceed with this book. I thank Professor Stuart Piggott for his support and advice, and Mrs Jessica Rawson of the Department of Oriental Antiquities of the British Museum for her help in getting at objects in the collections and in providing photographs; I am especially grateful to Mr Walter Cairns of the Edinburgh University Press for the thought he has bestowed and the pains he has taken in the preparation of this book.

ACKNOWLEDGMENTS
The author thanks the following persons and institutions for being allowed to make use of photographs and printed illustrations of objects in their possession: Dr O. N. Bader: plates 17, 26, 30; The Trustees of the British Museum: plates 5, 18, 19, 20, 21, 23, 26c, d, 27a, 29, 31, 33, 43, 44c, d, 48, 49, 54, 57b, 79, 81, 82, 83, 84, 86, 87, 91, 100, 103; Center of Asian Art and Culture, San Francisco: plates 6, 58; The Cambridge University Museum of Archaeology and Anthropology: plate 45; The Finnish Academy of Sciences: plates 25, 39; The Smithsonian Institution: plate 59; The Musée Guimet: plate 76; The Nelson Gallery–Atkins Museum: plate 60; The Oxford University Press: plate 88; Dr Paul Singer: plate 68: The Trustees of the Victoria and Albert: plates 52, 62. Further acknowledgments, including the sources of line figures copied here, are given in the captions.

WILLIAM WATSON
Percival David Foundation of Chinese Art
School of Oriental and African Studies
London, June 1970

Contents

Contents

List of Figures

List of Plates

In Memory of
Robert Scoular Watson

Introduction

THE CULTURAL CONTACTS of East Asia with the rest of the continent pass perforce through an inner zone of Asia which from Baikal to the Black Sea presents a picture of considerable climatic and geographic conformity. It is constituted by two parallel terrains: the steppe which passes at places into desert, and north of it the parkland, or wooded steppe, of south Siberia which is bounded on the north by the cold, dark-pine *taiga*. The long corridor of steppe and wooded steppe at various times is found to be occupied by a continuum of similar or related culture. As a broad unit in the cultural zoning of Asia it is a concept comparable to that of the Fertile Crescent of the Near East, which it fringes on the north; but the nature of the Fertile Crescent tended naturally to concentrate cultural growth in favoured regions – Egypt, Iraq, the Iranian plateau – while the steppe belt with its northern complement of parkland was a broad highway which encouraged and facilitated perpetual cultural travel. This is no less true of the pre-nomadic period in the steppes than of the age of the early nomads. The themes of pre-nomadic culture, the rise of nomadism, and the division of the nomadic cultures into an earlier pre-Scythic period and later Scythic period, provide a frame on which to build the classification of prehistoric culture in the whole of inner Asia. At either end of this corridor was situated one of the cultural luminaries: the western Asiatic states of immemorial antiquity in the west, and in the east the civilization of bronze-age China, the state of the Shang and Chou kings on the middle course of the Yellow river. These were younger than the earliest civilizations in the west, but they outmatched their western compeers in speed and vigour of growth, and in some important technical inventions.

Through the steppe corridor and through inner Asia, from time immemorial, trade had passed. Goods travelled often so far from their originators that they reached lands where these originators were known barely as such, were fabled creatures. If an archaeological interpretation postulates very distant travel of important artefacts, it only projects farther into the past the kind of cultural exchange which the classical writers describe, and which continued in later times, over routes no more passable and no less. It is characteristic of these inner Asian routes that communication, easily

B

established, was rapid and moved in both directions. Cultural ideas could travel, passing from one population to another, even when the range of each integrated community was small. Between populations such exchange required and provided a cultural unity in goods and ideas of a different order from that observed in the more isolating environment of temperate Europe. Only those things travelled for which there was an unambiguous demand, and we must suppose only things for which most of the people along the route themselves could find a use. But to this last there may have been exceptions. Jade may have had a ritual value more widely acknowledged than the find-places of the surviving material might suggest. Certain lade rings, for example, are located in China, Baikal and the Urals, and not in the intervening territory, yet there are grounds for thinking that they represent a single tradition of manufacture, trade and ritual usage.

The great antiquity of the human race in the river valleys of China cannot be doubted. Both lower and middle palaeolithic remains were identified at the famous site of Choukoutien, near Peking, the middle palaeolithic associated with the bones of *Sinanthropus pekinensis*. The so-called Upper Cave at the same site contained bones of *Homo sapiens* and a stone industry of upper palaeolithic type. Physical features still preserved in the modern Chinese race were found on the skull of Sinanthropus; and in a paper written in 1959 Wu Chu-kang and N. N. Cheboksarov tell us that at the end of the palaeolithic period the racial types of modern China and Indo-China are already distinguishable, with divisions between northern, eastern and southern mongoloids, and in the extreme south the australoids.[1]

A cultural unity embracing the more northerly parts of East Asia is first apparent in the upper palaeolithic. Much of the stone equipment at the Upper Cave of Choukoutien is virtually identical with the late palaeolithic of Siberia. In the Ordos region of north China, within the great loop of the Yellow river, similar tools occur with microlithic blade industries, in circumstances which show that this territory was then interrupted by lakes and marshy depressions which have since turned to desert. The Chinese industries, taking microliths and larger tools together, form a close parallel to those of Transbaikalia: we may think of the vast rocky plateau stretching between the most northerly point of the Yellow river and the Selenga valley as forming a single cultural province: a Sino-Siberian upper palaeolithic culture.

In contrast to the heavily wooded zone of Siberia, and to much of Europe also, this culture is remarkable for the manufacture of microliths in an early phase of its development. At the Ordos sites they are found in characteristically paleolithic levels. Gradually the microliths predominated in the stone equipment, no doubt being used to arm the edge of bone fishing spears and the like in the manner observed in Baikal, and the whole industry assumed an Azilian aspect. This trend is plausibly interpreted as evidence of an increased hunting of game on the move, with missiles, and eventually – as the Baikal parallel suggests for a like phase – with bow and arrow. In Baikal the adoption of the bow is taken by Soviet archaeologists as marking the beginning of the local neolithic, which in its earlier stages lacked pottery.

Eventually food production was introduced into the Ordos and the Gobi region from the well-favoured parts of the Yellow river valley where farming had begun and prospered early. But the Mongolias, Inner and Outer, never enjoyed the full measure of neolithic economy. Perforated stones, interpreted as weights for digging-sticks, have been found, but no stone knives – the hall-mark of the Chinese neolithic – or traces of village settlement. The lack of stratified finds in the Ordos and Gobi regions has hindered the classification of the remains. Pottery, even painted fragments, occurs on surface sites together with polished stone tools, larger chipped stones and microliths. These signs of contact with relatively advanced neolithic technique point inevitably towards central China, but the existence of this influence does not conflict with the recognition of the basic cultural affinity of the Ordos and Mongolia, which was with the steppe, with the Selenga valley and Transbaikalia, rather than with China. As the terrain dried, as in places rock was exposed by erosion and the sand sea began to form, the cultural structure became more complex. Judging from flint tools alone Maringer distinguishes four local groups.[2] Meanwhile one may question some generalizations currently made, as, for example, that 'the greater part of the Gobi microliths are neolithic in type' or that 'the end of the Gobi culture may be noted by its contact with the late neolithic elements from south of the Great Wall'. The facts do not yet warrant so much.

In central and north-west China itself the destinies of neolithic life were intimately governed by the properties of the loessic soil. The alkaline loess covers the whole of north-west China, blanketing hills and valleys alike, regionally in uniform thickness. It is the *huang t'u*, the yellow earth, essentially a wind-borne deposit blown from the Gobi for the most part, in the course of the cold climate desiccation and denudation which preceded the establishment of farming communities along the Yellow river. Over large tracts of Shansi the loess is comparatively thin, but in Shensi and Kansu it forms depths to 350 feet. Tending to a vertical cleavage the loess readily forms vertical banks and cliffs, water erosion over a long period producing in it a fantastic and characteristic landscape of deep ravines, narrow dark valleys, vertical walls. Along roads in the deep canyons one may travel for miles without seeing the surrounding country at all. Caves for dwellings are easily excavated in the vertical cliff-faces. Its importance for the early development of agriculture and of the village community in China can hardly be exaggerated. It is naturally fertile; being very porous it is unlikely that it was ever heavily wooded. Given adequate rainfall, the mineral elements in the subsoil are brought up by capillary action within reach of the crop roots. Thus it can be self-fertilizing, and by the erosion to which it is so liable the surface on slopes and near hills is continually renewed. Its one serious disadvantage is that it does not hold water well in small quantity. For the farmer there was a practical necessity to work near fairly large streams, or to carry water, or to construct irrigation channels. This last was probably achieved in the neolithic period. Irrigation encourages settlement in large communities and presupposes a considerable degree of social cohesion. If rice was grown in the Yellow river valley before the end of the neolithic, irrigation was indispensable; but the evidence for this crop is uncertain.

The loess afforded some minor practical advantages to the neolithic population. It is an eminently suitable soil for making clean mud-pies, for digging tunnels and niches, and the inhabitants of the great neolithic village of Pan-p'o in Shensi were in the habit of making the subsoil serve for all manner of interior conveniences in their huts: cupboards, cellars, wall-foundations, fireplaces and seats and beds. To the archaeologist the loess offers a boon in the ease with which it lends itself to the formation of earth 'ghosts' of perishable materials which have totally disintegrated after burial. The most celebrated examples of this phenomenon are chariot burials, ranging in date from the 11th to the 5th centuries BC (plate 40).

In spite of its immensely long coastline and its difficult hinterland, in its relations with neighbours and in all its territorial aspirations China has always functioned as a thoroughly continental country. It is a land of three great rivers. To the familiar Yellow river and the Yangtze we must add the Amur in the far north, which along all its middle course is the boundary between China and the Soviet Union. All these rivers lead through barrier mountain ranges into stretches of lower, more habitable country. Upstream the Amur leads outside China to the rolling foothills of Transbaikalia, a fact of cardinal importance for the cultural history of Manchuria. Manchuria itself is a rectangle of flattish land walled to north, east and west by mountain ranges, communicating with central China by a narrow passage around the coast of the gulf of Pohai into Hopei province. The Hsingan range rushes northwards and pushes up the middle of the Amur to the 54th parallel. This line of mountains is found to constitute a well-defined cultural boundary.

From the neolithic period onwards the nucleus of the Chinese development was the middle course of the Yellow river in Honan, the natural extension of this region westwards along the Wei river, and the flat country around the upper course of the Yellow river in Kansu. All of this territory belongs to the loess zone. The eastern and southern limits of the primary loess follow precisely the lines of the T'ai-hang range and the Ch'inling range. Rounding the east end of the Ch'inling mountains, a small area of loess protrudes south-westwards into Anhui. To the east of the T'ai-hang mountains the great plain consists of redeposited loess mixed with alluvium. The primary loess, including its offshoot into Anhui, was the realm of Yangshao culture, while the alluvial plain and the mountain mass of Shan-tung are the preserve of the neolithic culture of Lungshan. Beyond the headwaters of the Wei river the interlocking valleys of Kansu are separated by some considerable hills; here, however, the cultural boundary discernible between two varieties of neolithic culture is not physical, but only a human one, though the line is exceedingly well defined. To the migration of culture the Ch'inling range was impassable in the neolithic period. Both the Ch'inling and the Tapa range which doubles it to the south are at places forbidding barriers, but elsewhere some high valleys offer passage and even hospitable territory.

There is striking evidence of a survival of archaic bronze forms in the highland zone which is constituted by the region directly south of the Ch'inling and Tapa mountains. The western limit of this mountainous block is the mighty Tibetan massif. To the east its limit is less well defined – the map, however, shows it emphatically as a 'change of slope' – but in the cultural history this eastern edge marks a boundary. Another boundary is the line which defines the inland margin of the south-eastern massif of Fukien province. Between these two boundaries lay the broad corridor to the south which was taken by the gradual and normal expansion of the bronze age civilization of central China. Evidently the Nanling range extending west and east marks the line of a pause in the Sinic expansion. Chinese civilization only crossed this line and reached the south coast in the late 3rd century BC; and then the route of further penetration southwards, into North Vietnam, followed the coast of the Gulf of Tonking. In the south-western mountain massif are the flatter lands of Szechwan and Yunnan, to both of which the Yangtze gives access. The chronology of the prehistoric succession in China, still denied the advantage of radiocarbon dating, lacks a basis of comparison with the neolithic phases of the great riverine civilizations in the west, but with the inception of the bronze age more precision is possible. For in the period of the Shang dynasty, the beginning of which may be taken to coincide approximately with the adoption of bronze, dates transmitted by historians and deduced from epigraphy give initial limits. In a similar though a more limited sense these dates are to the student of the archaeology of inner temperate Asia what the dates and king-lists of Egypt and Mesopotamia are to archaeologists

concerned with the Mediterranean and Europe. The study of oracular inscriptions on bone excavated at Anyang has confirmed almost in its entirety
the king-list for the Shang dynasty as preserved in the histories. The
majority of questions put to the oracle asked if such and such a sacrifice of
animals would be acceptable to such and such royal ancestors. By the
collation of the ritual names of these ancestors a list of all Shang kings
dead at the time of the oracle, and of the pre-dynastic forbears of the Shang
kings has been compiled by Chinese scholars. The marvel was the close
correspondence of this reconstructed king-list with the list printed in the
histories. In 1927 the first reconstruction was made by Wang Kuo-wei,
who failed to match eight names with the extant list. Yung Tso-pin
later pointed out that the names of the last two kings were not likely to
appear, as they had not become ancestors at the time of the latest oracle
sentences recovered on the site. He supplied historical equivalents for the
remaining six, and of these the leading modern authority in mainland
China, Kuo Mo-jo, the president of the Academy of Sciences, appears to
question only two.

The chronological value of the oracle sentences and the king-list derived
from them is twofold. On a theory of Tung Tso-pin the oracle inscriptions
may be periodized so as to give a relative chronology for such of the Shang
political and ritual affairs as may be gleaned from the extremely terse
sentences. Since the bones cannot be related to other material objects
preserved at the site, the inscriptions unfortunately do not help to date
the strata of the site or any of the excavated material; but the unexpected
accuracy of the historical king-list compels scholars to treat even the earlier
sections of the historical chronological tradition with great respect. When
Ssŭ-ma Ch'ien wrote his history at the end of the 1st century BC, he
decided that dates supplied in his sources for events prior to a year equivalent
to 841 BC were not sufficiently reliable to be worth including in his chronological tables. The dates he gives from 841 BC onwards are now accepted as
wholly trustworthy; where astronomical checks can be made, they bear
this out. In the generations after Ssŭ-ma Ch'ien, Chinese scholars were at
pains to recover exact dates applicable to their early kings, and soon was
established the chronology due to be canonized in Confucian tradition.
It starts with emperors admittedly mythical, who are followed by a Hsia
dynasty which can be given no archaeological context and whose existence
many historians now doubt. Shang kings ruled, according to this chronology, from 1765 BC to 1122 BC. This chronology apparently went unchallenged until the discovery in AD 281 of the so-called Bamboo Annals,
in which dates differ slightly from those cited by Ssŭ-ma Ch'ien for the
period prior to 841 BC, but agree with his dates after that year. Still no
decision could be reached on the chief point at issue: whether the dates of

the orthodox system or those of the Bamboo Annals are more accurate. The text of the latter was soon impugned as a forgery, and then was again and finally lost. Today it is known only from quotations of it in other writings, now edited by Wang Kuo-wei.[3]

A crucial date for the chronology of the Chinese bronze age is that attributed to the fall of the city of Shang and the inception of the Chou feudal rule. The traditional date is 1122 BC; that of the Bamboo Annals is 1050 BC in the original recovered text, as quoted, but according to the text as reconstructed by Wang Kuo-wei, this date should be 1027 BC. Since Wang Kuo-wei's initial effort to rehabilitate the Bamboo Annals, many scholars have contributed to the arguments for accepting it in place of the Confucian chronology. In the east the most notable of these has been Ch'en Meng-chia, in the west Bernard Karlgren. From their calculations, which take chronological points from many texts, both incline towards the date 1027 BC as the year in which the rule of the first Chou king began.

The next advance is owed to the barely credible labours of Hector Dubs, who calculated the times of all eclipses visible at Anyang from 1400 to 1000 BC and published the results in 'A canon of lunar eclipses for Anyang and China, 1400 to 1000', *Harvard Journal of Asian Studies* x (1947). He chose oracle inscriptions as key material for deriving dates. The main deduction affecting the end of the Shang dynasty is that Wu Ting, 22nd Shang king, was ruling in 1189 BC. He was followed by eight other kings until the end of the dynasty. This makes the orthodox date of 1122 for the close of the dynasty quite impossible, and at the same time points strongly to 1027 rather than 1050 as the true date. Now in the Bamboo Annals we are told that 273 years intervened between the accession of P'an Keng – the nineteenth king, reported in history as the ruler who founded a new capital at the place near Anyang, the city called Great Shang – and the destruction of the last Shang king. This gives 1300 BC as the year of the foundation. The beginning of the Shang rule is 1765 BC according to the orthodox chronology, but reasoning based on the Bamboo Annals reduces this to 1523 BC. Archaeology shows the existence of another and earlier Shang city at Cheng Chou, still in Honan, but some 160 km due south of Anyang. We suppose that it was from here that P'an Keng moved his capital, that the site at Cheng Chou, which has been extensively excavated in the last ten years, was the city of Ao spoken of in the histories, and that its main occupation, corresponding to the earlier part of the Shang period, was from the late 16th century BC until about 1300 BC. In the contents of this book these dates are crucial in interpreting the contacts which may be traced between the bronze age of the Shang dynasty and the distant centres in inner Asia.

Despite such possibilities of estimating early dates on a tentative absolute scale based on objective criteria, and despite the official adoption in China of the Christian calendar, Chinese scholars are still reluctant to abandon the traditional categories of the histories, which are dynastic, or divide by historical dates established more by chance than design. Among archaeologists at least, the Hsia dynasty and its antecedent culture heroes are ignored; thereafter:

WESTERN CHOU: 1027 (1050, 1122)–771 BC
  ending with the eastward move of the Chou capital from Ch'ang-an in Shensi to Loyang in Honan.
PERIOD OF THE SPRING AND AUTUMN ANNALS: 722–481 BC
  that is, the period covered by Confucius' historical notes on the state of Lu.
PERIOD OF THE WARRING STATES: 481 (452, 403)–221 BC
  For the start three historical dates are taken, the middle one of which makes the most political sense; but in Chinese archaeological publication the upper date intended is seldom stated.
CH'IN: 221–206 BC
WESTERN HAN: 206 BC–AD 9
HSIN: AD 9–23
EASTERN HAN: AD 25–221

In this book dates are stated in centuries BC, and the lower Shang date is accepted as 1027 BC.

1

Neolithic frontiers in East Asia

THE IMPULSES WHICH created neolithic culture in Europe, often the result of considerable migrations, are traced ultimately to the eastern Mediterranean and to Western Asia beyond. Because of this client relationship the three main criteria of neolithic economy – polished stone tools, pottery and farming – tend to make their European appearance simultaneously, at a time when near-eastern centres had already reached an advanced stage of the neolithic. In Western Asia the coincidence of the three diagnostic activities is less apparent than in Europe; the beginnings of each are more difficult to define and patterns of cultural and ethnic migration do not emerge so clearly. In China the neolithic period, extending after 2000 BC even in the most progressive middle region, lasts longer than in comparable inventive centres in Western Asia, which it appears to resemble also more closely than Europe in the discrepant distribution in space and time of the basic techniques. Polished stone tools found widespread south of the Yangtze and in the south-eastern highland zone do not correlate with conspicuous signs of agriculture. Regarding the connexion between settled farming and ceramics one must take warning from Japan, where some seven thousand years elapsed between the adoption of pottery in the 8th millennium and the introduction of farming in the 2nd century BC.[1]

Thus far no incipient stage of neolithic culture has been clearly defined in central China, the scene of the earliest food production in East Asia. The classification into two successive phases of long duration, the Yangshao and Lungshan cultures, is justified stratographically, but in this sequence the lowest levels already witness to populous settlements and developed techniques. For millennia before this full neolithic economy was established along the Yellow river valley, China was occupied by food-gatherers, and eventually, we must suppose, by food-gatherers of a cultural level approaching that of the earliest Yangshao complex. One aspect of geographical distribution points to the existence of a pre-Yangshao phase of incipient neolithic character. The stone axes and the pottery with impressed decoration which are included in Yangshao and Lungshan neolithic complexes are not confined to the areas in which these cultures flourished. These artefacts were either selected from the equipment of more civilized neighbours and copied by the more primitive inhabitants of adjoining regions; or they existed and had been widely diffused before the rise of full neolithic economy even at the favoured centre, and were incorporated into the developed neolithic culture. The distribution and typology of the axes and pottery appear to favour the second hypothesis.

Varieties of poorly shaped and poorly fired vessels with simple ornament impressed from cords, matting or carved and moulded stamps are the most widely distributed ceramic in East Asia. This pottery appears at nearly all the neolithic sites of central China, and persists there into the bronze age (plate 1). No sites are yet known, however, along the Yellow river where it is the only kind of pottery made, and on present evidence it cannot be shown to belong particularly to an early neolithic phase. But comparable pottery decorated by cords or stamps occurs as the sole ceramic in all the habitable regions surrounding the central Chinese plain. It is difficult to see how this tradition came to be so firmly established in the main development of China proper if it had not been present in a pure form in the Yellow river valley at the very beginning of the neolithic period. The theory of a 'corded pottery horizon'[2] preceding the phase of advanced agriculture in central China is one which finds support from all the peripheral regions, in which neolithic civilization never attained the Chinese level, whether or not these regions are demonstrably under Chinese influence when the Chinese neolithic was well advanced. The fact that no pure corded-pottery level has yet been found on a neolithic site in central China remains, however, unexplained.

In South-east Asia corded pottery is associated with the polished shouldered stone axes of the latest (third) stage of the Bacsonian culture of Indo-China, and is the earliest pottery known there.[3] In the polished-stone cultures of the Yangtze valley and south China corded pottery and stamp-marked pottery of various kinds is prominent, and is the most abundant form on sites unaffected by influences from central China.[4]

Moving northwards from the Chinese central plain, into Mongolia, we find that corded ware is one of the wares represented by fragments on surface sites. At one stratified site in Inner Mongolia basket-marked and corded grey pottery is the only ceramic, with microlithic and polished stone tools of the so-called Gobi culture (figures 1, 2).[5] But it is not until we reach the Baikal region, a thousand miles distant from the middle course of the Yellow river, that the development of this primitive pottery can be related to well-defined stages of neolithic culture (figures 2-4).[6] There Soviet archaeologists define the pre-ceramic Khinskiy stage, in which the bow and arrow are first identified, as the opening of the neolithic period. The sites are on the 8-10 m terrace of the Angara river, and their date is estimated to be in the 5th millennium B C. In the following Isakovskiy stage

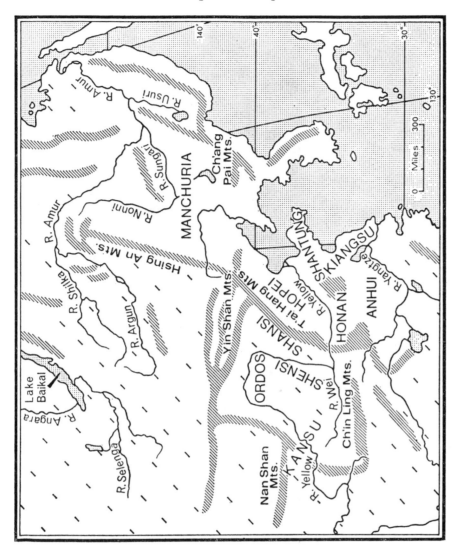

1. East Asia from the Amur to the Yangtze.

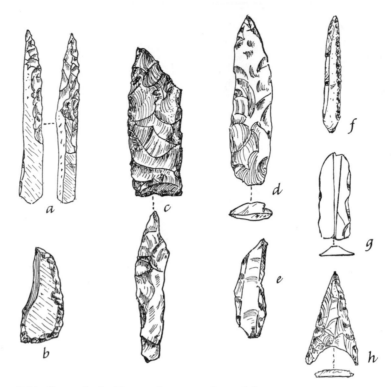

2. Neolithic flint tools. (*a, b*) *Serovskiy etap* in the Baikal region;
(*c*) Sha-la-wu-su, Inner Mongolia; (*d–h*) Hung-shan, Ch'ih-feng,
Manchuria.

bag-shaped pots are made, decorated with the impressions of netting, both
the strings and the knots of which are clearly visible on the pot surface.
Next, in the Serovskiy stage of the 3rd millennium BC the net is impressed
so lightly that only the marks of the knots appear, and now comb marks
from carved stamps and round pits are also used in the decoration. Stamped
decoration of this kind – patterns of comb markings – only comes to predominate in the Kitoiskiy stage, which centres on 2000 BC. This pottery
continues in use with little change in the Glazovskiy stage (*c.* 1700–1300
BC), when bronze (in the form of simple broad flat knives without a
distinctive handle) makes its first appearance.

Generally in East Asia, and no less within the boundaries of China itself,
there is a consistent regional variation in the styles of corded and other
impressed pottery. The close irregular cording seen in the Bacsonian and
in other fine and coarse pottery of south-east China is quite unlike the sparser
and well-organized patterns of the Baikal pottery. The earliest pottery of
Japan combines grooving with sparse cording. Stamping and round pits

Stage	Terrace	Date	Innovation	Pottery	Jade
Khinskiy	10-8 m.	v mill.	Bow	Nil	
Isakovskiy	6 m.	iv mill.	Polished stone pottery	Parabola shapes. Net marks	Knives Chisels
Serovskiy	6 m.	iii mill.	Compound bow	Mitre shapes. Combing pitting	
Kitoiskiy	4-2 m.	iii/ii mill.		Stamping relief rims	Rings
Glazkovskiy	2 m.	1700–1300	Copper	Grooving nail marks	Discs Rings
Shiverskiy	2 m.	1300–900	Bronze		

3. The periodization of neolithic and bronze-age culture in the Baikal region. After Okladnikov.

characterize the circum-polar region from Baikalia northwards. In the Chinese central plain the chief varieties of impressed ware are (1) corded pottery, (2) pottery impressed with basketry and matting, and (3) pottery impressed by a stamp carved with a small-scale chequer and the like. All these forms of decoration are used on soft grey and brown ware made by beating with paddle and pad, the method most widely used for handmade pottery in China and South-east Asia; but they persist also in the harder potteries produced as firing methods improved, and in the Yellow river valley had a notably long survival in a more sophisticated ceramic context. In central China, for a given area, the proportion of impressed wares compared with other styles of pottery remains fairly constant during the neolithic period, pointing to a continuity of population and a relatively undisturbed cultural development.[7]

In the central plain the impressed pottery increases in relative quantity on sites as one moves from Shantung westwards to Honan. Although the impressed ornament in the form of careful cording and mat-marking is found at the village site of Pan-p'o (plate 2),[8] this style of ware is nevertheless comparatively rare in Shensi, and occurs only near the Yellow river. In Kansu impressed ware occurs only in late assemblages of pottery, such as those of the Ch'i Chia stage,[9] which border on the bronze age and mark a cultural movement from central China. Southwards from Shantung through the maritime provinces the quantity of impressed pottery also increases; and both the corded and the chequer-stamped wares passed

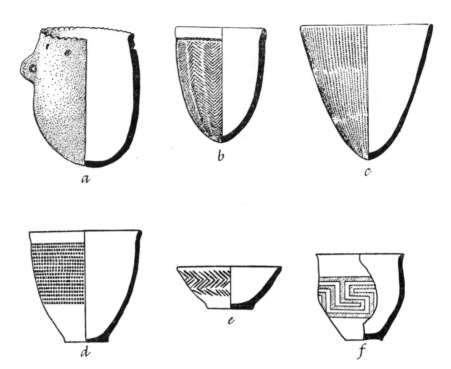

4. Neolithic pottery of the northern tradition. (*a*) *Serovskiy etap* at Mmayr', Baikal; (*b*) proto-Jōmon at Hanawadai, Kantō, Japan; (*c*) proto-Jōmon at Natsushima, Kantō, Japan; (*d, e, f*) Saisanovka I, Primor'ye, U.S.S.R. After Andreev, Okladnikov, Okamoto, Tozawa.

westwards into Szechwan along the Yangtze, and southwards into the north of Indo-China, where they contrast with generically similar impressed pottery of older local tradition. In this last area the impressed ware of northern affinity appeared only very late, accompanying the arrival of Chinese influence in the last century or two BC, but in the neighbouring territory of Thailand a local tradition of impressed ceramics subsisted from a much earlier period and, unaffected by the more efficient Chinese techniques, lasted until quite recent times.[10] The north-east of China shows an interesting disconformity: in the Liao-tung region the three Chinese varieties of impressed pottery appear to be absent; and on the north-west edge of the Manchurian basin, in the Hsi-lin culture, there is coarse pottery with impress of netting (figure 5).[11] This last marks the eastern limit of a neolithic province comprising Mongolia and the Baikal region, the first expression of a cultural frontier no less discernible in the bronze age; beyond it no distinct influence from central China ever passed.

In sum, the central zone of China presents an individual character even in terms of the most rudimentary tradition of pottery. To the north is

5. Pottery, flint tools and bone points from the neolithic site of
Ang-ang-hsi, Heilung-chiang, Manchuria.

another province, which connects in part with Baikalia, and to the south a
province which with minor variation extends into South-east Asia. There
are signs of the expansion of the typical central Chinese ceramic southwards
but not northwards. The proto-neolithic cultures of East Asia, of communities in which the extent of food production is uncertain and possibly still
quite subordinate to hunting and gathering, may in general extend back
beyond the 5th or 6th millennium B C. Their beginnings can hardly be later
than those of the equivalent culture in Japan.[12]

The Yangshao tradition of painted-pottery neolithic occupies the area
of the primary loess, from the western part of the central plain along the
middle course of the Huang Ho, the Wei river, through Kansu to the
tributaries of the upper Huang Ho in the north-west corridor. In Honan
the painted-pottery sites overlap the westernmost extension of the second
main tradition, that of Lungshan, whose eponymous site is a walled village
in Shantung and whose most characteristic pottery is fine, black, burnished,
wheel-made (figures 6, 7; plate 15). Already in the 1930s Wu Chin-ting
had correlated the sites where Lungshan lay over Yangshao: they were all
in Honan province. In the same province also the Lungshan could be shown
stratigraphically to precede the Shang levels, wherever the two occurred
together, though this is at a minority of sites. The question of the ultimate
relationship of the two neolithic traditions was left in abeyance.[13] Lungshan
had north-eastern and east-coast affinities, while the painted pottery
extended so far to the west that this alone raised a question of its possible

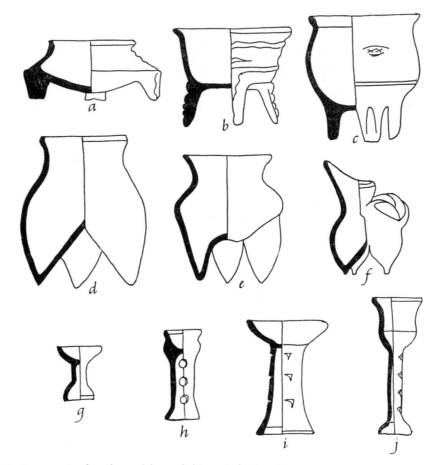

6. Pottery tripods and *tou* of the neolithic period. Yangshao:
(*a*) Miao-ti-kou I; 'transitional' Lungshan: (*b*, *c*, *e*) Miao-ti-kou II;
Lungshan: (*d*) San-li-ch'iao II, (*f*, *g*, *h*) Ching-chih-chen, (*i*, *j*) Hsi-
hsia-hou.

connexion with the Western Asiatic tradition of painted pottery. The
designs on many of the large Kansu funerary urns are broadly reminiscent of
those on the urns of the south-Russian Tripolye culture (cf. plates 20, 21);
but that was not encouraging to those who expected to find that the
Chinese painted pottery was intrusive, for a theory of ethnic movement
from south Russia to Kansu or *vice versa* would strain belief too far, and
pottery, even fine painted ware, was seldom an object of trade in these
early times.[14]

It is mainly excavation carried out since 1949 that has expanded this
picture beyond the limits of ceramic classification.[15] At the height of the
neolithic age the Yangshao farmers lived in Shensi and Honan in large

7. Pottery types of the Lungshan neolithic. The *tou* at the top left is of the 'transitional' type; the remainder are classic Lungshan shapes.

villages near rivers, but at some distance from the banks. The settlements could attain a size of 400 by 500 m, and the deposits could accumulate to a depth of 3 m. Their huts were sunk a short distance in the ground, the roofs raised on wooden pillars and covered with reeds and clay; these buildings left little permanent trace, and no foundation mounds were formed. The most thoroughly investigated Yangshao site, that of Pan-p'o in Shensi, has distinct areas for habitation, pottery and kilns, and burial. Agriculture was based on millet, of which three varieties have been identified; heavy cattle has been rarely found in excavation, but the remains of pigs, dogs, sheep and goat were comparatively plentiful on the larger sites.[16] The Lungshan neolithic area covers for the most part the alluvial eastern part of the central plain, Shantung and the part of the east coast immediately south of this province (figure 8). The sites more noticeably seek out low hills or mounds rising, if only a few feet, above the plain. Wheat was identified at a site in Anhui, and rice has been recovered at several sites in Hupei. To the domestic animals known to Yangshao, the Lungshan added the horse. The Lungshan houses are less well known than those of Yangshao, but appear to have been similar. At the eponymous site in Shantung and at Hou-kang in Honan traces of a considerable wall were found.

The implications of the stratification of Lungshan over Yangshao in Honan for the dating of the eastern province of Lungshan as a whole are still uncertain. It seems improbable that the Lungshan settlements of the eastern part of the alluvial plain of the Yellow river, of Shantung and the other coastal provinces, should all prove to be later than the Yangshao of Honan, or that the expansion of the Lungshan should have been wholly dependent on an extension of habitable land along the lower course of the

c

Neolithic and Bronze-Age Succession on the Yellow River

Shensi	*Shansi*	*Honan*	*Hopei-Shantung*
Chou	Chou	Chou	Chou
?	Shang	Shang	Shang
Yangshao	Yangshao	Lungshan	Lungshan
		↑ ↑⫯	↑
		Yangshao	?

C O R D E D   P O T T E R Y

8. Variation of the succession from neolithic to bronze-age culture in west, central and east China. In Honan the succession of cultures does not occur at every neolithic site.

Yellow river in a post-Yangshao period.[17] Apart from the introduction of metal, the Shang culture of central China grows naturally out of the Lungshan neolithic: in the most progressive area, on the middle course of the Yellow river and east to Shantung, the neolithic passes into the bronze age about the middle of the 2nd millennium BC. In the west the Yangshao neolithic of the Kansu facies continued until the introduction of metal, without the intervention of Lungshan culture. When a bronze industry was established in north-west China it was allied to that of the western Chou period of central China, and not to the Shang bronze culture which had roots in the Lungshan neolithic (figures 6-9).

The distributions of some elements of neolithic culture found in Yangshao and Lungshan are themselves mutually discrepant and fail to coincide even broadly with the geographic boundaries of the leading pottery types which are diagnostic in the accepted classification. Burial customs vary on a distinct pattern (figure 10, plates 11-14). In an area corresponding approximately to the extent of Yangshao culture, the dead are buried in earth pits, on the back and with the head to the west or the north-west (plate 14). In the western part of the Yangshao area there is a variation: in the Ma-chia stage of the painted ware, tombs occur with occupants placed on the right side with legs flexed, head to east and face to north (plate 13). A trail of flexed burials can also be followed along the river into central China in the early Chou period – sure evidence of an ethnic movement. At the eastern end of the Yangshao area, in Honan, a great

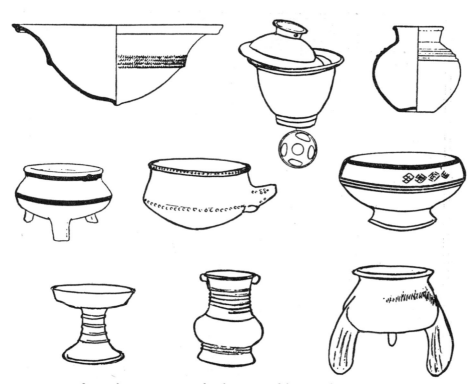

9. Pottery of east China representing local variants of the Lungshan tradition. Top row: Ch'ü-chia-ling culture; middle row: Ch'ing-lien-kang culture; bottom row: Liang-chu culture.

many burials are prone, with the same orientation (plate 12). These prone burials are in the neolithic associated with Lungshan pottery. Some burials of another kind have the same context. At Miao–ti–kou for example, 145 Lungshan burials were all supine, but oriented with the head to the south. In Shantung and on the east coast immediately to the south – in the areas where the Lungshan pottery occurs in its most developed and characteristic forms – the majority of the burials are supine with the head pointing to the east or the north-east (plate 11). There is thus sufficient regional consistency in the orientation of burials to imply discrete traditions, and to indicate two separate traditions within the sphere of Lungshan culture. The current theory of the origin of the Lungshan culture, discussed below, supposes a diffusion eastwards from Honan. Whatever form this cultural movement took, it cannot have been a predominantly ethnic movement, for it did not carry eastwards the burial rite associated with the Lungshan in Honan, while in Honan the prone burials of their rite persisted into the bronze age.[18]

Discrepancy of the same kind is to be seen in the distribution of polished

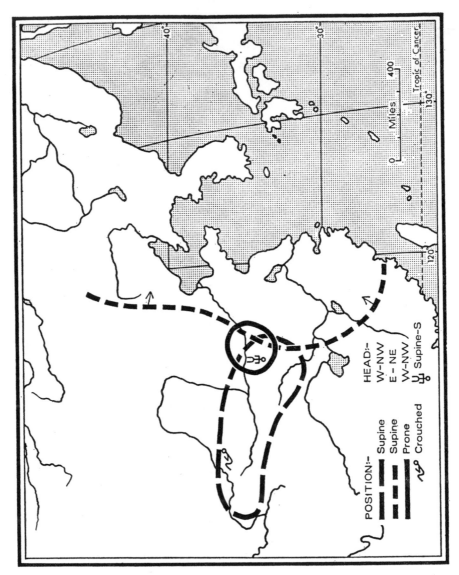

10. The predominant orientations of neolithic burials. The supine burials with orientation to east or north-east lie to the east of the close-broken line.

stone axes (figures 11, 12; plates 8, 9). The axe most characteristic of Yangshao is the all but universal form of neolithic axe: oval of section, slightly tapering, round-ended, 'walzenbeil' in the terminology of Heine-Geldern. The axe is found in central China and the north-west. It passes through the south-east corridor and then west to Szechwan. Most of this area of distribution of the rounded axe overlaps with that of thin, flat axes, oblong and often with oblique edge, which are generally perforated in the middle or towards one end. The area of the flat axe extends farther, to north-east, east and south-east. It is the axe most characteristic of Lungshan sites. But we notice a distinction: the flat axes of Shantung and the eastern seaboard tend to conform to a squarish, trapezoid outline, the finish is better and many pieces have a strongly curving blade. Unperforated flat axes are found with the neolithic of Manchuria. The area of overlap of the rounded axes with the superior kind of flat axes is comparatively small. Even less than the burial rite does the geographical pattern of stone axes support the idea of a movement of wholly integrated neolithic culture from the centre of China eastwards.

To the south and south-east is the realm of two strange forms: the segmented axe and the shouldered axe. The shouldered axes of China form a part of a very wide distribution of the type, reaching across Burma and into the South Seas. Their northern boundary in China lies along the Yangtze valley. The segmented axe or hoe has a more south-easterly distribution, and examples of this type are found farther north along the Chinese coast. These two carefully shaped axe forms are characteristic of the full neolithic in the south-east and south of the Yangtze, and the age of all of them may prove to be no earlier than the bronze age of central China. The stone axes which were still in use on the Island of Hainan in the 12th century AD were of this lineage and perhaps their descendants are still giving good service somewhere in the remotest parts of the southern archipelago.[19]

Most characteristic among the polished stone tools of the Chinese neolithic is, however, the knife or sickle (figures 13-15; plate 7).[20] It has two hafting-holes. The two leading varieties are the rectangular and the crescent-shaped; both are widely distributed in north and central China and both may be found on the same Yangshao or Lungshan site. Nevertheless, differences of distribution suggest that the two forms are not casual variants in a single diffusion. The most striking trend is the greater frequency of the crescentic sickles in the north and the north-east. The detailed distribution map shows, more clearly than the summarizing diagrams, that together the rectangular and crescentic sickles go with the Yangshao-Lungshan complex. They are rare south of the Huang Ho valley and only cross the Yangtze in a small area near its mouth. The crescentic sickle is

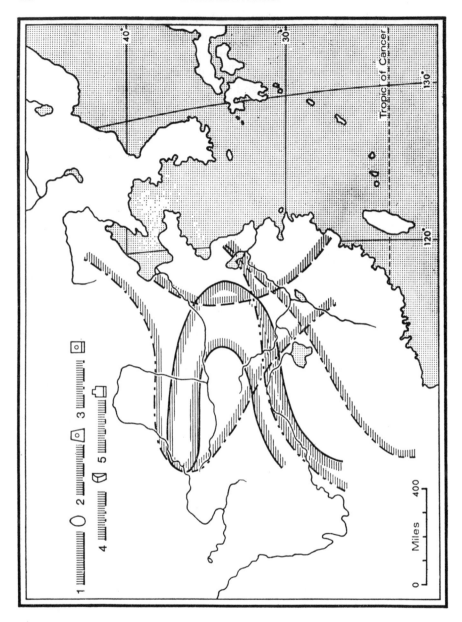

11. The geographic distribution of neolithic stone axes. (1) Rounded,
walzenbeil; (2) flat trapezoid; (3) rectangular; (4) segmented;
(5) shouldered. The distributions lie on the shaded sides of the boundaries.

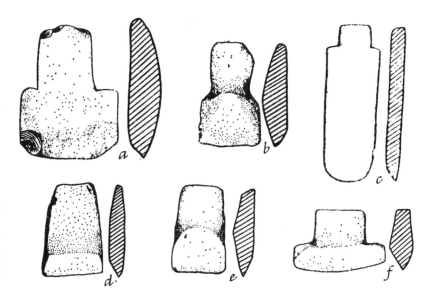

12. Southern neolithic stone axes (adzes). (*a*, *b*, *c*, *f*) Shouldered;
(*e*) segmented; (*d*) represents a common sub-rectangular type in which
the butt is often slightly tapered. From Hainan. After *K'ao-Ku*.

the only one found in the Manchurian basin. Another shape, a rough,
barely polished rectangle with notches at the sides for hafting instead of
holes, is also a northern variant. The hafting method in this case is the same
as that used for the stone hoes of Manchuria.

Its simultaneous connexions with China and the more northerly part of
east Asia make Manchuria one of the most interesting of the peripheral
regions. The provinces of Hopei and Liao Hsi form a corridor leading
around the shore of Po-hai bay and the wide, flat country through which
flow the Shara-muren and the Nonni rivers. From Harbin the latter, now
become the Sungari, leads through low hills into the low-lying basin of
the lower Sungari, which is continuous with that of the Amur forming the
present frontier between China and the Soviet Union. Both on the ocean
side and the continental side of this corridor are hills (in the west backed
by what is now semi-desert) which in early times ensured that the most
favoured cultural movement through Manchuria followed a north–south
line. The climate was almost certainly cool-temperate, the vegetation of
the wooded-steppe kind, yielding grassland with sparse growth of birch
and spruce. In the whole of East Asia the Manchurian basin was second
only to the Yellow river valley in the encouragement it gave to food
production and a settled life.

Four types of neolithic remains can be distinguished. The most advanced

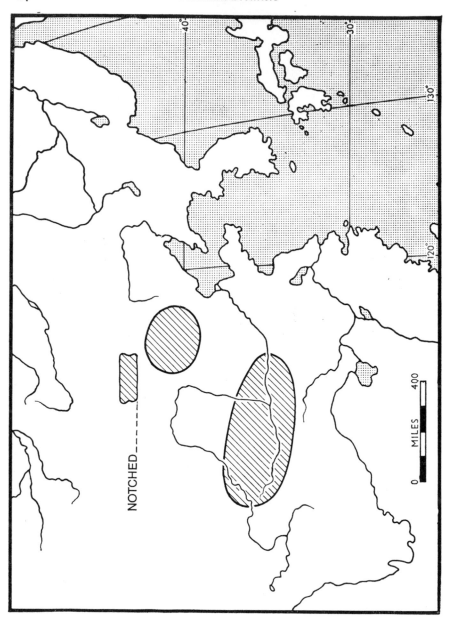

13. The distribution of stone knives of neolithic type in central and north China. Cf. plate 7. Generalized after An Chih-min.

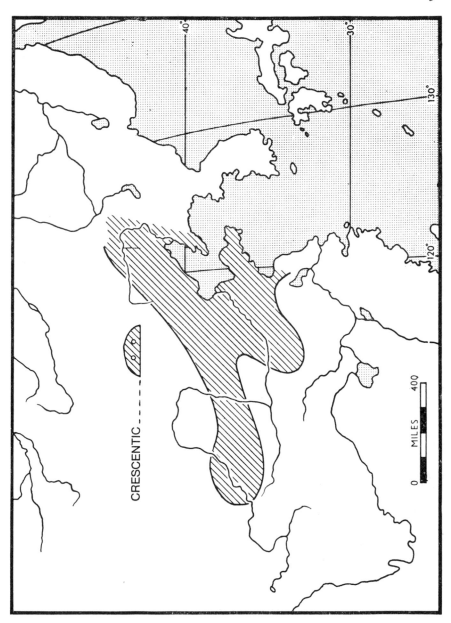

CRESCENTIC

14. The distribution of stone knives of neolithic type in central and north China. Cf. plate 7. Generalized after An Chih-min.

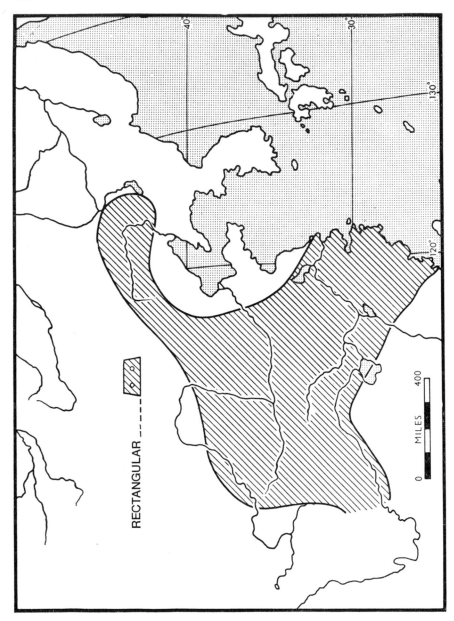

RECTANGULAR

15. The distribution of stone knives of neolithic type in central and north China. Cf. plate 7. Generalized after An Chih-min.

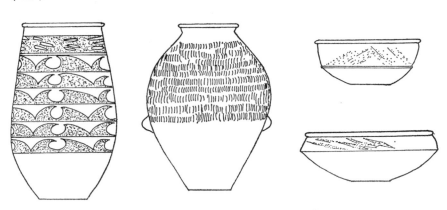

16. Impressed and black-painted neolithic pottery from Hungshan,
Ch'ih-feng, Manchuria.

of these is the Hung-shan culture of the provinces of Jehol and Liaoning
as represented at the type site of Hung-shan, near Ch'ih-feng on the Lao-ha
river in north Jehol.[21] Here were remains of a black earth overlying a rocky
terrace, giving evidence of erosion and denudation. This site produced
painted pottery which must derive from Yangshao, though the route it
followed, given the absence of painted pottery of any description in Hopei
province, remains mysterious (figure 16). The painted patterns only
generically resemble those of the Yangshao of Shensi and Honan. There
are tall vases of coarse ware not unlike that of Yangshao, and other vessels
in grey ware on a high foot (at Pao-t'ou) which are unquestionably of
Lungshan lineage. In the light of the view now propounded in China – that
Lungshan is a direct development from Yangshao – this mixture of traits
from the two neolithic traditions of central China is difficult to account
for. If painted pottery died out before the Lungshan stage in Honan, it is
curious that it should survive with Lungshan in Manchuria. No less important than these signs of southern connexion are clear links of Manchuria
with the north. The ceramic evidence is a tall beaker of coarse brown
pottery in the shape of a truncated cone decorated with grooved or incised
lines forming a broad herring-bone or zig-zag pattern (plate 22). This
vessel can be followed southwards into north Korea, northwards to the
lower Amur valley, the island of Sakhalin, and Japan. Some of the coarse
ware has analogies in the impoverished sub-neolithic of the Gobi. The
stone axes are the rectangular, flat kind, here without perforation, and
the sickles are crescentic, with two hafting holes. There are some flaked tools
marking the persistence of the mesolithic hunters' traditions.

The direct evidence for neolithic agriculture in Manchuria is of a striking
kind, and peculiar to the region. It consists of stone querns with rubbers of
various shapes (objects conspicuous by their absence in the high neolithic

of the central plain) and a characteristic large stone implement which must be a form of ploughshare, primitive in manufacture, but far from primitive in principle. The stone ploughshares appear to be unknown outside Manchuria and the adjacent part of inner Mongolia. What form of traction it required is not known, for the sites give no evidence for the existence of horse or water buffalo. The climate was almost certainly too cool for the latter. If the existence of a plough of some kind is questioned, some distinction must still be made between the tools interpreted as ploughshares and other implements, smaller and more roughly shaped, which have all the appearance of hoes. This ample evidence for agriculture in the Hung-shan neolithic of Manchuria is supplemented by the bones of cattle, sheep, pig and horse, excavated at Hung-shan itself, which attest the advanced animal farming which the geographical environment so clearly favoured.[22]

In the western part of the basin the Manchurian mosaic reveals its affinity with the Gobi microlithic culture. In the region of the city of Lin-hsi on the north side of the Shara-Muren there is at places a layer of black earth preserved under consolidated dune. Where the dune has weathered away, traces of ancient habitation are found on the surface of the black earth (figure 2). The pottery of this Lin-hsi culture was mentioned earlier for its connexion with the Baikal region, seen in the use of net impressions for decoration. The comb-marking of pottery, although less distinctive, belongs to the same northern tradition, which extends through Mongolia into Siberia. Stone tools associated with the culture point in the same direction. They are all worked by chipping: there is no sign of the polishing of stone or of the shapes of tools which only a hundred miles to the south at Hung-shan are sure indications of agriculture. Between the two regions, on a line following the edge of the Mongolian plateau, ran a firm cultural boundary. The inhabitants of the rocky highlands to the west could copy only the simplest equipment of the settled farmers and could not imitate their economy.

The third group of Manchurian sites is typified by the finds at Ang-ang-hsi, a town near Tsitsihar in the upper Nonni valley (figure 5).[23] Here too the microlithic element is prominent, with carefully shaped arrowheads, long rectangular blades and large triangular knives, all of which resemble the implements of the Baikal neolithic. The pots are thick and globular, with corded or simple incised bands.

If the kind of temporarily settled hunting and fishing communities represented by Lin-hsi and Ang-ang-hsi look culturally towards Baikalia and the north-west, the last of the Manchurian neolithic groups appears to connect rather with the north-east, the valley of the lower Sungari and the maritime province of the Soviet Union beyond the Amur river. This division of the Manchurian cultures is the least known and explored. The representative site, at Wei-k'en-ha-ta near Ilan, contained a pottery jar closer to vessels of the maritime province than those of China, a thick ground-stone axe, and jade rings and tubular jade beads identical with those found on the shell-mound habitation sites of the maritime province in the Ussuri valley between Khabarovsk and Vladivostok.[24]

That the germ of neolithic civilization reached Manchuria from the south, ultimately from central China, is hardly to be questioned. But the vigour displayed by the population of the north-east in receiving and adapting the agricultural economy, as compared for example with the hunting and fishing conservatism of the inhabitants of the Baikal region, needs some explanation. The reason is perhaps not entirely the more open character of the woodland in the Manchurian river basins. The recent work of Soviet archaeologists in the maritime province has shown the existence of comparatively advanced settled food-gathering communities in the flatter country on the left bank of the Amur and along the Ussuri.[25] The livelihood of these people was based on large-scale fishing. In the spawning season the rivers flowing into the Pacific teemed with salmon and other large fish, known in Russian as the *chevich* and *sima*. Villages of fishermen, who exploited the rivers from fixed stations and even ventured out to sea, sprang up in Kamchatka, on the Amur, in Sakhalin and in Japan. The catch was so easy that even bears took to a fish diet. Net weights, and stone clubs used for killing the larger fish, are important evidence in the archaeological record.[26]

The villages along the Amur consisted of houses built half underground, with roofs raised on pillars and covered with earth, reaching a depth of 4 m and a width of 30 m. The houses are in some cases adjoining, like the cells of a honeycomb.[27] The tradition of sunken houses lasted long in the north-east: in the 3rd century B C a Chinese writer notes that the inhabitants of this region reckon civic dignity not by the height of their houses but by the depth, a descent of nine steps denoting the noblest rank.[28] The pottery was decorated with stamps which are a formalized version of net impressions (plate 100), and cloth was woven of vegetable fibres. Examples survive of an ancient art of spiral figures in the form of rock carvings. These signs of settled life distinguish the ancient inhabitants of the maritime province from the forest huntsmen farther west, whose itinerant food-gathering is reflected through the successive stages of the Baikal neolithic. A population bred to the comparatively fixed and reliable livelihood of the Amur fishermen was likely to be more ready than the hunting tribes to learn methods of food production.

AN HISTORICAL EVALUATION of the inner Asian relations of the Chinese neolithic depends ultimately on conclusions reached on the connexion of the Yangshao and Lungshan cultures in central China. It is not certain that the alluvial plain along the lower course of the Yellow river was at any stage of the neolithic period as populous as the middle course and the valley of the Wei river, which is its natural geographical prolongation to the west. Probably the difficulties presented by deltaic vegetation and the wandering of the river itself limited the scale of neolithic life in the east. In the west, in Shensi and Kansu, settlement appears to have been almost as dense as on the middle Yellow river, in spite of the steeply ravined terrain of the western loess and the consequent difficulty of water supply to fields of any size. Neolithic fields were terraced, as they are at the present day, in the steep valley walls; water must have been carried a considerable distance from the stream below, or a system arranged to catch torrential rain. The neolithic remains in Kansu in places imply a greater population and agricultural activity than may be seen today.

Many facts speak against the theory of a far-western origin for the Kansu-Yangshao culture. No known painted pottery in Western Asia – least of all that found in the rudimentary bronze culture of south Turkestan – provides a convincing source for the vessels or designs in the Ma-chia and Ma-ch'ang stages of the Kansu succession which correspond most closely to the form of Yangshao found in central China. In the 3rd millennium BC copper was being used in Turkestan, and in Sumer and Elam bronze was manufactured. Neither metal appears with the earliest painted pottery in Kansu. Mud brick was widely used in Western Asia, but not in Yangshao. In western Asia from the 6th and 5th millennia BC, the staple crops were barley and wheat, and the chief domestic animal the goat. In the Chinese neolithic these are replaced by rice and millet, dog and pig. Thus in the light of current archaeological research the painted pottery of China stands isolated.

Andersson, the first excavator of Yangshao remains at the eponymous site, insists on the differences between the Kansu and Honan traditions of the culture, regarding them as connected; but he could reach no certain conclusion on their relative dating.[29] The differences are palpable: not only the shape of vases, but the use of colour and such details as the employment of a white slip on the Honan vessels, and the avoidance there of ornament painted inside the bowls. He recognized too that the two different groups met in the T'ao valley of south Kansu (figures 17, 18).

In recent years, however, the chronological scheme based by Andersson on a rather hazardous correlation of river terraces has been corrected by better stratigraphical evidence. His Ch'i-chia culture, with pottery shapes reminiscent of Lungshan, which he regarded as oldest, is shown to stand

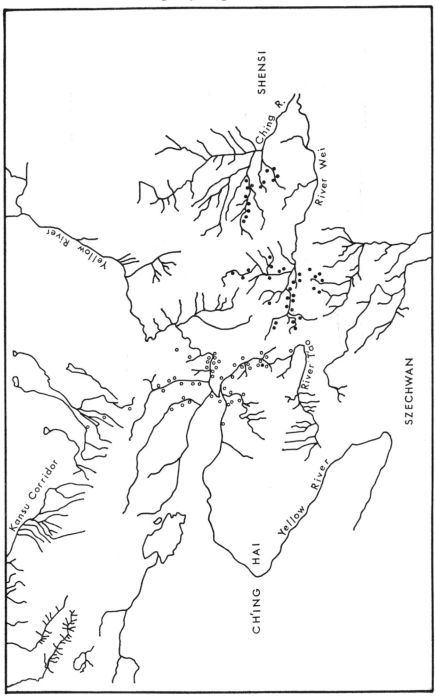

17. Neolithic sites in Kansu with painted pottery. (●) sites of the central
Yangshao tradition; (○) sites of the Kansu Yangshao tradition. After
Chang Hsüeh-cheng.

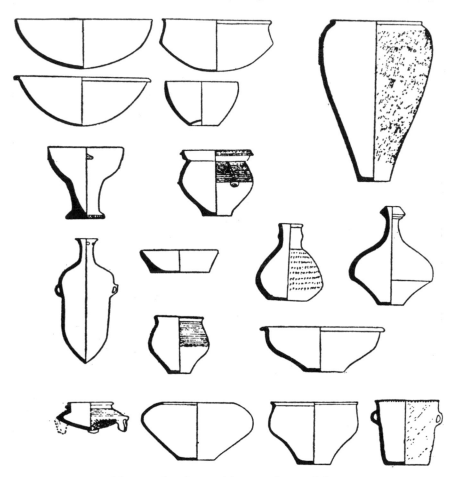

18. Pottery types of the central tradition of the Yangshao neolithic.
Bottom row from Miao-ti-kou, the remainder from Pan-p‘o.

at the end of the neolithic development of painted pottery, though it
precedes other stages of painted pottery culture which extend into the bronze
age and are contemporary with the western Chou period (figure 8). At
Ch‘i-chia-yao in the T‘ao valley painted pottery of the Yangshao tradition
allied to that of the central plain lay stratified beneath painted pottery of
the true Kansu variety.[30] The priority of the central Chinese tradition would
thereby appear to be vindicated, and the Kansu tradition would appear to
be a retarded province of the eastern Yangshao, prolonged in varying but
unbroken descent well into the period of the central bronze culture. The
area of overlap of the two traditions is comparatively small, lying between
the sources of the Wei river and the middle course of the T‘ao. In it are
some sites with a mixture of elements, but these are not such as to justify

recognition of a transitional phase. The Kansu tradition occupies the Yellow river valley in west Kansu (the western corridor) and the T'ao valley. East Kansu and the valley of the Ching river is the preserve of Yangshao culture closely allied to that of central China. The ceramic boundary could not be more clearly drawn: the nature of the cultural cleavage that it represents, apart from the difference of age, cannot yet be further elucidated (figure 17; plates 18-21).

From the eastern watershed confining the T'ao valley eastwards to Honan, the Yangshao potteries are fairly consistent in their forms, whether of the fine painted ware or the grey and coarser red ware which accompany it. A few vessel shapes are peculiar to subdivisions of this Yangshao sphere: an amphora with pointed base, in hard red pottery, is found only in south Shensi (plate 18); and an idiosyncratic version of the *ting*-tripod, linking with the characteristic Lungshan vessel without resembling it closely, does not occur outside Honan, and is there comparatively rare (figure 6*a*).[31]

In Honan the Yangshao tradition confronts that of Lungshan. The problem of the relationship of these two cultures has dominated neolithic research since the Lungshan culture was identified at the eponymous site in Shantung in 1935. The new view promulgated in China is that Lungshan simply developed from Yungshao in south Shensi and Honan, then spread east and south-east, laying the foundations of neolithic culture in all the low-lying and accessible parts of China. This strongly diffusionist interpretation is based upon observations made at the neighbouring sites of Miao-ti-kou and San-li-ch'iao in Honan. These lie respectively south and north of a river, about one and a half kilometres apart. The settlements were both very large, 240,000 and 180,000 sq.m respectively, of which only 4,480 and 1,526 sq.m were excavated (figure 18).

At each site Lungshan lies above Yangshao, in the manner often found on Honan sites. The crux of the problem lies in relating levels which are separated by the river. The new feature is the claim to have defined a level precisely transitional between Yangshao and Lungshan. The postulated successive levels alternate between the two sites, as shown in figure 19. At Miao-ti-kou a lower level with typical Yangshao pottery is followed by a level containing pottery of distinct forms and fabric which has been classified as transitional between Yangshao and Lungshan. The succession is denoted for the most part by the intrusion of the later pits and other features into the Yangshao deposits, the boundaries being sharply marked, without indication of gradual change or of a mixture of the styles of pottery. The excavators argue that habitation at Miao-ti-kou was not interrupted, so that we witness there the emergence of the Lungshan ceramic tradition from the Yangshao. Unfortunately it was not possible to demonstrate the relation of the transitional to the fully developed Lungshan stratigraphically,

D

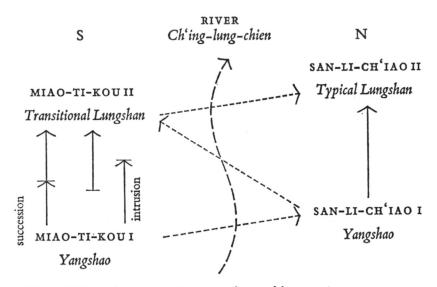

19. The neolithic sequence in west Honan: a scheme of the succession at
Miao-ti-kou and San-li-ch'iao. The solid arrows stand for observed strati-
graphic sequences, the broken arrows for the inferred typological
relation of the two sites; the curving line represents the river.

since deposits representing the latter were absent at Miao-ti-kou and
present only at San-li-ch'iao across the river Ch'ing-lung-chien, where they
overlay typical Yangshao without the intervention of a transitional stage.[32]
    The transitional pottery shows no sign of the use of the potter's wheel;
it includes none of the very thin burnished black ware which is characteristic
specially of the eastern Lungshan, and it still preserves a degenerate form
of painted ware. But two diagnostic Lungshan forms are present: the *chia*-
tripod and the tazza called *tou*, which was destined to have a varied history
in pottery and bronze from the 8th to the 4th centuries B C. The *ting*-tripod,
rare and of eccentric shape at Miao-ti-kou, is commoner, and assumes the
characteristic Lungshan form in the transitional level, Miao-ti-kou II. But
the *li*-tripod, typical of Lungshan in the central provinces, is absent from
the range of transitional pots, although the *chia* which these include is
related to it. The classic Lungshan *li* appears at San-li-ch'iao II.[33]
    Before the excavation of Miao-ti-kou and San-li-ch'iao, and the promul-
gation of An Chih-min's new view of Lungshan origins based upon them,
deposits with mixed Yungshao and Lungshan characteristics had been noted
at a number of Honan sites, and attributed to the contact and blending of
two neolithic traditions which were partly contemporary in central China.
The new view is not fully vindicated in terms of the Honan stratigraphy. On
at least six extensive sites in the centre of this province, and at most of the

sites in its northern part, typical Lungshan is found resting directly on the local Yangshao, and the stratigraphy indicates a discontinuity, whereas a transitional phase, such as is now postulated, would be expected to leave its traces over some considerable area. It is claimed, however, that a transitional level is present at some half-dozen important sites in west Honan, and at a few sites in Shensi and Shansi. To the east and north-east of Honan the transitional level seems not to occur; to the south-west we enter a region of eccentric local cultures in which the terms of the problem are different, although in general the pottery is more like that of the transitional levels than that of typical Lungshan.

Before the implications for the whole Lungshan area of the theory of a Honan origin are considered, the regional variation of the typical Lungshan culture should be noticed. The so-called classic black ware, which is thin, black right through the fabric, burnished on the surface and very skilfully potted, is most typical in its forms and most abundant on the Shantung sites where never an echo of the Yangshao is to be detected (plate 15). As we move west and south from Shantung, the black ware becomes rarer, the inner fabric browner, the forms less sharply characterized, although rarer typical pieces are still found both in Honan and Kiangsu. This distribution points to a spread of the fine black ware outwards from Shantung, the easternmost province of the Lungshan culture. The alternative and less plausible hypothesis is to suppose that the black ware improved technically and was produced in ever more sophisticated forms as it spread from west to east. A regional comparison of other leading Lungshan ceramic types no more supports the theory of a simple extension of Lungshan eastwards from the west-Honan area of the 'transitional' pottery. The three-lobed and four-lobed jugs of Lungshan are hardly found beyond the confines of Shantung (plate 16). Whether these so-called *k'uei* were a special adaptation of the three-lobed *li*, or its progenitors, remains uncertain and perhaps to be determined eventually by closer datings; but it is noteworthy that the *li* is virtually unknown on the Shantung sites, increases in frequency towards the west and is commonest in Honan, though absent from the transitional levels, and there survived into the bronze age as a standard coarse-pottery form. The *chia* found in the transitional level at Miao-ti-kou is a peculiarity of Honan. The distribution of the *ting*, which never has the lobed sides and hollow legs of the *li*, makes a simpler pattern: it occurs over the whole area of Lungshan, its only Yangshao appearance being in the rare eccentric variety noted at Miao-ti-kou.

These aspects of the Lungshan neolithic tell against the theory currently favoured in China of a single cultural impulse diffusing from a generative centre in south Shensi and west Honan, an eastward migration of the integrated Lungshan culture spreading the practice of agriculture and

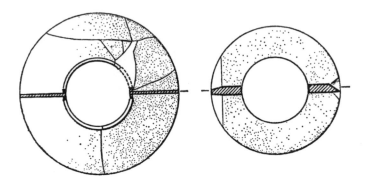

20. Nephrite rings, *pi*, from Shang tombs at Anyang. The ring with internal flange measures 135 mm in diameter. 14th–11th century BC. After Shih Chang-ju.

carrying with it an integrated complex of pottery and stone tools. The facts of distribution of ceramic forms, tools and burial rites combine to give east China a unique character which cannot be satisfactorily explained by a simple diffusion from the centre, and by complete derivation from Yangshao tradition. The geographic distributions point either to north-south connexions along the eastern seaboard, reaching at the extremities into Kiangsu and the Manchurian basin, shown by stone axes and knives, and the burials; or, like the pottery forms, support no marked cultural movement from west to east, but in many details suggest the contrary. This is not to deny that neolithic civilization based on settled farming was first created in the middle course of the Yellow river and advanced there-from to the limits of the loess and beyond to the eastern seaboard; but in subsequent cultural history the individuality of local tradition in east, north-east and south-east was a decisive factor.

If we suppose that there was no neolithic culture in east China before the date of the transitional levels in Honan, how are the characteristic stone axes of the east to be accounted for, since they are not found in the Yangshao region? We should perhaps picture Yangshao influence, chiefly on farming technique, moving slowly eastwards from Honan through a milieu of more primitive farming communities which still relied to a great extent on hunting and fishing, especially the latter. The economic tradition of the eastern seaboard and the adjacent areas inland, already ancient, combined with cultural affinities and possibly ethnic affinities which lead far to the north-east. The quasi-settled tribes of fishermen in territories extending to the mouth of the Amur and beyond, pressing southwards towards the east China coast, must explain the idiosyncrasies of Lungshan civilization. This variety of northern influence is detectable in the Manchurian basin; the spiritual ties of the eastern Chinese population with the far north are symbolized by the arm-rings and chisels of nephrite which are found in the Lungshan culture, for these objects, or the material from which they are made, were imported from Baikalia, and surely by no other route than the Amur and Sungari valleys (figure 20; plate 17).

Yangshao and Lungshan influences appear in Anhui and Kiangsu, but hardly any farther south beyond the limit of the loess. In Kiangsi, Chekiang and Fukien ancient local tradition continued unaffected by the farming culture of central China until long after the beginning of the bronze age in the north, when the Chinese were actively penetrating the southern territories. We then witness a curious phenomenon: the superior firing technique developed in central China was applied in the south-west to pottery decorated with impressed ornament in the primitive manner. From about the 8th century B C the south-eastern corded and stamped pottery was fired to a hardness comparable to that of the northern wares.

2

Isolation and contact in the high bronze age

BRONZE FIRST APPEARS in East Asia on sites in China which are dated on good evidence to the period of the Shang dynasty.[1] It was therefore unknown before about 1600 BC. Some twelve centuries then elapsed before iron came into general use. In the interim we witness the growth of a bronze-age society typical in all its manifestations. The vigour and speed of its advance compare with the rise of the younger bronze-using cultures in the eastern Mediterranean, the Phoenician and Aegean civilizations. But in its essentials, apart from the higher quality of its bronze work, the Shang state more resembles the states of ancient Mesopotamia: kingship and priesthood, sacrifice and oracle-taking, the bow and the chariot, the hypertrophy of the funeral rite, with human sacrifice; and beneath it all a vast peasantry hardly advanced beyond their old neolithic economy.

The history of Chinese metallurgy begins with the casting of thin bronze vessels with fairly elaborate relief ornament, such as those found at Cheng-chou in Honan. These date to the earlier half of the Shang period (plates 33, 48).[2] So far no trace has been found in China of a rudimentary bronze industry which might represent a stage equivalent to the chalcolithic of the Near East, or the early bronze age of temperate Europe. Simple knives and awls of copper, such as belong elsewhere to an initial stage, have been discovered in Kansu in a context of the Ch'i-chia culture, and thus date immediately after the local neolithic succession.[3] But even apart from the forms, which do not answer closely to any of the Shang finds, the manufacture of the awls by hammering cold metal and the use of pure copper are both alien to the central Chinese tradition. Moreover, the date of the Ch'i-chia culture can hardly be earlier than Shang itself. The later stages of the Kansu painted-pottery culture – the Hsin-tien, Ssŭ-wa and Sha-ching cultures – are also associated with similar small bronzes, and the late bronze-age date of the tombs in which these are found is generally acknowledged. Between this Kansu appearance of copper tools and the adoption of bronze casting in Honan – whether the latter is independent invention or in some sense derived from elsewhere – must be drawn one of the cultural frontiers which are the theme of this study: the two spheres betray no sign of interaction.

21. Painted pottery and bronzes of Namazga III, south Turkmenistan.
3rd millennium BC. After M.E.Masson and V.M.Masson.

Unpalatable though it may be to some theorists, an inescapable conclusion from the facts thus far established is that the comparatively sudden rise of metallurgy in central China must follow a cultural borrowing. This influence from elsewhere in Asia may have been no more than the basic idea of bronze smelting and casting. It does not follow in such cases that any considerable packet of cultural influence – still less a migration of people – reached China simultaneously with the technical information. The archaeological record shows that this did not happen.

If we consider the possibility of a cultural migration of any size into East Asia the obvious starting-point of such a movement is Western Asia. Yet the fundamental isolation and independence of the Shang bronze-age culture is made only the more striking by comparison with the nearest considerable bronze centre of like age: the early cities of south Turkmenia.[4] Here we reasonably look for analogies with Shang. The tradition of hand-made, richly painted pottery dating from the neolithic period, the large, undefended villages of farmers who cultivated intensively, with irrigation, give as close a social and economic parallel to the Yangshao culture of the Huang Ho valley as may be found anywhere in Asia. Metal appears in south Turkmenia early, and its immediate derivation is certainly from the neighbouring culture of the Iranian plateau beyond the Kopet Dagh. Were China ever in a like client-relationship to a metal-using neighbour, we might have expected the artefacts to show a similar progression, but in fact nothing of the kind is found. In Turkmenia, in the periods of Namazga II and III, small awls and needles, and a few very simple flat spearheads were made of copper. These stages mark the true chalcolithic. In Namazga III, corresponding approximately to the 3rd millennium BC, metal spreads farther, but pieces with a tin content are rare. Tin was distant and perhaps difficult to obtain from the ore. The metal artefacts are still mainly of pure copper, though a minority now have traces of arsenic and antimony. The predominance of tinless metal continues even in Namazga IV and V, which brings us into the 2nd millennium; but by now some true bronze was made (figure 21).

As for Shang China, there is contrast with this Turkmenian metallurgy at every point: tin and lead were alloyed with copper from the start, multipart casting moulds of baked clay were in regular use and the level of skill displayed in producing thin-walled vessels with fine and exact relief ornament surpassed anything achieved in Turkmenia. In any case there is little sign that the influence of the south Turkmenian chalcolithic and bronze culture spread beyond the narrow belt of watered or irrigable territory flanking the north side of the Kopet Dagh. To the north, in Khorazmia, the food-gathering Kelteminar culture lasted until about 2000 BC, the Namazga IV period of the south. North of the Aral Sea and east of the Caspian a vast flat territory was occupied by a sparse hunting and fishing population of Kelteminar or south Uralian affinities which was equally incapable of absorbing Namazga influences, even supposing that these reached them. On the other hand – a fact of importance for east-west connexion – they were able to absorb bronze-using culture in the form in which it reached them through contact with the Andronovo culture. The latter sphere of small, little-settled communities of farmers flourished in the 2nd millennium BC with remarkable uniformity in their artefacts and burial customs. It is not clear whence the Andronovans derived the forms of their bronze products. Influences emanating from the Caucasian bronze-using centres may have given the first impetus towards metallurgy, but no connexion is discernible between the Andronovo tradition and the cultures of south Turkmenia.[5] The line of separation ran east and west: on the northern side it was the Andronovan bronze-smiths who diffused

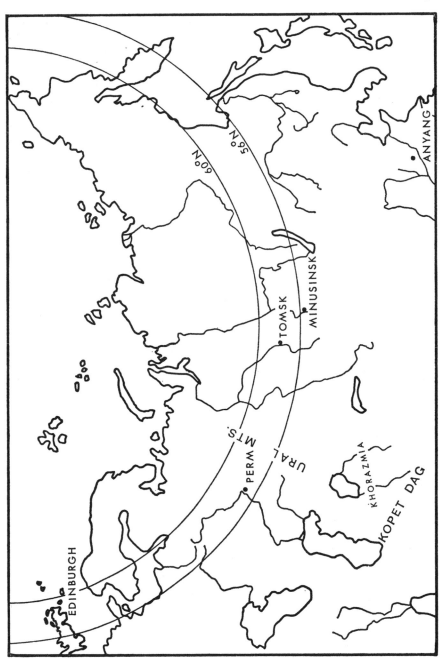

22. The zone of movement of the southern margin of the woodland steppe in the 2nd millennium BC.

the knowledge of their metal through the grassed and forested territory stretching from the Ural river to the Minusinsk basin. In the Andronovo culture we see the first expression of the cultural unity of the Siberian steppe zone which is the most striking feature of the inner Asian bronze age: by 1500 B C it embraced the whole zone from the Caspian to south Siberia; but China lay far beyond its eastern limits and no formal connexion with the Chinese bronze age can be established. Before describing the evidence that can be adduced for Shang cultural contact with inner Asia there is a climatic factor to be considered.

Soviet Russian climatologists believe that the forest-steppe boundary through Asia east of the Urals in the comparatively recent past ran much to the north of the present line (figure 22).[6] Archaeology adduces further proof of a temporary northward shift of the southern limit of the forest zone, the Siberian taiga, by pointing to the alternation of agricultural and food-gathering populations in certain latitudes. In the zone of the middle Ob and Irtish rivers, approximately between the 56th and 60th parallels, are situated sites characterized by grain-rubbers, bones of sheep, horse, cows, bone cheek-pieces and a southerly type of incised pottery. The presence of these remains necessarily implies a much lighter vegetable covering than the present heavy woodland, the taiga. Moreover, the cattle-raising, agricultural tribes whose passage is thus recorded had displaced cultures (typified by Samus III and IV) dependent on a gathering economy and characterized by pottery of a northern forest type, with impressed designs. It is estimated that the boundary of forest and steppe (or wooded steppe) lay at its northern limit, along the 60th parallel, around 1250 B C. Around 1500 B C it stood some 200 miles farther south, along the 56th parallel. A north-south division of pit burials (forest tradition) and kurgan burials (steppe tradition) which belong to the later 2nd millennium B C also runs approximately along the northern steppe limit, and the same line marks the approximate edge of the distribution of the rich degraded black soils on which the agriculturists throve.

The period of improved climate corresponds to the sub-boreal of Europe. According to Kosarev the archaeological material indicates that the northwards encroachment of steppe on forest started earlier and went farther on the middle Irtish, in the higher-lying region nearer to the Urals.[7] This circumstance, in the first centuries of the 2nd millennium B C, favoured the creation of a well-defined area of chalcolithic culture along the middle and lower course of the Irtish river. The western and northern edge of this area approached the Urals in the region of Sverdlovsk and Perm (Molotov). Immediately to the south was the frontier with the northern province of the Andronovo culture, which is well represented in the region of Tobal. Thus a cultural sphere was created through which influence from the steppe,

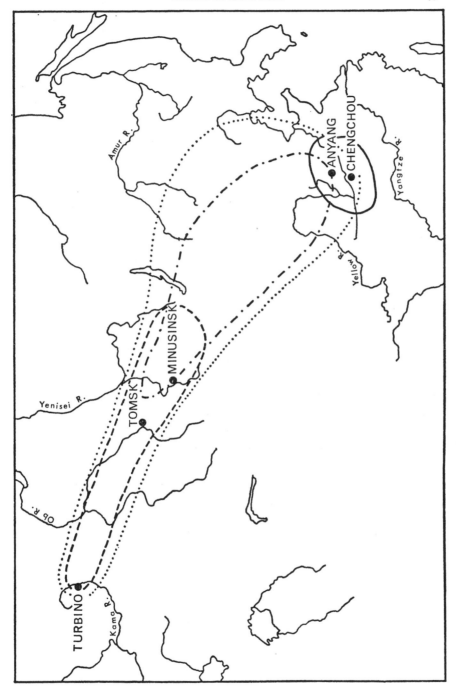

23. The geographic distribution of bronze types in east and inner Asia
1600–800 BC. The zones of diffusion are: (.....) socketed axes and
spearheads; (—·—·—) long-bladed axes, ibex-head knives, daggers
with notched guard and standing animal; (———) knives with standing
animal; (———) the Chinese *ko*-halberd.

by this time carrying with it the knowledge of bronze working, was able to reach to the eastern slopes of the southern Ural mountains. Here, in the Perm-Sverdlovsk area, arose the first bronze industry of importance in northern Asia, which culminated in the production of spearheads, battle-axes and socketed axes of the types associated with the cemeteries of Seima and Turbino on the western edge of the middle Urals (figure 23).[8]

From the Seima-Turbino centre two cultures of full bronze-age character, the Suzgunsk culture and the Yelovsk culture, spread along the middle and lower Irtish, and thence along the middle Ob, some five hundred miles farther east. The presence of this widespread continuum of bronze-using culture – and one which in north European terms was comparatively advanced – is of some importance in considering the foreign relations of the Chinese bronze age.

The west Siberian sphere of bronze culture extended from the Urals to Tomsk on the middle Ob, while the influence of Shang China was strong in the Minusinsk valley of south Siberia. The distance separating the boundaries of these two spheres of influence was a mere three or four hundred miles, only a tenth of the whole distance between the central plain of China and the Seima-Turbino centre of bronze production. The zone of latitude between 60° and 56° runs north of Lake Baikal and reaches the sea in the east in the northern part of the Sea of Okhotsk, north of the Amur mouth. Consequently movement both ethnical and cultural between Manchuria and the Minusinsk basin, along the flat land of the middle Amur, must have been easier during the climatic optimum than it was either before or afterwards. Except during the brief period of improved climate the cold forest descended to the mouth of the Amur. In China there are indications from the Shang capital at Anyang in Honan that a markedly warmer climate was enjoyed there during the last few centuries of the 2nd millennium B C. Animal bones excavated there include those of elephant, rhinoceros, tapir, water-buffalo and other warm-climate species which were not known later in the Yellow river valley, and the oracular questions engraved on tortoise-shell and animal spatulae at the Shang capital are so much concerned with rain that one suspects an incidence of drought greater than in later times. While a zone of wooded steppe existed between the 56th and the 60th parallels, communication between bronze-age China and inner Asia was unusually favoured. The germ of metallurgical knowledge may have reached China by this route towards the middle of the 2nd millennium B C rather than along a more direct line from Western Asia, and certain forms of bronze weapons and tools were undoubtedly transmitted through Siberia.[9]

But if Shang China opened a narrow window towards the inner Asian steppes, it nevertheless remained a culture singularly isolated and self-sufficient. The continuity of the bronze-age culture with the Lungshan neolithic is very clear. In the latter are anticipated some quite specific features of Shang civilization. One of these is the technique of reading oracular answers from cracks caused in flat animal bones – usually shoulder-blades – by applying heat (plate 31). In the Shang period at Anyang the technique is refined and the answer perhaps controlled to some degree. An oval cavity was gouged on one side of the bone and heat applied to the edge of it with a bronze point. On the other side of the bone, beneath the cavity, a short crack was caused, generally with a still shorter spur branching off. On a principle not known to us the answer to the question put to the gods and spirits was read from the cracks as merely yes or no. The questions were often inscribed on the bones near the oval cavities, and sometimes the answers also. Oracle bones have been found on a number of Lungshan sites, including the eponymous site in Shantung, but on these there are no inscriptions. Uninscribed oracle bones have been found on sites (some of them are only tentatively dated to the Shang period and may possibly be earlier) in Hopei, Shansi, Shantung, Hunan, Anhui, Kiangsu, Liaoning and Liaotung, as well as at Chengchou in Honan. Some of these provinces lie outside the area of characteristic Shang culture. The absence of inscriptions suggests too that the writing found on the oracle bones at the capital at Anyang, which was founded half-way through the life of the dynasty, about 1300 BC, was not known in the earlier Shang period.[10]

In various techniques, apart from the introduction of bronze, a similar local continuity from the neolithic is to be seen. The potter's wheel, first used in the Lungshan period, is now more widely applied in pottery, but the basic methods remain the old ones of coiling and beating. The similarities of bronze vessels to certain Lungshan pottery shapes underline the independence of Shang metallurgy even in its initial stage. The most characteristic feature of Shang architecture, the building of foundations and walls by pounding earth in successive thin layers, is a development of the neolithic custom of carving the lower parts of houses out of the soil itself. Over these foundations rose wooden buildings: the use of bricks, fired or not, was not known.

Two extensive city sites constitute the most important remains of the Shang period: at Anyang in north Honan, on the Huan river, and at Chengchou, about a hundred miles to the south.[11] Between the two, much nearer to Chengchou, flows the Yellow river. At both places the Shang remains overlie neolithic levels, so that the two cities between them appear to cover the five hundred years or so of the dynasty's existence. The historical tradition that Anyang was occupied by the nineteenth king P'an Keng is supported by the king-list constructed from the names of former rulers appearing as recipients of sacrifice in the oracular sentences.[12]

According to the historical chronology (in its revised form) the main features of the Anyang site fall in the period from 1300 to 1027 BC; the Shang occupation at Chengchou must extend back at least through the previous two centuries.[13]

The remains at Chengchou appear to be those of Ao, an earlier Shang capital which history reports to have been built by the tenth king, Chung Ting. Exactly to what extent Ao was abandoned in 1300 BC is not yet certain: the excavators found no clear sign of destruction, but the absence of any of the objects characteristic of the late, Anyang, phase of Shang seems to be good evidence for the abandonment of the site or its decline to insignificance after P'an Keng's move. The reason for the move may have been of a superstitious kind (the early Japanese emperors were itinerant for such reasons) or it may have followed a political trend, for the main expansion of Shang rule was towards the north-east and the west.[14] In the time of the twenty-second king (Wu Ting), Shang controlled the southern half of Shansi, then after a setback in the west extended its power again in that direction during the last few reigns of kings recorded in the oracle sentences. The limit of its western influence was in the region of the middle Wei river. To the north-east Shang sites are recorded as far as the middle of Hopei. Through the gap to the south-east Shang influence passed into the north of Anhui, and sites occur along the south bank of the Yellow river, but it is clear that neither the material culture of Shang nor its political control reached far south of Chengchou itself. A capital at Anyang was more suitably placed than Chengchou as Shang affairs stood in the second half of the dynasty.

At the southern city, Ao, on sites both within and outside the ancient wall line, a stratigraphy of intersecting trenches and foundations was established, and the sequence is borne out by typological development, especially of the pottery.[15] The latest level at Chengchou corresponds with the earliest material found at Anyang, but the stratigraphy at the northern site is not clear enough to allow a precise correlation. It is argued there that three levels may be distinguished, and these have been quoted, without comment, by many writers:

 I   The earliest level, above the layer with black Lungshan pottery but below the level corresponding to the rammed-earth foundations of the buildings.

 II   The building foundations, representing the *floruit* of the site.

 III   The latest level, overlying the foundations and equated by the excavators with some burials.

It is possible that the last level represents a limited post-Shang occupation of the site, since the great buildings whose destruction preceded the formation of level III may be presumed to have survived until the overthrow

of the Shang dynasty by the Chou confederacy in 1027 B C. But no indubitable post-Shang material seems to have been excavated at Anyang;
if there was any occupation there at the beginning of the Chou period it
must have been quite brief. The stratigraphical division proposed for
Anyang unfortunately throws no light on the relative dating of material
belonging to the later Shang phase represented by the northern capital,
for none of the groups of finds – bronzes, pottery or oracle bones – was
clearly related to any of the three levels. It is certain, however, that the
latest material obtained at Chengchou marks a stage earlier than the latest
phase at Anyang, possibly by as much as two centuries. This will be of
importance when inner Asian contacts are considered.

The tombs of the Shang period are no less distinctive than other aspects
of the civilization, though they follow broadly a practice widespread in
Asia. In inner Asia at large there are two traditions, each with its elabora-
tions. One tradition is of cists built of stone slabs, or earth graves placed
within hedges of slabs set on edge. The classic examples are in south
Siberia. The other tradition starts from a well-formed rectangular pit or
shaft. Either may be covered by a mound. Pit graves covered by mounds
were the rule in south Russia and reached their greatest splendour in the
classic kurgans of the Scyths. There were two bronze-age variants in the
west: the earlier, which gave its name to the Srubnaya or timber-frame
culture of south Russia, is a pit reinforced by a structure of timbers. The
Srubnaya culture was confined to a rather small area between the Volga
and the Dnepr. The succeeding bronze phase is that of the Catacomb
culture, which extended farther east and north to march with the western
limit of the Andronovo. Here the two practices met, on the line of the
Ural river, for the Andronovo rite belonged essentially to the tradition
whose variations took the slab-built cist as the point of departure. The
catacomb tombs are so called because the burial chamber was placed to one
side of the shaft, in a more or less elaborate annex, whose original purpose
was presumably to foil robbers (figure 24).[16]

All of these tomb types, except the cists with elaborate kerbs, are found
in China proper. Tombs of the essential Chinese tradition are variations of
the pit-grave and the shaft-grave. The type of the superior Shang tomb is
found already at Chengchou, dated to the latest phase, though in modest
dimensions: for example, 21·5 m deep and 2·9 by 1·17 m in plan. The
rectangular pit has a step in the wall near the bottom, a feature perhaps
originally used to avoid a collapse of the pit wall, but which has now
become a ritual prescription. Similar steps are seen in pit-graves dug into
kurgans in south Russia. When, in China, the pit is furnished with a burial
chamber, this is of well-jointed timbers, and sunk in the floor of the pit
so that its top comes level with the step. The usual practice was to make

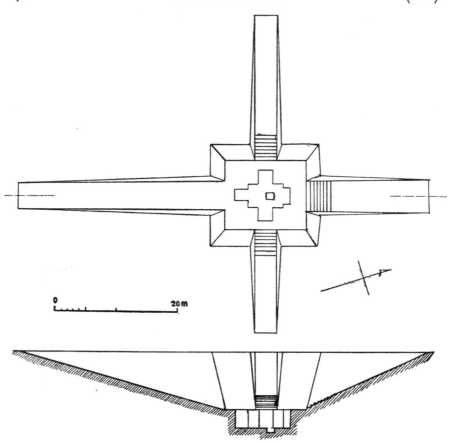

24. Plan and section of a Shang cruciform shaft tomb, no. 1400, at Hsi-pei-kang, Anyang. 12th–11th century B C.

this structure double walled, like a double coffin rather than a chamber, the space between the two walls being reserved for the grave goods, and the whole protected from the filling by the cover of timbers. The *kuan*, or inner coffin, and the *kuo*, outer coffin or coffin chamber, were funeral institutions which were destined to spread throughout China and survive in this original form until the present day. When no coffin was supplied, the ritual of the step in the pit was still observed. Grave gifts were placed in the pit and on the step whether or not a timber coffin was present. The smaller tombs, dated to all periods of the settlement, lack the step and the coffin, and many casual burials were in irregular pits.

A few cremation burials in small globular jars are recorded, but this rite, in the Shang period as later, was quite exceptional in China before the arrival of Buddhism in the 2nd century A D.[17] In some half of the formal burials, and often in the informal ones, the corpse was laid prone. This custom was observed in the Honan region in the neolithic period, and now it is good evidence of continuity of the same population into the bronze age. There seems to be no parallel to this method of burial elsewhere in Asia. Few of the more formal burials lack another peculiar feature: a small pit in the centre of the floor, below the coffin, in which was placed a sacrificed animal, usually a dog, or even a human being.

In the aggrandizement of the Shang tomb the pit was enlarged and deepened, the wooden burial chamber was elaborated and an access ramp was constructed leading to it. A great tomb excavated near Loyang had such a ramp with a right-angle turn at its centre.[18] Of the eight tombs at Hsi-pei-kang near Anyang whose dimensions and contents seem to warrant their loyalty, the burials of Shang Kings, seven are cruciform in plan. On three sides a ramp descended to the level of the step and the top of the timbered burial chamber, and on the south a ramp, which was in each case the entrance to the tomb, led to the floor of the burial chamber.[19] Human victims had been sacrificed: in two cases a man was buried with the dog in the basal pit beneath the chamber and four kneeling men at the corners of the pit. All the ramps except the southern had further small sacrificial pits and steps in their line of descent. On the steps of the northern ramp of one tomb human skulls were laid in rows of ten.

The royal tomb excavated at Wu-kuan-ts'un in 1950 had suffered less depredation than those at Hsi-pei-kang. The outer chamber was decorated with a painted and inlaid wooden canopy (this seems to have been a pre-rogative of royalty), and pottery, jade ornaments, bronze vessels of the ritual shapes and bronze weapons were scattered between the two walls of the chamber. But the barbaric splendours of these burials are outdone by the lavish slaughter of animal and human victims, whose remains were excavated around the building foundations of the city. Some of these burials were related clearly to the buildings, either as foundation offerings, or as guards and servants buried with their vessels and weapons to continue the functions of this world in the next (plates 33-35).

In the Shang funeral observances there is no reason to see any close or direct link with practices elsewhere in Asia, since the cruciform plan and the stepped profile of the pit are peculiar to China; but the Shang rite is sufficiently in keeping with a broad Asiatic tradition to suggest that in this case the cultural boundary which isolates ancient China is not sharply drawn. It is important to note that the design of tombs is an innovation and not inherited from the neolithic. Only in one particular, the continuation of the prone burial, is the influence of the pre-metallic age apparent. For the Shang royal tombs, the shaft-graves at Ur supply the obvious comparison. In similar societies the funeral megalomania of bronze-age kings led inevitably to similar holocausts.

E

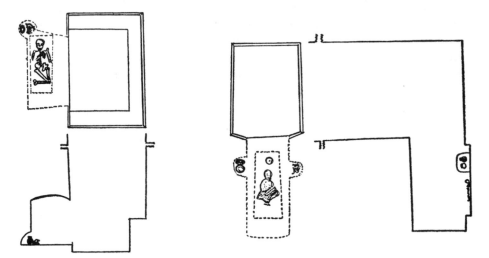

25. Annex tombs in plan and section, at Pan-p'o, Honan.
5th–4th century BC.

The bronze-age tombs of central China are in some degree related to
traditions of tomb structure which established themselves in the western
steppes, but the absence in China of mounds, stone cists, kerb-stones and
other stone settings, shows that the connexion is not close. There is one
exception to this generalization: the catacomb tomb. But this does not
appear in China until long after the Shang period; in the 5th century BC
such tombs are common, particularly in the western part of central China.
The dating shows that the south Russian catacomb tombs are much older
than the Chinese ones. The adoption of this tomb form in the east is clearly
the result of an external influence (figure 25).

    In the art of the Shang period we find the same mysterious cousinship
with the practice of inner Asia as we trace in tomb forms and weapons.
There are two manners. One is a naïve realism, seen in the profile jade
plaques of birds, hare, tigers, fish and the few full-face representations of
the human face (plate 32). This style was little developed: the artist's
ingenuity went into the elaboration of the conventional animal designs
which were cast on the bronzes and carved in bone and wood. Chief
among them is the *t'ao-t'ieh* mask, a monster lacking a lower jaw, with
lateral extensions which are in part at least a duplicated representation of
the body behind the head (plate 58). In most treatments the *t'ao-t'ieh* is
divisible into two halves about a vertical line running down the nose.
These halves are then called the *k'uei* dragon, apparently a one-footed
creature, which entered also independently into the bronze decoration.
Some apparently non-representational motifs may derive from reality, like

the blade-shaped pattern on socketed axes which is a stylized cicada. Of the *t'ao-t'ieh*, dragons, cicadas, birds and a few other creatures which peopled the obsessive imagination of the Shang artist, many symbolistic interpretations have been given, based either on the notions of primitive animism or on fragments of later moralizing explanations preserved in Chinese literature. Some of the designs possibly refer to the gods and demiurges who make rare appearances in the oracle texts, and are generally apotropaeic in intent, but nothing more can be said that is valid for the Shang period.

Being based in the main on linear and not plastic form, and tending to ever greater graphic elaboration in which mere symmetry is avoided, this art is akin in the broadest sense to the traditions of inner and East Asia, but its like is nowhere found outside China, nor, in a strict sense, outside the Shang domain. Some rare naïve drawings of fish (plate 3), birds, a human face, found painted on Yangshao pottery hardly furnish satisfactory antecedents for it. The art appears in Shang times in what seems an evolved form, even when the relatively simpler *t'ao-t'ieh* of the Chengchou period are considered. If it did not spring complete *de toutes pièces* from the Shang soil we must assume that its style and motifs were formed previously in perishable media and are lost to us in their more elementary expression. The style as we know it fits well with the wider context of early Chinese art as it developed after the Shang dynasty, but we cannot say that it necessarily had its origin at the centre of the Shang state in Honan.[20]

In its criticism of the chronology which was established for the Shang dynasty in the early Han period, placing it between 1722 and 1166 BC, modern scholarship has argued persuasively in favour of 1027 BC as the lower date. No collateral evidence can be found in history, however, in support of the year 1722 BC, and the doubt evidently entertained by Ssŭ-ma Ch'ien himself in Han times can no more be resolved today. For reasons not altogether clear Russian archaeologists have generally taken a date of *c.* 1600 BC for the beginning of bronze in China when they estimated the age of the Siberian bronze age through its eastern connexions. This figure, whether explicitly stated or not, is influential in most of their reasoning on Siberian chronology, their philosophy of *stadial'nost* having meanwhile tended to draw the teeth of absolute datings in any case.

In examining the inner Asian contact with Shang we must now take into account the situation created by the recently established relationship of Anyang and Chengchou. Two important Shang bronze types are knives with handles terminated by animal heads (horse and ram) and spearheads: these have not been reported from Chengchou but were found in fair numbers at Anyang (plates 30*a*, *b*, 37*b*). Arguing from the revised historical chronology we should therefore infer that these bronzes were not made in

China before the 13th century BC. We may speculate further: since the knives and spearheads were not found in the Chengchou levels which are claimed to correspond with the postulated early phase at Anyang (that is, Chengchou Jen-min Kung-yüan), it is conceivable that they were not made until the latter part of the Anyang occupation, after *c.* 1200 BC. In either case we may associate the spearheads and knives with the other important innovations which mark off the Anyang period of Shang: the use of the war chariot, the flowering of art, the invention of a system of writing consisting of ideographs which, like the scripts of ancient Mesopotamia and Egypt, employ phonetic as much as visual elements.

But two important bronze types were already manufactured in the Chengchou period: the *ko*-halberd and the socketed axe. The halberds, which have no parallels outside China,[21] come from graves attributed by the excavators to the 2nd and 3rd phases, that is, from the period immediately preceding the Anyang occupation and the period corresponding to the early phase at Anyang (plate 28). We may therefore place their first appearance *c.* 1400 BC at the latest, and allow that it may have been a century earlier. The socketed axes from Chengchou belong to the Ehr-li-kang site, but the report does not record whether they are attributed to the upper or lower level. Therefore the socketed axe may have been made during the first phase of the southern city, perhaps not long after 1500 BC, and on this evidence date to a time before the appearance of the socketed axe in western Europe (plate 27).

The Chengchou axes are of a distinct type.[22] The transverse section is neatly rectangular, with sharp edges, and there is usually a heavy collar at the mouth. The longitudinal section seems to be symmetrical. The ornament consists of crossed lines in relief. In a few specimens there are two small bosses which add 'eyes' to the cross. The later Anyang specimens are usually decorated with a series of triangles hanging from the mouth, each triangle may be filled with a design resembling a stylized cicada; or there may be a broad band above the triangles decorated with a *t'ao t'ieh* mask. The collar at the mouth tends to be wider and less raised than on the Chengchou specimens, and many are distinctly adze-like in profile.

These phenomena bear an interpretation which concerns the problem of culture movement in inner Asia at the beginning of the bronze age. It can hardly be questioned that the Chengchou socketed axes were the progenitors of the axes made at Anyang. Specimens comparable to both of these groups from central China have been found, unfortunately without datable context, at widely scattered points in Inner Mongolia, and they extend even into Manchuria. On the dating suggested for the earlier Shang phase at Chengchou, *c.* 1500–1400 BC, the Chengchou axes bid fair to rank with the earliest examples of this tool made anywhere. Any view of the diffusion of the socketed axe must take into account the possibility of a movement starting from central China and bringing the axes along the zone of wooded steppe to the region of the middle Urals and thence to Europe and its late bronze age. In a paper published shortly before his death, written while the impressions of study of new material in China were still fresh, Kiselev took up this standpoint.[23] Already in 1949 Gordon Childe was near to it, though he could know nothing of the Chengchou evidence, and finally he denied the priority to China.[24] This was because he believed that an axe form with the beginnings of a socket but open to one side at the lower end (cf. plate 25, top right) was transitional to the socketed axe proper. He had observed, correctly, that this supposed transitional form is not found in China: but it is questionable if the open-sided axe was in fact the first kind to be manufactured.

The other pivot in the argument about the Asian diffusion of socketed axes is the existence of the well-defined group named the Seima-Turbino type after the sites on the western side of the middle Urals.[25] There is no questioning the claim of these axes to be the oldest in Europe, but their date has been a subject of debate among scholars during the half-century that they have been known. Until recently it was assumed that they are the prototypes of the whole widespread family of socketed axes, ultimately responsible for those found in China as for those which diffused through Europe and became, on its outer fringes, the hall-mark of the western late bronze age. As to their paternal relation to the Chinese axes, the early date of Seima has always been deemed sufficient proof. Even when the Anyang phase in China was dated back to the 15th century, Seima could still be argued to have a century or two in hand. Minns was content to place the Seima tombs in the middle of the 2nd millennium. Estimates based on the western material rely on analogies between Seima and the spearheads and axes in the bronze treasure of Borodino, because features of this last can be related to bronzes from the shaft-graves at Mycene. Reasoning on these lines, Loehr would accept only a broad dating, between 1700 and 1400 B C. Gimbutas finds grounds for narrowing this to the century between 1450 and 1350. Merpert reached the conclusion that the Borodino treasure, the Seima and Turbino graves and the Pokrovsk stage of the Srubnaya culture of the lower Volga all belong to the 16th century B C, the date assigned by Wace and Mylonas to the Mycene tombs. A few years earlier Bader had argued a date of 1550–1450 for the Seima-Turbino complex. Merpert operates only with the western evidence, while Bader allows weight to the Chinese parallels. But Bader attributes socketed axes to Anyang only, thinking they cannot be earlier than the 14th century B C. Piggott dates Borodino to the 15th century.[26]

This summary of a chronological debate affecting the theory of the origin of one of the chief tools of the ancient world sets in relief the importance of conclusions reached on the dating of the Shang remains at Chengchou. If socketed axes were made there in the 15th century BC they are hardly later than the date attributed by the majority of scholars to the Seima-Turbino axes. Could the principle of the socketed axe, with its comparatively sophisticated casting requirement, be conveyed five thousand kilometres through inner Siberia between the western and eastern bronze centres in a mere half-century or a century? All that we learn of cultural movement in inner Asia and central Asia, both in the early bronze age and in the later period of full steppe nomadism, predisposes us to accept the fact of almost incredibly rapid transmission of types of metal artefacts over great distances. If the socketed axe travelled in this fashion through the sparse woodland-steppe populations of inner Asia this was because it answered a real need. As pastoralists possessing the knowledge of bronze, if only by trade, were attracted to move farther north by the northward advance of the wooded-steppe zone, their need of wood-working tools would be greater perhaps than before. These tribes provided the cultural continuum through which contacts between China and the Urals became possible.

Bader thus describes this situation: 'The predominant links of the population of the Seima-Turbino historico-cultural region lay in the east, beyond the Urals. There, as in the neolithic period, was a population related to that of the slopes of the Urals. This population extended to the middle Ob and maintained close ties with the Ural region until the beginning of the second half of the 2nd millennium BC. At this point these ties were weakened or even destroyed by the expansion of southern steppe tribes of the Andronovo culture, who penetrated far to the north.'[27] By extending the cultural continuum of pastoralist bronze-users as far as south Siberia the Andronovo expansion can only have promoted further the distant intercourse between the Urals and central China.

It is interesting to note the varied cultural structure implied by differences of distribution of the travelling bronze types. The socketed axes extend from the Urals to Chengchou, but the path is marked by successive groups of local design (figures 26, 27; plates 25, 26*a*). The axes which occur in the Minusinsk basin and the Baikal region form in each case individual groups, distinguished particularly by the ornament of lines and simple geometric figures cast on them. The comparison of shapes and ornament does not strongly suggest that one group derives from the other, or that either is sprung directly from the socketed axes of central China. In each region, we must assume, a local development took place after the tool had been adopted. Yet on the whole the Baikal group stands closer to the Chinese

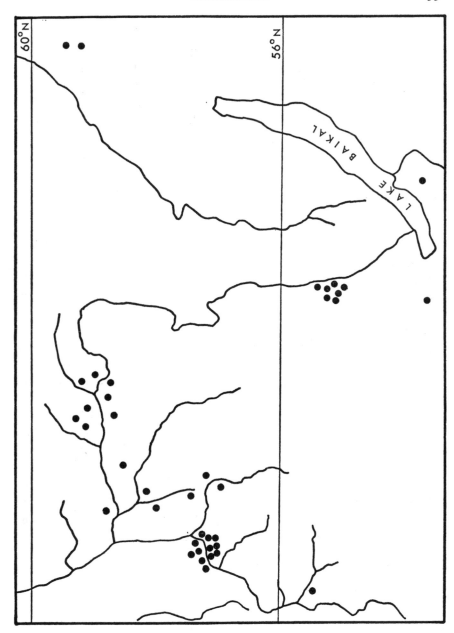

26. The distribution of finds of bronze socketed axes in the Baikal region. *C.* 1500–800 B C. After Maksimenkov.

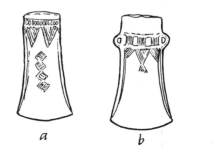

27. Bronze socketed axes from west Siberia (*a*, *b*) and the eastern Baikal region. C. 1500–800 B C. After Bader and Maksimenkov.

specimens, and therefore suggests an east-west movement for the travel of the socketed axe from one bronze-producing centre to another, and points to central China as the place of origin of the tool type. The specimens found along the Angara and its tributaries in Baikalia have (i) ornament of hanging triangles and of vertical lines with eyes, both of which can be paralleled in China; (ii) include an isolated group (type VIII) differing from all the others by their more elongated shapes (figure 27*c*, *d*). The latter type, absent in the Minusinsk basin and farther west, is close in proportions to Chinese specimens made in the Chengchou and Anyang periods of Shang.

It is certain that no considerable influence reached Siberia from Shang China before the latter part of the Shang period. It is to this influence that Kiselev ascribes the rise, from *c.* 1200 B C, of the Karasuk culture, marked by an unprecedented expansion of the south-Siberian bronze industry. Since bronze weapons and tools were rarely placed in Karasuk graves, the composition of this part of the Karasuk inventory is deduced from scattered finds of the bronzes, but the correctness of the attribution is hardly to be doubted. The initial transmission of the socketed axe through inner Asia, a movement which on the present evidence appears to have begun from central China, took place in pre-Karasuk time. According to Kiselev, the manufacture of socketed axes both in Minusinsk and Baikalia belongs in the main to the Karasuk period and so dates from *c.* 1200 B C. But on the hypothesis of a Chinese origin, the first socketed axes in south Siberia, and particularly in Baikalia, may have been somewhat earlier, and would imply an earlier date for the formation of the Karasuk bronze culture. Debets' study of crania indicated a movement of mongoloid people into the Minusinsk basin during the Karasuk period, a fact which Kiselev connects with the derivation of essential cultural elements from China. Broadly speaking, the advent of the Karasuk in south Siberia substituted a culture with south-eastern structural relations for another, the Andronovo, with western connexions.[28]

The other bronze type which connects China with the middle Urals is the spearhead with leaf-shaped blade and deep socket of rhomboid section (plate 30*c*).[29] The Uralian specimens, represented by finds in the Seima cemetery, have the projecting part of the socket made with a round cross-section. About half of the Shang specimens continue the rhomboid section of the midrib to the end of the socket. The Seima spearhead regularly has a single loop on the socket, whereas the Chinese model has two loops, and the latter never displays the three-ribbed moulding at the base of the blade. The outline of the blade in China approximates to an isosceles triangle, whereas the western blades are more nearly oval in shape. These differences are in no case fundamental and are in the order of those distinguishing various groups of socketed axes. When all allowance is made for them, the conclusion that the spearheads of Shang and of the Urals are connected in origin is inescapable.

Since the bronze spearhead seems not to have been made in China before the Anyang period of Shang, possibly not before the latter part of this phase, we infer that the travel of the spearhead was not closely tied to that of the socketed axe; and in view of the dating of the Seima-Turbino complex (taking even the lowest estimate) there is a presumption that the migration of the spearhead type was from west to east. The separation in date of the appearance of axe and spearhead in Shang China further enhances the possibility that the axe originated in China, a possibility which the purely chronological argument on balance favours. The Seima type of spearhead is, however, not the only one that was made in China. Hardly less frequent among the Shang spearheads is the design in which the lower part of the blade is extended down the socket to incorporate the loops, which appear as perforations in the lower edge of the blade. This most eccentric of spearheads is peculiar to China and to the Shang period and sphere. It is an elaboration of the leaf-shaped type, unaffected by further external influence, and well illustrates the free and inventive treatment which borrowed ideas received in China.

From the west spearheads related to the Seima type can be traced as far as Tomsk, on the upper Ob. Here there existed a bronze-casting centre which played an essential rôle in the traffic of ideas through inner Asia. Probably from the middle of the 2nd millennium B C it was in contact to the east with the Minusinsk bronze industry. Eventually there is clear evidence of a migration from Minusinsk to the Tomsk region, involving ceramics as well as bronzes characteristic of south Siberia.[30] In the Minusinsk basin itself the spearheads are not recorded, but the reluctance of the

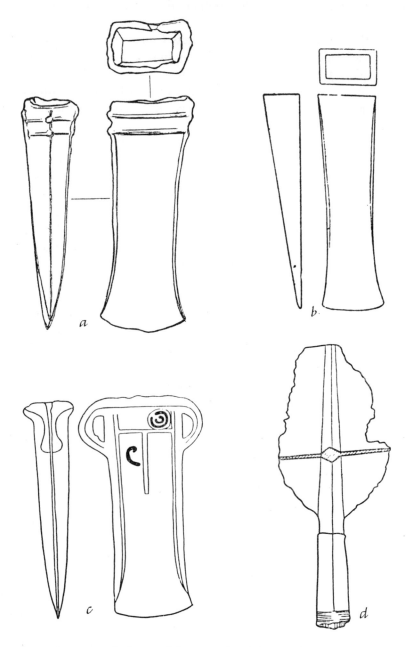

28. Bronzes from central China and the Primor'ye. (*a*) From the habitation site at Chang-chia-p'o, Feng-hsi, Shensi, 10th–9th century BC; (*b*) found in a grave at Shang-ts'un-ling, Honan, 9th–8th century BC; (*c, d*) found near Kazakevichevo, Primor'ye. After Okladnikov.

population of this region to place weapons in their tombs at all may be sufficient explanation. As evidence of the travel of the Uralian spearhead farther east there is one important piece to be cited. It was found, together with a socketed axe, near Kazakevichevo on the Ussuri river in the Soviet maritime province (figure 28*c, d*).[31] Okladnikov is disinclined to date it before 1000 B C, but there seems to be no reason why it should not be earlier. Since the spearhead is not of the form made in the northern region of China or in Manchuria, the Kazakevichevo specimen suggests a western prototype. That the Uralian spearhead should have had an influence in this remote valley near the Japan Sea is even more remarkable than its having reached China.

The rings of nephrite which were cited earlier as linking the Lungshan neolithic tradition to Baikalia are in their further distribution in China and west Siberia no less indicative of bronze-age contacts. Rings of green and white jade which occur at the site of Turbino resemble those of the Pribaikalye sufficiently to indicate that they were made by a similar method. No certain source of nephrite has been identified in the Urals, and there is a presumption that the technique travelled west with the material itself from the sources in the Vostochny Sayan mountains of south Siberia. The inner Asian route which saw the passage of bronzes was probably followed also by a trade in jade. The nephritic stone, we must suppose, was valued for its rarity and beauty, and no doubt for magical properties of the kind attributed to it later in China, when it is credited with the power to prevent the putrefaction of corpses.[32] The rings are mostly of similar proportions, with a wide central perforation which in Shang China was sometimes furnished with a low flange projecting on both sides. With and without the flange the ring was consecrated in the Chinese official ritual tradition as the *pi*, which the emperor used in sacrifice to heaven. In Shang China jade-carving was practised in the two capitals, the material being almost certainly imported. It is generally assumed that it came from the same places as supplied jade to China in recent times: the districts of Khotan and Yarkand in Hsinkiang.[33] But a more acceptable hypothesis is that the Shang jade was obtained in the first place from a source lying in a region where it was already used to manufacture rings. This would point to Baikalia, whence it might reach Shang China by the same route along the Amur valley as was followed by the bronzes. The Shang custom of burying *pi* with the dead was inherited from the Lungshan neolithic, a culture with connexions extending far to the north-east. In Baikalia the rings were cut from a ground, thin sheet of jade using a template and a flint graver. This method was used for rings found on a Lungshan site in Shantung (where they may be imports from the north) and is similar to that adopted in the manufacture of hardstone (quartzite) rings in south China in the earlier

1st millennium BC. In the Shang sphere a bamboo borer was employed and the edges of the rings are squared.

The method of manufacturing the jade rings, using a hard sand as abrasive, can have differed little from China to the Urals. There is no reason to think that the Baikalian rings were not local products. Kiselev was convinced that the jades found at Seima and Turbino were made of the Baikal nephrite, even if they were made in the west. The differences between the two groups point to more than one centre of manufacture. Bader holds that the stone used for the Turbino rings was obtained in the west, a possibility which has not yet been either excluded by petrological assay or confirmed by the discovery of suitable nephrite in the Urals themselves. The weight of opinion is against him: the probability remains that Baikalian nephrite was traded to west and south-east, reaching the Urals and central China over similar distances; and the trade may have blazed the trail through the wooded-steppe zone that was later to be a channel of communication in the bronze age. But the lack of finds of jade at places along this route, in the Tomsk region for example, is an awkward fact. The Glazkov stage in Baikalia, in which the rings first appear, places them there in the initial bronze phase. Okladnikov dates this phase to the 17–14th centuries BC. In the Urals and in Lungshan and Shang China dates within these limits are acceptable.

The Sino-Siberian relationship is further demonstrated by the bronze knife with decorated handle. It first appears in China at Anyang, where it regularly accompanies the burials of chariots with their charioteers (plate 37*b*),[34] lying near the other bronze equipment of the charioteer.

Usually the knife has a ridge at the root of the blade, the grip may be slotted, and the terminal is formed of a somewhat schematized horse head or ram head, or of a ring, or of a hollow sphere with slotted sides. Often the tip of the blade is bent backwards. But the knives which link north China most clearly with south Siberia are not those most typical of the Anyang, but the ram-headed and the ringed types. They are found also north of Shang, in the zone which includes Inner Mongolia, the Ordos region, Sui Yüan and the northern tracts of Shensi and Hopei, a distinct cultural area, with windows open towards Mongolia rather more than towards central China.

This Northern Zone was the home of pastoralists perhaps already semi-nomadic in Shang times, where the power of the central Chinese state was felt only intermittently, where bronze was cast near the camp fire and not in skilled workshops, a client subregion of the Chinese sphere where metropolitan tools and weapons were rarely imported, but regularly copied. Bronze forms were varied for reasons of local tradition and taste, or the shortcomings of the bronze-smiths. In the late Shang period onwards, it was from this Northern Zone, and with the modifications applied to them in this zone, that Chinese forms of weapons and tools passed beyond to inner Asia; and ideas reaching China from without went through a corresponding transformation on the northern frontier. The connexions of south Siberia with China, established through the Northern Zone, can be followed also well into the post-Shang period. Developments in bronze equipment which took place in central China during the western Chou period, in the 10th–8th centuries, were diffused through the cultural continuum joining Siberia to the south-east. We cannot yet determine whether the path of these influences lay principally through Mongolia or along the Manchurian valleys. By the 8th century BC they had effected the general change in south Siberia which led to the first phase of the Tagar culture.

The bronze knives with ram-head terminals found at Anyang and in the Northern Zone have analogues in the Ordos, in Mongolia and in the Upper Yenisei valley of south Siberia, all of which must be dated to the Karasuk period: they may be as early as the closing centuries of Shang in China, and cannot be later than about 800 BC. In the same period in Siberia local types were developed, in particular knives with terminals in the form of small standing rams or horses. These extend to the Baikalian region, but not to China. One such piece comes from the Turbino cemetery, but the animals it depicts are wild sheep, which were never to be found in the Urals, or nearer to the Urals than the Altai mountains (plate 37a). It is most probably an import from south Siberia, or at least it copies such an import. The bronze knives were never at home in west Siberia and the Urals.

These facts have a curious import for the theme of cultural frontiers: the bronze age of south Siberia participates in the distributions of fundamental bronze types which differ on the one hand by their varying extension to the west, and on the other by the degree, in their south-eastern extension, to which they include the territory of China. Two phases are to be distinguished in these contacts: an earlier, involving spearheads and socketed axes, which linked central China with the far west; and a slightly later one, with the knives as the leading item, which did not extend far west of the Yenisei, and is fundamentally linked with the Chinese Northern Zone and not with the Yellow river valley. Apart from the single Turbino knife with mouflons decorating the handle, the bronze knives conform to the second, more limited area of diffusion. Another type similarly confined is the long-bladed axe with shaft-hole known from south Siberia and from the Chinese Northern Zone (plate 23).[35] It occurs only rarely in the heart of Shang territory, and is perhaps to be regarded as a Northern Zone adaptation of the *ko*-halberd in the first place. Karlgren explains these axes as a case of simple derivation from central China; but then, as Loehr

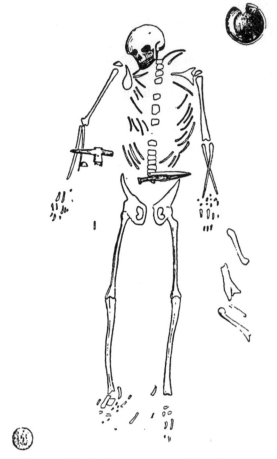

29. Burial at Ujunjul, south Siberia, showing the position of a bronze knife at the waist and of a *pickelaxt* at the right side, the latter having had a shaft three or four feet long. 10th–7th century BC. After Tallgren.

remarks, immediately there arises a difficulty: the derivatives do not resemble the prototypes. If a simple spread of Shang and western Chin metallurgy accounted for the phenomenon of the Northern Zone, we should expect to find there some of the typical Chinese forms: the *ko* and the tanged axe. But these weapons did not establish themselves in the north. The only answer to the problem is to recognize (as Loehr was first to do) that the Northern Zone was a region of primary invention also, competent to adapt any useful ideas which reached it from the higher civilizations lying far to north and south.

In south Siberia the long-bladed axe became the *pickelaxt*, with the shaft-hole near the middle and the upper part sometimes extravagantly decorated (plate 39; figure 29). In post-Karasuk (Tagar) time it travelled west to the

Sauromatian territory south of the Ural mountains. An individual type of dagger – a weapon seldom made in China – was also a product of the Northern Zone and south Siberia, and appears as far west as Tomsk, but no farther. The specimens from the Ordos, judged typologically, look the oldest. In this case there is no question of a central Chinese prototype, and we must accept the dagger as an invention of the Northern Zone.

Thus the later phase of east-west contact demonstrated by the bronzes tends to show that the true cultural boundary between the civilization of the Yellow river valley and inner Asia lay not through the barren and rugged Gobi desert, but along the southern edge of the Northern Zone. This is the country of the Great Walls, which the Chinese began to build in the 4th century B C, monuments to cultural incompatibility. The frontier was not determined by geography. On a line through the middle of the modern provinces of Shansi and Hopei were confronted the civilization of peasants living in large settlements and the culture of tribes of less settled life, in whose economy stock-raising played a bigger part. It looked out to the north across the grasslands which, briefly interrupted by the desert zone (a tract which had not yet reached its present size), stretched to the hills of north Mongolia and Siberia, and it connected with the rich lands of the Manchurian basin and beyond with the parklands of the maritime province of the Soviet Union. It was the Northern Zone also which later was receptive to cultural influences traversing inner Asia from the west, particularly those called Scythic in a later chapter.

Of all the Shang themes which lead to a discussion of ancient Chinese relations with inner and western Asia the war chariot is the most intriguing in its suggestion of a specific contact which cannot be fully substantiated by archaeological evidence (plates 40-42). There is no sign that it yet existed in China in the earlier half of the Shang dynasty.[36] Neither burials of chariots nor the bronze parts of chariots were found in the excavations at Chengchou. The best described of the chariot burials at Anyang is that excavated at Ta-ssŭ-k'ung ts'un in 1953 (plate 42).[37] The chariot had been buried intact and the trace of the timbers was preserved. The only bronze structural parts present here are the axle caps. There are bronze cheek-pieces on the bridle, and the position of the head-harness is recorded by the rows of convex bronze discs which were originally attached to it. The lie of the traces (if there were any) and the course of the reins are uncertain. The horses were attached to a yoke by V-shaped pieces – clad with bronze here – which rested on their necks. The precise manner in which the draught was applied remains obscure. Probably it was entirely at the yoke, the V-shaped members being tied to the horse's neck and shoulders by straps which have left no trace in the tombs; and in this case the harness could hardly have avoided the choking effect such as also hindered the horses'

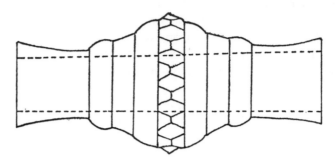

30. Bronze mount for a chariot-wheel hub, excavated at Hsin-ts'un, Honan. The mount is divided into two halves longitudinally, being designed to reinforce an inner wooden hub and the spokes radiating from it. Length 403 mm. 10th–9th century B C. After Kuo Pao-chün.

draught in the harnesses of ancient Mesopotamia and the Mediterranean civilizations.[38] In other burials were found bronzes combining tubes and plates which served to attach, or to decorate the attachment of the shaft and axle to the driver's box. The attention given to the design of the hub is a measure of the technical skill which went into the structure. It is seen best in the bronze-clad hub parts from a chariot grave of the 9th century B C at Hsin-ts'un in Honan. It is composed of six parts, the inner two clasping the whole hub of the wheel. The end of the axle tapers slightly (figure 30).

It is clear that this chariot in general resembles the construction of the near-eastern chariots of the 2nd millennium B C and later, but there are fundamental divergences which have to be taken into account when the origin of the Chinese design is considered. The chariot of Tiglathpileser III of Assyria in the 8th century B C and that of Argishti I of Urartu in the 7th both have massive wheels with wide rims and six or eight sturdy spokes;[39] and an important difference from the Chinese model is the placing of the axle at the back edge of the driver's platform. The shaft is set high over most of its length, at about the level of the horses' shoulders, and the draught is very clearly taken from the animals' necks, which have a broad band of leather or stuff wrapped around them.

In structure, balance and harnessing these chariots are all different from those of the Shang vehicles, and they look much heavier. The peculiar feature of the Chinese design is the yoke harness, with V-shaped pieces resting on the horses' necks, suggesting a later harness used for oxen. That this harness was the only one used in Shang and early Chou times is shown by its appearing regularly in the elaborate ideograph for 'carriage', which is used in inscriptions cast on bronze vessels. Down to about 400 B C, the date of the latest burial of chariots which has been excavated, the construction of the chariot varies not at all in essentials. In many ways it resembles the construction of the four-wheeled marriage or funeral carriage excavated in the 5th Pazyryk Kurgan in the Altai. All these chariots were intended for pulling by two horses. There is a tradition that in his campaigns against barbarians in the north-west, the 9th-century Chou king, Hsüan, used a team of four horses in each chariot. An example of this harness—all four horses under one yoke beam—was excavated at Chang-chia-p'o in Shensi, at a site of western Chou date; but two horses were the rule.[40]

For all its individual design, indeed the superiority of its design and certainly the superiority of its construction, the conclusion seems inescapable that some historical connexion must exist between the war chariots of the Near East and those of Shang, and since there is no question of China having supplied the model for the western chariots, the influence can only have travelled from Western Asia before the design with rear-placed axle, first used *c.* 1600, had become universal. The earliest bridle bits of Shang date, survive only in the cheek-pieces, which are rectangular plates. Through the holes at the centre, and through the horse's mouth passed a bit of perishable material, horn or wood or leather. Another type reflects the method of keeping the bit more firmly in place by attachment at two points to a divided head-strap, the rein coming from the centre. This was the device favoured in Assyria in the 9th–7th centuries B C. In the west the cheek-pieces were by this time already combined with a linked bit. The linked bit duly appears in China, probably in the 8th century B C, but has only rings at the ends into which plain bars, also usually of perishable material, were inserted and lashed in place, there being no holes or lugs for the attachment (plates 44, 45). The circular flat cheek-pieces which were so beautifully decorated in China are not found with bits fixed in them, although this combination was used in the west; and the ring-ended bits were not paired with bar-shaped cheek-pieces. In short, the phenomenon we observe in the case of the chariot itself is repeated: the basic form copies something manufactured in the west, but its treatment in detail by the Chinese is independent and inventive.[41]

In the sequel to the establishment of the Shang state and culture on the middle course of the Huang Ho, the interplay of the two spheres, the central plain and the Northern Zone, provide much of the groundwork to the cultural development. As we know from the oracle sentences, the Shang state had faced hostile territory in the west, and in 1027 B C it was overthrown by an attack which came from this quarter. Material characteristic of the Shang sites of central China is not found much to the west of the junction of the Yellow river with the river Wei. Beyond this frontier neolithic levels of settled sites are followed by pottery and other material which in central China can be shown to follow Shang and so to belong to the western Chou period. One of the most pressing unresolved problems

F

of Chinese archaeology is the question whether the earliest bronze-using culture of the home territory of the tribes who moved east under Chou leadership was contemporary in date with the whole or part of the Shang period of central China, or postdates Shang entirely as is generally assumed.[42]

In the development of the bronze age of China proper, in central China, the great turning-point was the defeat of Shang by the Chou confederacy in 1027 BC. In the branch of bronze production which has been most intensively studied, the ritual vessels and their decoration, a sudden change is seen, coinciding with the beginning of Chou rule. The change is such as no theory of mere distortion of Shang styles can explain; it can only be accounted for on the assumption that an independent tradition of bronze-founding had been forming on the territory neighbouring Shang to the west, at a time no later than the Anyang period of Shang. This is no more than is claimed for the rise of an independent tradition in the Northern Zone; but in the north there is no reason to suppose more than temporary foundry sites, where tools and weapons were cast as need arose. The switch from Shang to Chou styles in central China upon the fall of the Shang bastion is only satisfactorily explained by assuming that comparable bronze-work was already executed in the Chou territory before the advance of the Chou rulers into the central plain.

But any closer discussion of this problem lies outside the limits of this book. The Shang oracle sentences, in which the inhabitants of the western region sometimes figure as enemies, give hints that these peoples were pastoralists: we may speculate that the Shang supply of horses came from the uplands of Shansi and Shensi, both of which were included in the cultural sphere of the Northern Zone and the latter of which was Chou domain. It is noticeable at Anyang that the animal-headed knives and the curved bronze bow-mount (as it is interpreted, and which occurs also in south Siberia in Karasuk and Tagar contexts) are specially associated with chariot burials, in which perhaps the men of the west and north are buried with the horses they brought to Shang.

3

Technology

IN THE ANCIENT WEST, from Iran to Erin's Isle, we recognize a reasonably uniform sequence and analogous rhythms of technological events. It is from just such facts that the diffusionist theory draws its strongest proof. But any inclination we may feel to regard the western development as more or less determined in the order of nature is discouraged by what we see in China. In the first place, over East Asia as a whole, and even in central China itself, the categories of stone, bronze and iron are of less value in archaeological periodization than they are in Europe and Western Asia. Bronze was employed for essential tools and weapons long after iron was available; but at all times bronze tools were rare, rarer than in Europe. Nothing in China proper or in the Northern Zone resembles the hoards of the itinerant European bronze-founders. In metropolitan China we neither trace the growth of metallurgy from the rudimentary stages known in the west, nor discern the effects of successive waves of technological influence coming from elsewhere. In pottery, metalworking and armament the precocity and speed of progress are exceptional, and the persistence of primitive features in all of these techniques hardly less so. In this chapter some early aspects of Chinese metallurgy and architecture are discussed. These unrelated techniques both demonstrate the vigour and isolation of the Chinese tradition. In both, and specially in metallurgy, the cultural boundary was closely drawn around the region of central China on the middle course of the Yellow river. Here the foundations of the metropolitan Chinese tradition were laid.

The early success of bronze-casting in China was the direct outcome of experience gained with pottery kilns of advanced design, such as existed already in the neolithic period (figure 31; plate 47).[1] Kilns of both neolithic and Shang date have been preserved almost intact on a number of sites through their being built partly underground. In design they are similar. The floor of the chamber in which the pots were fired was at ground level more or less, perhaps a little lower, and the furnace and heat-flue were hollowed out in the soil beneath. All that is lacking from the kilns that have been investigated at Yangshao, Lungshan and Shang sites is the walls and roof of the firing chamber. But judging from the circular plan of most of

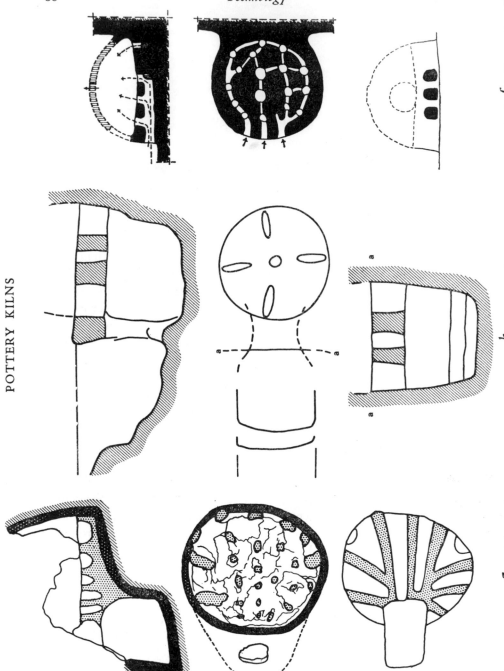

POTTERY KILNS

31. Pottery kilns. (a) Miao-ti-kou: Lungshan neolithic; (b) Pi-sha-kang, Chengchou: late Shang period; (c) Sialk, Iran: late 4th millennium BC. After Ghirshman. Scale c. 1:25.

the chambers and the lower part of walls remaining on some, we can be sure that the covering was usually dome-shaped.

In the history of ceramics in general the principle of the clear separation of furnace, heat-flue and firing chamber is one mastered at an advanced stage of development. In China it was the rule from Yangshao times on. At Pan-p'o in Shensi six kilns were found in the excavations. The simpler type has a broad, short flue leading obliquely upwards to the firing chamber. Another type has the firing chamber set vertically over the furnace, with which it communicates by a shorter, narrow flue. The vertical flue and the longer slanting flue represent two traditions of different origin. The latter principle was to survive to the present day in China, Korea and Japan, in the 'dragon kiln' (*lung yao*) consisting of a succession of communicating kilning chambers built up the slope of a hill, while the vertical arrangement can be matched in Western Asia.

A further refinement of the kiln produced changes in the arrangements for the access of the flame to the firing chamber. Still in the Yangshao period, at Lin-shan-chai near Chengchou, we find the simplest version of the branched flue which tends to spread the flame more evenly through the firing chamber.[2] Here a central partition dividing the flue into two main branches helps to support the pots, but the fuller development of this idea required a pierced floor for the chamber, and this device is attested for the Lungshan period, both at the eponymous site in Shantung and in the latest neolithic level at Miao-ti-kou. The fuel was placed in a sunken space only a little removed from the firing chamber. The flues, as short as is compatible with this arrangement, are many-branched and communicate with the firing chamber by many small and rather irregular perforations in the floor. Two examples of kilns of Shang date are built on the same principle, but the furnace extends farther under the firing chamber, so that the flues become mere vertical openings in the floor, no branching of the flue being necessary. It is the latter form which presents such a remarkable parallel to a pottery kiln excavated at Tepe Sialk in northern Iran, although here the furnace is a little farther separated horizontally from the firing chamber (figure 31c).[3] It would be satisfactory to be able to distinguish among these kilns those destined for oxidizing flame and those for reducing flame, making them correspond to the light and dark coloured traditions of pottery, and to suggest the design, destined to produce a reducing flame, which led to the smelting furnace. Unhappily no such distinction seems possible.[4] It has been suggested that a kiln excavated on a Shang site at Hsing-t'ai in Honan may have been intended to ensure the reducing atmosphere required for dark-surfaced pottery. In either case the advantage of the kilns was that they made direct use of flame and gases at their maximum temperature for firing pottery. The primitive method of kilning by heaping fuel over the pots, as may be seen applied today in south-east Asia and Africa, could never fully exploit the effect of the flame.

Kilns of this design were capable of very high temperatures. The vitrification point of the fine, hard Yangshao pottery varies between 1,000°C and 1,100°C, and the firing temperature was probably between 950°C and 1,050°C. The Yangshao potters were aware of the difference in colour caused to their wares by the use of lime-rich or lime-poor clays. Therefore, seeking a rich red or buff surface they avoided the limey loess, which in any case has a comparatively poor plasticity, and used the natural clays underlying the loess. This preference is less marked after the neolithic period and the quality of much of the pottery is poorer in consequence. In the Shang period the greatest feats of firing are the fine white ware and the thin, hard ware of which a proportion is glazed. The white ware, which was used only for noble vessels, is made from kaolin, but lacks the felspar and silica which later made this clay the basis of porcelain. Analysis has shown that the white pottery of Anyang has undergone a change in firing which can be simulated only by heating for some ten hours at a temperature of 1,125°C. Probably the ware was fired at a slightly higher temperature still, between 1,180°C and 1,200°C.

One consequence of this firing skill was remarkable: the discovery of a felspathic glaze and the method of controlling it. The thin, lemon-coloured or brownish glaze which covers the pottery–a thin fabric of stoneware hardness–has the appearance of a high-fired glaze deliberately applied. Available analyses include the clay body with the glaze, but only high-temperature fluxes are present. The importance of this achievement cannot be exaggerated, for it laid the foundation of the unique ceramic tradition of recent times. The belief that hard glazes were a later invention than the soft lead glazes of the Han dynasty is now wholly disproved; and with that goes Laufer's theory that the lead-glazed wares 'rendered the manufacture of the porcellanous ware possible' (plates 60-62).[5]

Copper melts at 1,083°C. When potters could raise temperatures well above this figure the bronze-smiths can have had little difficulty in designing kilns to smelt and pour their primary metal, or of reaching the lower temperatures required by bronze alloys. Potters' work supplies one reason for the sophisticated level from which the first Chinese metallurgy was launched. In removing oxygen from metallic ore a strongly reducing atmosphere was no less important than temperature: reduction firing had long been a strong point with the Chinese potter. There is a hint from a character occurring in oracle sentences that furnace bellows were employed in the Shang period (figure 36). The control of temperature and furnace atmosphere was evidently very efficient.

There was no problem in the supply of the necessary ores to the Shang

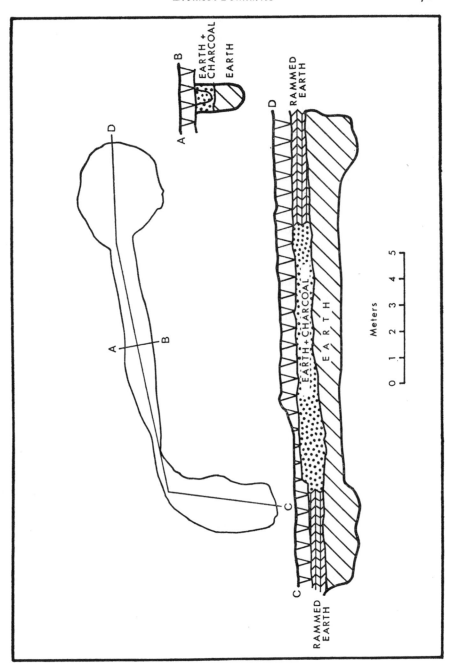

32. Plan and section of a bronze-founding floor at Hsiao-t'un, Anyang.
13th–11th century BC. After Shih Chang-ju.

capitals. Within a 300 km radius from Anyang old records assembled by Shih Chang-ju list a score of places where copper ore has been obtained. That distance stretches the area of probable direct political control by the Shang to its limits. If we take the radius to 3,000 km, so as to embrace the metalliferous region of the south-west, the Tibetan plateau and the mountains of Transbaikalia in the north, the number of possible sources rises to 124. Northwards at least the possibility of trade to that distance must be allowed. The figures for tin are 11 sources within 300 km and a further 6 within 400 km.

At Anyang a foundry floor was investigated in the fifth and sixth seasons (figure 32).[6] Much clay baked with an admixture of straw was found, and fragments of the conical crucibles called 'generals' helmets', made of coarse clay with a middle part containing a notable quantity of straw; also slag and a quantity of malachite. Only the oxidized ore has been found on Shang sites. There was no sign of tin-smelting, but it is plausible that this metal should have been refined at the source and imported in ingots. There was also a distinct trace of a melting furnace. We must suppose that the furnace, possibly quite similar to one of the pottery kilns, was situated at the higher end of the run. The unusual length of the run is proof of the high temperature attained in the firing. The structure is supported by rammed earth at either end, and along the run there are still traces of the charcoal bed that lined it. With the high temperatures available we may assume that the smelting method also allowed for the metal to be tapped, and not recovered merely in ingot form. It is significant that no copper ingots have been recovered in China. The excavation of a foundry site at Chengchou was even more promising, but it has not yet been published in detail.[7] The summary report describes an area of 1,000 sq.m over which more than a thousand fragments of clay moulds lay scattered. There were two intact crucibles, and much evidence of the casting of arrowheads. In one small room with a *pisé* floor some two hundred mould fragments were found.

Discussion of the casting method followed by the Shang bronze-smiths has been unduly influenced by the confident statement made by Yetts in 1929 that the *cire perdue* method was chiefly employed,[8] an opinion that is still repeated in many books. But in 1935 Karlbeck studied some of the beautifully exact parts of clay piece moulds found on Shang sites and demonstrated that they had been in contact with molten metal (plate 49).[9] While the heart of the clay was red, the surface, often sooty or glossy, was grey or black. A particle of bronze was lodged in a minute cavity of a design. Contrary to a view held previously, these multipart moulds had not served only to impress a wax model for investing with clay, nor can such mould parts, fitting precisely together with dowels and sockets for

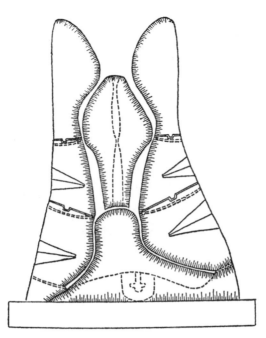

33. Multipart ceramic mould for casting a bronze *chüeh*, as reconstructed
by Shih Chang-ju. Height 250 mm. Late Shang period.

positioning, be what remains over from *cire perdue* casting. Yet the perfec-
tion of Shang bronzes in detail of ornament, thinness of vessel walls and
overall complexity of design, had even to specialists seemed hardly feasible
without recourse to the wax procedure. It seemed hardly credible either
that China should have remained ignorant of a technique of miraculous
efficiency and ease which was known so widely in the west.

In fact the evidence strongly favours direct casting, the molten bronze
being poured into a mould prepared without recourse to a wax model. In
the majority of fine bronzes, particularly in the ritual vessels, the seams
which are to be expected to mark the joints of the mould pieces are quite
lacking, or to be detected only after close and sceptical inspection. They
were either removed with the greatest care after the vessel was cast, without
leaving file marks, or avoided in the first place by lining the mould joints
with clay – a most difficult procedure – before the metal was poured.
Nevertheless, many traces of seams can be found, in places which argue a
plausible structure of the mould components (plate 48). The vertical flanges
cast on many vessels coincide with the joints, or the joints run up a handle
or follow a vertical line of the ornament. The astonishing ingenuity of the
mould-maker was first discussed and illustrated by Shih Chang-ju in 1935
(figure 33).[10] His case was unanswerable, and more recently Barnard has

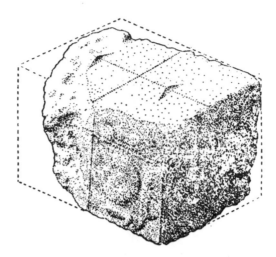

34. Part of a positive model for forming the mould sections for casting a bronze vessel, showing a *t'ao-t'ieh* mask. Hsiao-t'un, Anyang. The longer side measures *c.* 100 mm. 13th–11th century B C (cf. plate 58). After Shih Chang-ju.

elaborated the argument and drawn diagrams of possible moulds for nearly all the known vessel shapes.[11]

    We still lack adequate information on the foundry finds made at Cheng-chou. But here as at Anyang it is noticeable that the number of mould parts reported to be identifiable with parts of surviving bronze objects are few in comparison with the scale and variety of production that must be assumed. The mould parts belong to vessels (those of the *ku*-goblet are remarkably frequent), but they poorly illustrate the array of different pieces that must have been needed to cast vessels of intricate projecting ornament, handles bearing monster masks, etc. It appears therefore that the mould parts, particularly complicated ones, were normally destroyed when the cast metal was removed from them, being left in small fragments which escaped the excavators' notice or are not capable of reconstruction. To avoid damage which may occur to the bronze in cooling, especially when there is fine relief work on the surface, it may have been the custom to knock away the clay mould while the casting was still very hot. All of this would indicate a procedure in which one main advantage in the employment of direct casting and piece moulds, the possibility of producing several castings from a single mould, was of no account. The moulds would thus as a rule be manufactured afresh for each operation.

    The manufacture of the clay moulds presupposes the use of some kind of positive model at the start.[12] For this purpose a finished bronze would serve, or the model might be carved in any suitably soft material. But among the abundant material recovered from the Anyang tombs, in which many pieces closely resemble each other, there is no record of cases of exact resemblance arguing use of the same mould or model. Whatever the standardization of the mould making, it still allowed for some variation in individual pieces. On the cast vessels many details of ornament exactly match those in other vessels, even when their disposition and accompanying decoration differ somewhat from one vessel to another. A few positive clay models of parts of vessels recovered at Anyang throw light on the procedure followed in preparing moulds. One of these is plainly part of a *hu*-vase; the other is covered with ornament and represents the middle part of the bronze casket called *fang yi* (figure 34). Some of the design is raised in the clay, but it is clear that these birds have themselves been impressed from moulds. We glimpse the provision for mass-production which determined much of the method. But the surface around the birds, and the birds' bodies, are painted in red with detailed ornament of the usual kind. It must be supposed that the paint is a guide for carving the smaller relief of the mould. The clay is baked but soft. From this positive model, when the ornament had been completed, the mould was to be made, no doubt merely by wrapping it in clay and cutting the wrapping at convenient places.

It is often noticeable that the relief of the inside of a vessel follows that of the outside fairly closely: the bronze wall is kept economically thin. It is tempting to guess at ways of achieving such close correspondence between the mould and the mould core, and many scholars have yielded inventively to the temptation. Cores do not survive, for they are shattered when they are removed from the bronze. Since it is likely that the mould parts were drawn from the casting while the latter was still suitably hot, it is likely that the removal of the core was left until cooling was completed. The base, hollow legs, etc., of vessels often retain much of the core material. Contemplation of the problem presented by the core has prompted one suggestion involving wax; that a layer of wax was placed on an approximate model of the intended casting and either carved or impressed with the desired ornament: this model was then used to produce the mould, so that afterwards, the wax being melted off, a core of just the right size and modelling was left. If this method was ever used it is difficult to believe that the mould-maker should not have discovered the *cire perdue* routine as a short-cut to his goal.

Some other features besides the record of mould joints point to the direct pouring of bronze into piece moulds. These are perforations explicable as devices for holding the mould core in place, and fragments of bronze spacers ('chaplets') inserted beforehand which became incorporated into the side of the vessel (plate 54). In the case of the *ku* a pre-cast disc serving as a bottom to the goblet was inserted into the mould before the bronze was poured; and there are cruciform holes, or depressions covered by the thinnest web of bronze, just under this bottom. A theory advanced by Karlbeck that the cruciform holes were intended for a key which was passed through them to position the mould core in both the horizontal and the vertical planes, has not been proved, although no other explanation of the curious feature has been suggested. But it is noteworthy that the cruciform perforations appear also on an ivory goblet of Shang date, where it is difficult to attribute any meaning to them at all. It is just as likely that they are symbolic or ideographic as that they should preserve a minor technical device of the bronze goblets.[13]

Other traces of a technical procedure which still defies explanation are the taut lines raised in sharp, low relief on the base, within the foot-rim, of bronze vessels of Shang and early Chou date (plate 52). Typically there are two sets of parallel lines, intersecting so as to divide the base into small diamond-shaped figures. The lines cast in the bronze are the reversed image of lines scored on soft material – the unbaked clay of the mould core which formed the footrim – with a sharp point. Often the nature of the scorings indicates a point of the kind that can be cut from bamboo. Possibly these scorings helped to hold in place a sheet of wax serving the same purpose as the metal spacers used elsewhere in the mould, that is, to hold apart core and outer mould parts before the metal was poured. In this instance the wax would separate the mould cores which formed the foot and the basin of the vessel. If indeed wax was used in this way, the failure of Shang bronze-smiths to hit upon the technique of *cire perdue* casting is still more surprising, and their isolation from the all but universal tradition of bronze-age technology all the more peculiar. On a few vessels of Shang date, which are contemporary with vessels having the intersecting parallel scorings, the base is decorated with similar thread-like lines raised in relief forming geometric designs derived from the rhomboid figures of the intersecting lines. There are instances from the early western Chou period of figures freely drawn; such as the coiled dragon on the base of a *p'an*-basin (plate 53). In most cases the lines would still serve the purpose suggested for them above.[14] Eventually the lines are broader and in rounded relief, indicating possibly that their original intention was forgotten, and it is in this form that they were imitated on archaistic vessels cast in much later times.

Cire perdue casting was known in Western Asia by the early 3rd millennium BC. It spread to temperate Europe in the middle bronze age, and there, as in the Mediterranean civilizations, wax-casting became the method for all elaborate and artistically sophisticated work. When was it adopted in China? Since the routine of wax-casting does not leave recognizable

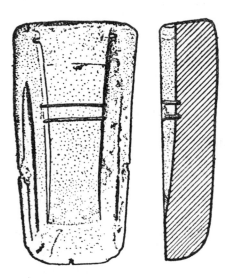

35. Stone mould for casting a bronze socketed axe. Hsiao-Kuan-chuang,
T'ang-shan, Hopei. Length 130 mm. 6th century BC. After An Chih-min.

debris, its use at Anyang may have been overlooked. Whether the method
was employed to a minor extent, or in some way combined with the use
of piece moulds in the production of the fine-cast ornament, it is certain
that the prevalent technique was that of direct casting, into moulds prepared
wholly or mainly without the intervention of wax. Barnard's opinion that
wax-casting did not reach China before *c.* AD 200, when it was introduced
from the west by Buddhists for the production of their cult images, is
hardly defensible.[15] Such objects as the ram heads of Shang knives or the
handles of an 8th-century bronze vessel (plates 37, 55), while they at first
sight suggest the wax method, may only witness to the extraordinary
refinement achieved in the use of multipart moulds. But a pair of openwork
handles belonging, at the latest, to the 5th century BC, are unthinkable
without the clay investment of wax models, and an *ajouré* strap mount of
the 9th–8th century BC is already suggestive (plates 56, 57). Not all the
moulds used in central China were assembled from components of burnt
clay. A trickle of finds of mould parts carved in stone, from the Shang
period onwards, is proof that the method common in inner Asia was sometimes followed also in China. A small fragment of a two-part stone mould
was found at Anyang: moulds of this type were probably employed for
axes, knives and *ko*-halberds. Specimens of the bivalve stone mould (including a number for the socketed axe) have been found at places on a line
strung through inner Asia, along the route postulated for the Sino-Uralian
contacts discussed in the last chapter (cf. figure 35, a mould of post-Shang

date, but representative of the northern tradition). If a form of spearhead made in the middle Urals was copied in China it is likely that the western method of casting was also adopted. The distinguishing technical require-ment of the socketed axe: the accurate positioning of the inner mould core, is a device thoroughly in keeping with Chinese casting practice, and may be added to the other arguments for the Chinese origin of this tool.

The largest bronze casting of Shang date so far discovered is the ssǔ-mu-wu *ting*, a four-legged rectangular vessel for sacrificial foods, which was excavated from the great tomb at Wu-kuan-ts'un near Anyang in 1950 (plate 32).[16] It stands 1·33 m high and weighs 900 kg. The metal for it must have filled some eighty of the 'helmet-shaped' clay crucibles of the kind found on Shang foundry sites. A work of these dimensions argues a foundry of some size and organization, and probably a sustained furnace temperature, well above the melting pointing of the alloy, in order to allow a fair flow or portage between the furnace and the site of the huge mould. The *Chou li*, a work compiled in the 3rd century BC from much older material, in which forms of ritual, social organization and even industrial practices are reduced to rule, names six clans for metalwork, each prescribed a special task. Apart from this and other references in ritualistic texts of late Chou and Han date, little can be gleaned about the industrial organization: but it appears that certain clans or guilds enjoyed a monopoly of their part in the process of bronze manufacture. This would be in keeping with the oriental tradition that required such groups of artisans working in the capital to be put under the control of the govern-ment. The similar and historically better known system in force in the early dynastic period in Japan, where forms of governmental and official organization imitated China, corroborated the information given in the *Chou li*.

Of greater interest, however, are Shang oracle texts investigated by Satō Taketoshi,[17] which name clans in contexts suggesting connexions with industry, in some cases clearly with metallurgy. Thus the *t'o* or *ya t'o* clan is designated by an ideograph whose linear descendant, by the 2nd century AD (in the *Shuo wen chieh tzǔ*), had come to be glossed as *nang*, a bag (figure 36). It is plausibly argued that the ideograph represents bellows. Even if the Shang pottery kiln could generate enough heat to melt bronze easily, in the processes of smelting, refining and casting there would be great advantages in a blast furnace activated by bellows. A system of clans each charged with one part of the procedures of bronze manufacture, from securing the ore to cleaning up the casting, could hardly be improved upon as a means of perpetuating a technique unchanged, even of resisting the advantages offered by the wax process. At Hou-ma in Shansi, where recently a profusion of mould parts and positive clay models were dis-

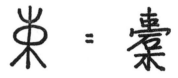

36. Rubbing of a relief depicting iron-making, excavated from the site of a tomb of the 1st or 2nd century AD at Hung-tao-yuan, T'êng-hsien, Shantung. The section on the left shows what appears to be a large air pump; in the central section iron is being forged. The operation in progress on the right is not clear. The ideographs included in the figure are a Shang form occurring in the oracular sentences and its argued equivalent in the current script, i.e. *t'o*, 'bag opening at both ends'. After Wen-wu.

covered in excavations, the routine differs little from that inferred for Shang (plate 50).[18] A reason for the speedier and wider spread, as compared with East Asia, of bronzes of uniform quality through bronze-age Europe lies in the 'detribalized' and itinerant status which its bronze-smiths seem to have enjoyed. No such phenomenon is perceptible in China, where bronze hoards of the kind found in the west are unknown.

The isolation of the Chinese metallurgical tradition is no less apparent in the composition of bronze. This is far from observing the standard of about one-tenth tin to nine-tenths copper which was adopted so early and maintained so constantly in Western Asia and Europe. In China lead was much used, but even when it is absent, the proportion of tin may still vary between 10 per cent and 20 per cent; and even combined with tin, the proportion of lead varies between 1 per cent and 18 per cent. No satisfactory explanation has been found for these vagaries: so far no significant correlations of the ingredients have been observed. Yet it does not appear that the lead-bearing and tin-bearing ores were used indiscriminately, being indistinguishable to the Shang bronze-founders. Nor can it be said that lead was a cheaper substitute for tin in castings intended for burial with the dead; or that it entered into the composition of decorative work, while tin, which hardens the alloy better, was reserved for weapons and tools. The presence of lead (which remains mixed, not dissolved, in copper in the form of minute droplets) helps towards a flawless casting; but it contributes less than tin towards the lowering of the melting point of the alloy. The advantage to art of a lead-rich bronze, which Greek sculptors appreciated, was in China probably fortuitous.[19, 20]

In the manufacture of weapons iron superseded bronze in China only in the course of the earlier Han dynasty, in the last two centuries B C.[21] Before that, in tombs of the Warring States period (4th–3rd centuries B C) iron objects are fairly common, but they are confined to knives, tools – including hoes and spades – and occasional ornaments, such as the hooks which attached belts, swords and quivers. The finest of these iron hooks are encrusted with gold (plate 68). At the western end of the steppe belt iron appears in graves which represent the transition from the Andronovo to the Scythic culture. From the late 6th century the expansion of the Scythian and the allied Sauromatian culture in the territory between the Black Sea, the Urals and the Caspian Sea, went hand in hand with the spread of iron metallurgy.[22] The relation of China to this phenomenon is still uncertain; but whether China was a recipient or an instigator of the knowledge of iron which was so rapidly communicated through central Asia and south Siberia, we should expect to see the first signs of iron there in the 6th century B C. But so far satisfactory *archaeological* evidence for so early a date of iron is lacking in China, where the nomads' readiness to adopt iron for swords was not imitated. Until the eve of the Han dynasty the bronze sword remained the normal Chinese arm.

The iron tools found in Chinese tombs of the 4th–3rd centuries B C have all the appearance of *cast* iron. Whether they are adzes or socketed axes their shapes do not suggest forging. A passage in the *Tso chuan* is much quoted as proof that iron, and in its cast form, was well known in the later 6th century, that is, somewhat earlier than the earliest time to which we can attribute iron on archaeological evidence alone. In the year 512 B C a minister of state of the northern state of Chin is reported to have levied from the people a quarter of a ton of iron for the casting of tripod vessels on which penal laws were to be inscribed.[23] The casting of the *ting* would be a skilled operation, and iron must have been a common commodity to make the levy worth while; so it seems reasonable, if this literary evidence is accepted, to put back the introduction of iron metallurgy at least to the beginning of the 6th century. This conclusion agrees with a curious argument: that the spade-shaped coins which circulated in the 7th–6th centuries in all the northern Chinese states except Ch'i, presuppose the existence of iron.[24] Here it is assumed that a bronze currency would not be issued while

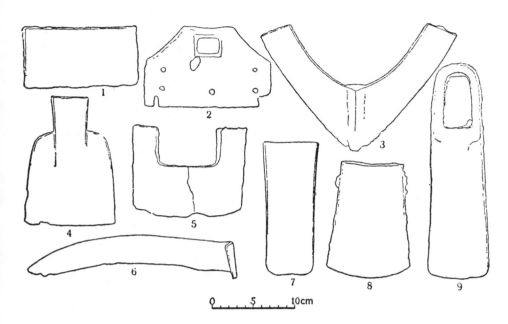

37. Iron hoes, spade edges and axes. No. 2 excavated at Shao-kou,
Loyang, Honan, the rest from Ku-wei-ts'un, Hui-hsien, Honan. 5th–4th
century B C.

bronze was still the staple metal, and that the spade money must copy iron
spades, since only iron could be plentiful enough to supply farmers with a
common tool. But this reasoning would indicate iron no less in the Shang
and western Chou periods when bronze socketed spades were buried in
the great tombs.[25] In such early times the bronze specimens, of reduced size,
can only have been meant as symbols of the wooden spades, or bronze spades
employed in excavating the pits.

It is doubtful if the *Tso chuan* testimony should be accepted. The character
'iron' in this passage seems not to have been questioned by modern scholarship, but the identity or meaning of almost every other character in the
sentence has been questioned and variously interpreted. While archaeological corroboration is lacking, final judgment on the *Tso chuan* record is
best suspended; and the coin argument can only be substantiated by a find
of iron spades in suitably early context. This has not yet occurred, and
archaeological evidence does not at present warrant dates for iron much
before the mid-5th century B C. Certainly there is no unquestioned find of
iron dating so early as 600 B C.[26]

The iron tools discovered in recent excavations consist for the most
part of hoes, socketed axes, spades and a few sickles (figure 37). As a rule

G

collections of these tools placed in tombs have not included knives, and indeed these, like the swords, are not commonly found before the Han period. The origin of the tool shapes presents no difficulties. The axes copy the socketed bronze type which continued in use in central and north China from the Shang dynasty until the 5th or 4th century B C. Often these are shaped as adzes. The spades are of the type already attested for the late Shang period by a find at Ta-ssŭ-k'ung-ts'un (plate 51). Rare as finds of the bronze spades are, we must assume that they persisted in use through the western Chou period. It is not unlikely that a wooden spade of similar form was made, with some kind of reinforced socket. In many instances the surviving iron tool is in any case only an edging which must have been mounted on wood, arming an axe, spade or hoe. A fully formed iron axe with cast shaft-hole is conspicuously absent from the array of tools. There are examples on the other hand of narrow and broad types of hoe with comparatively thin blade and a collar strengthening the shaft-hole. The ploughshare is represented only by the reinforcement of the edge, designed rather elaborately. There is care to save metal by keeping the blade thin and stiffening it with a moulding: in hoes a little extra weight would not perhaps have been a disadvantage. These tools clearly do not follow stone predecessors closely, although the narrower hoe recalls Lungshan stone tools. Only one form is a simple transference into iron: reaping-knives reproducing the stone crescentic knife with two holes and the trapezoid knife with a single hole. These iron specimens both come from a northern site, in Liaoning, where they hardly antedate the 2nd century B C.

Iron tools of the types described above have been found in most of the northern provinces of China: Liaoning, Honan, Shansi and Hunan. This distribution suggests that iron metallurgy reached south China slowly, hardly spreading there before the 2nd and 1st centuries B C. In the south agriculture was less advanced, and the frontier of neolithic economy retreated slowly. The iron tools do not appear in humble graves. Their presence may indicate the grave of a monopolistic iron master: some measure of monopoly seems to have existed even before the Han period, and Han politicians urged the government to take iron production into its own hands. We are fortunate in possessing a number of iron moulds destined to produce tools similar to iron specimens which survive. These were excavated at Hsing-lung in Hopei, and are themselves masterpieces of casting.[27] The two valves of the moulds are hinged at the lower end and each is supplied with an iron core. There would be no difficulty in casting from such moulds provided they were heated beforehand. Traces of core-clay still adhere to some of the iron tools, pointing to clay moulds, while others are completely clean, in a state comparable with the employment of metal moulds in their manufacture. Some pieces upon laboratory

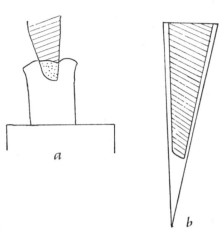

38. The forging of an iron socketed axe. (*a*) The heated iron held for forming by cold punch; (*b*) the finished axe. After Sun T'ing-lieh.

examination proved to have a crystal structure caused by over-rapid cooling, a fault to be expected from the employment of metal moulds.

The first scientific investigation of excavated iron tools, published by Sun T'ing-lieh in 1956, contained an unexpected conclusion: that, in spite of the improbable shape, some of the implements with deep sockets were fashioned by forging (figure 38).[28] His first observation, made on a socketed spade, was that particles of impurities were scattered through the metal, each particle being encased in an oxidized layer. Had the metal ever been in the liquid state for casting, these particles, in themselves lighter than pure iron and rendered still lighter by their coat of oxide, would certainly have come to the surface of the melt and would not have appeared in the finished article. The iron of the spade thus had never been molten: it was melted at a low temperature and refined by hammering from a bloom. The other evidence was supplied by layers of decarburization on the surface, and the confused state of the metal structure at some places. The decarburization (argues Sun T'ing-lieh) was the result of secondary work, by long hammering, carried out wholly in an oxidizing atmosphere. It was concluded that the shape was achieved by forging; yet only a faint hint of forged seams appeared in the structure of the metal, and no continuous line. Either the forging was of a superb kind, which avoided all unwanted oxidization of the metal (unlikely in view of the decarburization) or the piece was hammered to shape without having to fold and weld. This could have been done by driving a suitable wedge-shaped tool into the hot metal, and is a method which was still employed in China in recent years. But these findings did not dispose of the problem. Analysis carried out in 1960 on 4th-century iron (a hoe from Liaoning) showed that the metal was a *cast* iron made workable by mixing with a wrought iron, so that in the microscopic structure features typical of each metal remained. This process of 'softening' iron (there are modern instances in China) may explain the use of the word *chu*, meaning to cast or pour, in texts which apply it even to such uncastable objects as swords.[29]

As a result of these tests the history of early iron working in China is placed in a more intelligible context. Archaeology gives no support for iron before 500 BC nor despite what has been said, does it furnish proof that casting preceded forging. It would appear rather that both treatments were practised from the first. This conclusion has surprising implications. In the west, for some two thousand years after its discovery, iron was obtained from the ore as a bloom, an impure lump, from the furnace, and purified and shaped by hammering. In China it was obtained at the start either as a bloom, or poured and cast: here, if any interval separates the adoption of the two methods, it is short and not yet perceptible in the archaeological record.

If the new metallurgy was first practised in central China, it is natural that the simpler of the two techniques, forging, first found its way to the southern provinces. Iron conferred a military advantage by making possible the manufacture of long and strong swords. But in China one discerns reasons why this advantage was not seized upon at once, particularly in the metropolitan centre. Here military conservatism, the habit of horse-riding, the increasing arming of infantry with the crossbow – all this may account for the evident delay in exploiting fully the capabilities of the iron sword. There are indications that this weapon was first made in quantities in the south: pre-Han tombs of the state of Ch'in at Ch'angsha and Heng-yang in Hunan have produced a total of 33 specimens. They are long and narrow: no longer the short stabbing weapon of the horseman, allied to the akinakai of steppe tradition, but swords a man wielded on foot. Sekino Takeshi has enlarged on the change of tactics which this implies.[30] He suggests that the possession of the long sword more than any other military factor aided the armies of the Ch'in state to conquer the whole of China in the mid-3rd century BC. The histories speak of more than a million of Ch'in's enemies beheaded in the war. Whether the comparatively light iron sword was specially efficient in decollation is questionable, but its adoption throughout China certainly coincided with Ch'in's rise to power.

The iron swords are of two kinds. The two-edged type shows no influence in its design beyond that of the bronze short sword. The guard and terminal are similar, made of bronze or even jade, and passed over the narrow tang of the iron blade. The other is a single-edged sword, remarkably light, which has a ring as terminal. It is little more than an enlarged version of the ring-handled knife whose history in the north goes back to the western Chou period. A few of these swords were made of bronze: the terminal of the grip could be made separately, and was often adorned with bird-heads within the ring, and gilded. Such a sword terminal was found in a lacquer toilet box in a tomb of about 200 BC at Ch'ang Sha. Swords of this general type passed eventually to Japan and there founded the tradition of the iron sword removable fittings.

ARCHAEOLOGICAL RESEARCH in the last decade has thrown light also on the early history of architecture. The Chinese style of wooden trabeate building shows an unusual uniformity wherever it has spread: in Japan, where some of the earliest examples are preserved, in Korea and Vietnam. The principles underlying the construction are uncompromising: once the style was established in the last few pre-Han centuries the essential features remained unaltered to the present day. It is not a style easily adapted to or hybridized with other building traditions, so that the limits of its geographic distribution are sharply defined. The high-raking roofs, deep overhanging eaves and elaborate brackets springing from pillars engaged in the walls symbolize China to the world more effectively than any other branch of its art. Architecture in stone was in almost every respect subservient to the wooden style, to a degree which almost deprives it of significance: its ornament could only imitate wood, and size alone could not confer on it the impressiveness of wooden pillars and beams.[31]

The curve of roofs was a fashion established by the T'ang period; it is absent in Han buildings, where gables and eaves have straight lines. In other respects the essential characters of the buildings, simple in principle, were well established in Han times. A building consists of a setting of pillars, their lower ends resting on some sort of stone foundation, not engaged in the ground. Their tops are linked by beams. The wide eaves of the tile-clad roof project beyond the outer pillars so much that their weight must go far towards balancing the weight of the rest of the roof, the line of outer pillars acting as the fulcrum. To support the eaves brackets project from the tops of the pillars, or rather from blocks set on top of these which act as capitals. This statement covers all the structural principles of Chinese buildings through their whole history. No use is made of immovable triangular frames in the roof supports, side-thrust being minimized by building weighty eaves.

Since the lower ends of the pillars are not buried in the ground there is a natural tendency to place all important buildings on a stone or brick platform, which is larger than the floor of the building itself and provides a walk around the building. Naturally it is convenient to enclose this walk under cover of the projecting eaves, and the building may thus become surrounded by a continuous ambulatory. The walls of the latter, and the walls filling the spaces between the main pillars, will be decorated with a variety of openings, or lattice work, confined to certain bays or repeating in the bays; but the chief ornamental resources, strongest in purely architectural effect and a touchstone of one's appreciation of the whole style, was the bracketing showing beneath the eaves, and the jutting eaves themselves emphasized by the lines of terminal tiles. The multiplication of layers of brackets went to great lengths in post-Han times. As purely functional devices they often look, and almost certainly are, unnecessary; like the vaulting of Gothic buildings, not every piece is an engineering necessity, and some pieces may be no more than a statement, more or less fantastic, of the stressed system of the whole building. The walls have no structural importance and are given no notable architectural rôle. They could be made of lath and plaster, or of mere wooden panels.

Most of these customs in building can be traced back to the feudal period, and some of them even earlier. Even the design of the neolithic houses is not irrelevant to the later tradition. The houses at Pan-p'o conform approximately to 5 building levels, and the more elaborate buildings belong to the later levels.[32] At levels 5 and 4 (numbering from the bottom) most of the houses are nearly square in plan, and sunk four steps below the surface. The steps lead down to a threshold which separates the interior from the entrance. The flanking post-holes show that the entrance was roofed, forming a long porch. The position of the fireplace varies: in the simplest houses it is placed a little to one side, because the centre of the floor was occupied by a single roof pillar, which implies a conical or at least pyramidal roof. But others have a central fireplace, which implies a different arrangement of roof-supports, presumably with a short roof ridge; and here the porch was weighty, resting on four stout pillars (figure 39). In level 3 there is a hut with the interior post-holes preserved: we see that the roof ridge was at right-angles to the entrance. The lie of the burnt timbers surviving on the floor suggests the slope of the rafters – they sloped up from all sides to the short ridge. The roofing here was of combustible material, probably rush thatch; other houses had a thick layer of clay over the thatching, which was baked when they burned and was found strewing the floor.

The largest building excavated on the site was nearly square in plan. It belongs to the later level (no. 2) and seems to mark the most advanced

39. Reconstruction of a neolithic round house from the evidence of excavation at Pan-pʻo, Shensi. After *Hsi-an Pan-pʻo*.

stage of house construction. Its size – almost 16 m wide – suggests that it had some communal rôle. The main structure consisted of four massive pillars, each about 450 mm in diameter set in the sunken floor some distance from each corner. This arrangement gave the greatest amount of clear space in the centre of the room. But the lines of small post-holes on the edge of the higher level around the sunken floor indicate that the eaves of the roof still descended close to the ground, as is assumed to be the case with the smaller huts. Here the post-holes are reasonably good proof of this, for the small posts cannot have taken the full weight of rafters at any height, or even close to the ground. Here and there some of the eaves supports were stouter posts, and set a little farther in – further proof that the roof sloped down to a level close to the ground.

But the greatest interest of this house lies in the massive pillars which appear to have stood in the room. They must have supported stout beams carrying the main burden of the rafters. Thus already the central problem of Chinese wooden architecture must have been envisaged: the means of keying the tops of pillars to the horizontal beams. Eventually there were three sets of beams to be locked together over the tops of pillars: the transverse and longitudinal beams in the horizontal plane, and the major rafters sloping down from the ridge. The subsequent history of Chinese architecture is broadly governed by the complication of this problem and its solution.

In the Pan-p'o house attention is paid to the footings of the pillars. The post-holes were found surrounded at the lip by a double fillet of carefully kneaded clay. This device was intended to protect the ends of the pillars from damp and rot. It cannot have been very effective. Later the solution was to avoid burying the ends of the pillars altogether.

The round houses at Pan-p'o were built on lines similar to the rectangular ones. One of them, in level 4, is reconstructed from a foundation particularly well preserved. Around the edge of the floor (which is not sunken) is a line of close-set post-holes, 80-120 mm in diameter. Taken with the four larger pillars rising from the middle of the floor, leaving space between them for a fireplace, the outer fringe of small pillars again points to a roof sloping on all sides to a level fairly close to the ground. There are also two lines of post-holes extending inward for a few feet from the entrance. Along the greater part of the line of the outer post-holes and those at the entrance is the remains of the lowest few inches of an earth wall which encased the posts. In their reconstruction the excavators have shown this wall rising a considerable height to meet the eaves. Since the floor is not sunken, one would expect the eaves to be held higher above ground level. In the case of a round hut with sunken floor, it is assumed that the eaves reached down to the ground. The roofing was a thickish layer of clay tempered with straw. Fragments of this material were found strewn on many of the house floors.

In the Shang and Chou periods our knowledge from archaeology of ordinary dwellings is thus far poor, but something can be said of the more pretentious edifices. The houses of the Lungshan culture, in general resembling those of Yangshao as excavated at Pan-p'o, have one distinguishing feature which persisted into the bronze age: the preparation of foundations by pounding earth. The wall at the site of Lungshan was also built by this means. In the alluvial area of north China, beyond the loess region, the soil conditions were perhaps less favourable to the house with sunken floor; the construction of *pisé* foundations, and the raising of these slightly above the general ground level, had distinct advantages. At Anyang *pisé* foundations were made on a large scale. The method was to spread layers of soil, presumably within timber frames, to a depth of an inch or two, and to pound it hard with an instrument measuring no more than two or three inches across the face. Both the lines dividing the original layers and the impressions of the ram on the surfaces of layers were visible to the excavators.

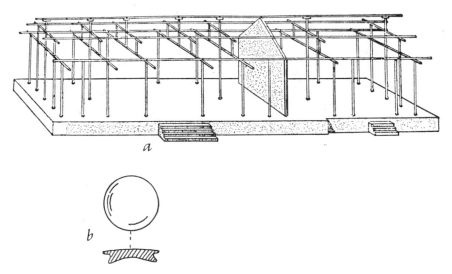

40. (*a*) Reconstruction of the timber framing of a building on a podium of rammed earth 20 m long. Hsiao-t'un, Anyang, sector C; after Shih Chang-ju; (*b*) bronze footing for a wooden pillar from the same site, 150 mm wide. C. 12th–11th century B C.

A number of oblong foundations some 20–40 m long and about 8 or 9 m wide were discovered on the site. One such platform was made of particularly clean yellow earth, had no traces of a superstructure, and was interpreted to be an altar. On others the siting of pillars was indicated by the disposition of large stones – river boulders – on which the pillars had stood. For the method now was to stand a pillar on a stone buried with its flat surface flush with the surface of the podium of *pisé*. In a few places pillar footings of bronze were found, circular, with a depression to receive the end of the pillar; but these were rare (figure 40*b*). Sector C of the site was distinguished by the immense number of slaughtered human victims buried in graves sited in relation to buildings. Of these a certain number, perhaps five or six, were raised on *pisé* platforms; and on the platforms alignments of stones recorded the positions of pillars and the spatial division of bays. Some alignments suggest long buildings with projecting eaves on one side, with subdivision into rooms of different size, as indicated by a double row of posts at one side; others are set closely together in double rows certainly indicating gateways. But these regularities still do not permit a reasonable reconstruction.[33]

In the north part of the site, however, one foundation platform with pillar footings allowed reconstruction to a useful degree of certainty (figure 40*a*). The total length is 28·4 m; the wider part is 8 m across and the narrower 7·3 m. It is clear that the stones have not been much disturbed:

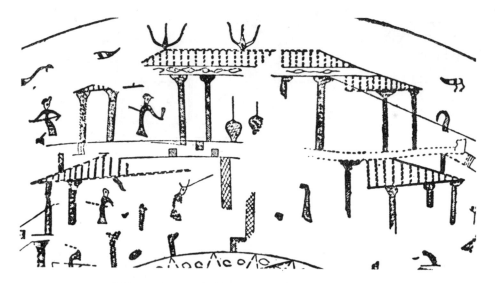

41. Detail of design on a bronze bowl excavated at Hui-hsien, Honan, showing a building raised on a high podium, surrounded by a gallery at a lower level. 5th–4th century B C.

only one was found seriously out of place. Evidently there was not a gallery down one side, as in some of the buildings in sector C. It is noticeable that, except for the ends, the spacing of pillars is for the most part about 3 m. One may allow that the stones had been disturbed to some small degree when the building fell in ruin or was despoiled. The intervals between the stones are sufficiently regular – about 3 m – for us to suppose that the pillars were originally equally spaced around the perimeter.

Giving due weight to the four close-set pillars at the ends, Shih Chang-ju assumed a roof structure raised in three stages. Some such explanation certainly is called for, but one might object to his reconstruction that it requires bearing beams some 6 m long to bridge from side to side at the places where no central pillar is recorded by a stone. This is excessive: more probably pillar footings are missing for some central pillars, and the whole building was composed of equal bays, measuring 3 m square; but if we accept the long tie-beams postulated by Shih Chang-ju, the places which *have* a central pillar may have been the positions of walls dividing the building into several rooms.

There is no reason to think that the outward appearance of Shang buildings was necessarily as rustic as Shih Chang-ju shows it; but the ground plans are simple, and it is clear that the potentialities of pillar and beam design had been little exploited. It is not until some seven centuries later that we have direct evidence of the shapes of roofs. This consists of pictures

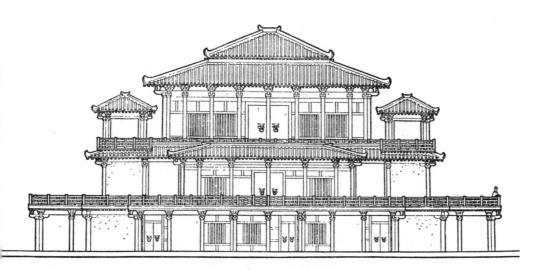

42. Reconstruction of the elevation of a ceremonial building excavated
in the southern suburb of Ch'ang-an, Shensi. 1st–2nd century A D.
After Wang Shih-jen.

of buildings engraved on bronze vessels of the 5th–4th centuries B C, of
which that found on a bronze bowl excavated at Hui-hsien is typical
(figure 41).[34] In all these scenes the buildings are the centre of festival or
ritual performances, and it is possible that they are temples. They are
certainly intended as august buildings, and they display some new features.
The roof is tiled: the tiles themselves are found and dated at least as early
as the 4th century B C. The pillars are surmounted by expanding capitals
and evidently painted. But the main peculiarity of these bronze drawings
is that two buildings appear to be placed one above the other; though the
relationship of the two is not clear, it is not merely a whim of the artist
or a conventional perspective. The explanation of the drawing is clear if
one glances at the structures surviving on some city sites of the late Chou
period. The most prominent feature at the capital of the state of Chao in
Hopei, the Chao Wang Ch'eng, is a stepped rectangular platform with a
base measuring 210 by 288 m, rising to 13·5 m (plate 63).

Crowned with a pillared building and skirted by one or more continuous
covered galleries beneath on all four sides, a mound of this kind would
have resembled the type of building depicted on the bronzes. A tradition
of royal buildings consisting essentially of a high platform had subsisted
from the time of the Chou conquest. Wen Wang, ruler of the Chou
confederacy in the west, on the eve of the conquest possessed such a *ling-t'ai*
'spirit platform'. To this tower the king resorted for solemnities. The ritual
institution it served and the shape of its construction were imitated, it is

43. Pottery models of houses raised on pillars, found near Canton.
1st–2nd century AD. After An Chih-min.

alleged, by the feudal princes of later times, notoriously by Ling king of
Ch'u whose *chang-hua-t'ai*, or resplendent adorned tower, was castigated
by the Han commentator as incorrect by the canon of the ancient Chou
emperor. The principle of the building with a solid core of earth and
presenting two or three storeys in the elevation was to survive at least to
the mid-Han period. Judging from the representations on bronze the
buildings of the 5th–4th centuries BC had achieved a certain sophistication
in the design of the roof (figures 41, 42). The line of the eaves of the lower
roof shows interlocking tiles. The relation of this level to the upper one
is intelligible if one assumes that a *ling-t'ai* type of building is intended, for
the upper pillars would hardly otherwise be sited over the intercolumnar
sections of the beams resting on the lower pillars. The lower edge of the
tiling of the upper roof appears to be hidden behind a low vertical facing
which is decorated, and at either end of this 'upper storey' are further
extensions of the eaves, forming lateral galleries on the upper level. These

upper galleries correspond to the gallery at the lower level that surrounds the solid foundation block which we have supposed to exist. Only in the case of the smaller pillars supporting the gallery roof may one be certain that the support is near the edge of the eaves; but it is to be presumed that there was no great overhang of the eaves of the main roof either; for otherwise the roof would surely have appeared higher in the drawing, and the capitals of the columns would probably have been hidden. This archaeological evidence, admittedly slight, suggests that architects had not yet adopted the principle whereby eaves and roof were balanced about the main columns and the need for tie-beam triangulation avoided.

The development of the eaves principle was necessarily accompanied by the elaboration of the support springing from the columns (figure 42). In the case of the *ling-t'ai* of figures 41 and 42 the capitals are simple, apparently spreading the thrust only sideways along the eaves beam. The next step was to build the area of support outwards both longitudinally and transversely. The pottery models commonly found in tombs of the eastern Han period record the first growth of this bracketing. The fortress-like building of plate 66 has indeed no place for wooden columns, but the decorative devices associated with their capitals appear at the windows of the corner towers. In some cases, as in the model from Inner Mongolia (plate 67), one suspects that pillars and brackets have been eliminated to simplify the design for the modeller, for the raised lantern roof is a scheme more natural to the method of counterbalancing eaves and inner roof than a system of triangulation. The brackets seen on the tower shown in plate 66 mark an initial stage of which the forms shown in figure 44*a*, *b* are a logical development. The design shown in figure 44*a*, intended to spread the support mainly along the line of the eaves beam and to a lesser degree forward to the eaves, appears to have been standard practice in the eastern Han period. Brackets of this kind appear on Wang Shih-jen's reconstruction of a ceremonial building of this period; in it the solid core of the *ling-t'ai* is assumed, and the suggestion of a roof with raised centre is taken from the tomb models. The elaboration of eaves has begun, but has not yielded the engineering principle which the later tradition was destined to exploit so ingeniously.[35]

It appears therefore that the pillared and trabeated wooden house, built on the surface of the ground or raised only slightly above it on a solid platform, descended in central China from the remotest antiquity. There is no trace from early times of any distinct building method competing with wooden houses and palaces. If the stone and brick edifices of Han times, whose design and ornament derive from the work in wood, had any considerable ancestry in the preceding feudal period, archaeological investigation has not yet produced any evidence for it. In the early post-Han

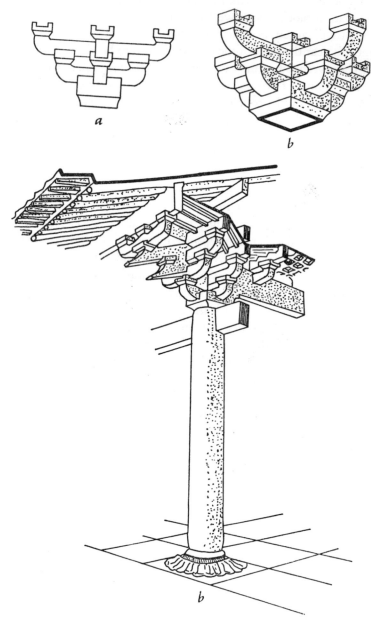

44. Bracketing, *tou-kung*, supporting the roof above one of the main
pillars of a building. (*a*) The simpler form as developed by the end of
the Han period; (*b*) the elaboration of the principle as used in buildings
of mediaeval and later date, with 'great rafters' penetrating the console
complex and supplying further cantilever support. After Andrew Boyd.

centuries the spread of Chinese civilization to Korea, Japan, the southern seaboard and Vietnam carried with it the art of building in wood at the evolved stage which it had reached by that time. The ambition of the expanding Buddhist church no less than the political emulation of the rulers in the adjacent countries ensured that the costliest and most impressive Chinese buildings were imitated abroad from the start, often at the hands of Chinese architects. In Korea no independent native tradition of formal architecture appears at all; in Japan neither the ancient tradition of farmers' houses with low walls and thick thatched roofs, nor even less the ground-framed wooden houses of the Ainu exercised any influence on the construction of sophisticated and solemn buildings in wood, except that eventually the great thatches were placed on buildings otherwise constructed in versions of the Chinese style.

In the south and south-east, however, a local building tradition successfully resisted the encroachment of Chinese standards of architecture. It is interesting to find the contrast revealed archaeologically from the 1st century BC. At Shih-chai-shan in Yünnan and in the newly acquired provinces south of the Nan-ling houses were then built raised above the ground on posts after the manner of all the houses of valley dwellers in South-east Asia today. The little bronze house which decorated the top of a drum-shaped 'cowrie container' at Shih-chai-shan (plate 64) has the projecting gable which may be seen on palaces and temples in Thailand; and the generous space of the raised platform lying outside the house walls is in keeping with the modern village houses of Thailand and Cambodia. The pottery models of raised houses found in Han graves in Kuantung lack the external platform, but they witness to the same far-spread non-Chinese tradition (figure 43).[36]

4

China and the nomad heritage

THE SUBJECT of this chapter is one that has been treated enthusiastically in the west. To us, as to the Greeks, the mounted nomad is a good fellow. Herodotus on the nomadic Scyths of south Russia is echoed by Lawrence on the Bedouin: both admired what they regarded as the nomad's breezy freedom, his scrupulous avoidance of the lies of civilized life. In the east Herodotus' loving account of the Scyths is matched by Ssŭ-ma Ch'ien's no less appreciative chapter on the Hsiung Nu in the *Shih Chi*. Though he has not the Greek's keen interest in ethnography, Ssŭ-ma Ch'ien gives unusually full information on Hsiung Nu customs and institutions. Herodotus had remodelled the initial plan of his history in order to include, among other things, a description of the Scyths who had so unexpectedly frustrated Darius' attempt to invade their territory. There is something of similar admiration for military success, against the Chinese in the 2nd century BC, in Ssŭ-ma Ch'ien's account of the Hsiung Nu.[1]

The Chinese of that time did not clearly distinguish the Hsiung Nu from other peoples situated beyond the northern frontiers who had been periodically in conflict with the northern states of China from the beginning of history.[2] From the Shang dynasty and through the Chou feudal period dealings with them had been unrelentingly difficult. Before the Han period the northerners without the Chinese pale were designated by regional rather than ethnic names. They appear to be unrelated to the Hsiung Nu; and whereas the latter's nomadic way of life is clearly described in the *Shih Chi*, that of their predecessors on the Chinese marches is not clearly recorded. The Chinese view was of a conflict of barbarian and civilized; the modern historian sees a cultural cleavage, hardly admitting compromise, between a settled, taxed peasantry and a nomadic tribal population. As the northern feudatories of the Chou Empire extended their boundaries northwards and took measures to increase the number of their settled farming subjects, the barbarians replied by raid and plunder.

Under their kings T'uman and Mote at the end of the 3rd century BC, the Hsiung Nu had succeeded in organizing a state and an army which controlled territory from Tzungaria to the Hsing-an mountains, including all the grasslands of the Mongolian hills and the lower country south of

the Gobi desert extending to the zone of the Great Wall. Like their predecessors in the same region, the Hsiung Nu took a hand in the wars of the
Chinese feudatories. In the early 3rd century BC they joined a coalition
of eastern states in opposition to the north-western state of Ch'in, whose
growth threatened to engulf the whole Chou confederacy. Soon after they
appear allied to the Tung Hu and the Yüeh Chih. After Shih Huang Ti of
Ch'in had conquered and unified the feudal states under his sole command,
he turned his attention to the Hsiung Nu, and in 214 BC defeated them,
expelling them from their headquarters in the Ordos. The Hsiung Nu for
a short space were under the domination of the Tung Hu, their eastern
neighbours who occupied territory on the east slopes of the T'ai-hsing-an
range (Manchuria). On their western boundary they were contained by
the Yüeh Chih, who ruled Dzungaria and the steppe zone of Kansu as far
as the Ala-shan.

Five years after this defeat – such was the speed with which coalitions
of the nomad tribes could reform and collect their strength – Mote, the
second Khan of the Hsiung Nu whose name is recorded, killed his father
and brother, assumed rule and consolidated a steppe state. He reorganized
the army, subjugated the Tung Hu in the east and the Chiang in the
Kokonor region of the west Tibetan massif, and obtained the allegiance of
tribes in the Sayano-Altai region and of the Wu Sun tribes in Kansu.
Consequently the Yüeh Chih were forced to move westwards, and the
Ordos was retaken. The Hsiung Nu hegemony in the eastern steppes continued, in spite of the efforts of Wu Ti, the most warlike of the Han
emperors, until the beginning of the 1st century BC. By the middle of this
century their political structure was undermined and thereafter they constituted no threat to the Chinese.

The far-flung, if ephemeral, ascendancy of the Hsiung Nu in the eastern
steppes, the readily formed, if unstable, tribal coalitions on which their
power rested, the ease with which defeat was accepted and repaired – all
denote the possibilities of a political structure raised on a common economic
basis, that of intensive pastoralism. Chinese sources concur in stating that
stock-raising was the main occupation of the Huns, and that they moved
from place to place in pursuit of grass and water. But there are mentions
of crops and ploughed land in the 1st century BC. In the Hsiung Nu tombs
in the Noin-ula hills of north Mongolia and at Il'movaya Pad', grains of
millet were found, and an iron ploughshare was excavated from the floor
of a house at the Ivol'yin fortified site (a *gorodishche*). But the extent of
this agriculture was small. It is probably the result of the close contact
which the Hsiung Nu centre enjoyed with China, and gives no proof that
agriculture was practised by other nomadic tribes. The farmers may have
been emigrant or captured Chinese, or perhaps natives of Turkestan

H

specially brought for the purpose. General prosperity depended entirely on herds and flocks.[3]

The Hsiung Nu lived in tents or in wheeled huts, were perpetual horse-men, expert with their bows of compound structure and armed with short swords similar to those which had already been long current in China. To these swords they accorded a religious cult.[4] They swore oaths while drink-ing a mixture of wine and the participants' blood (in one instance drinking from the gold-mounted skull-cup of a Yüeh Chih chieftain). They im-ported luxuries, especially silk stuffs from China, and bought or stole food-stuffs as best they could at the sealed frontier. Only in 152 BC did the Emperor Cheng Ti authorize markets there for their convenience.

Anyone who reads Herodotus' fourth book and chapter 110 of Ssǔ-ma Ch'ien will be struck by similarities in the habits and equipment of the Scyths of the 6th and 5th centuries and the Hsiung Nu of the 3rd and 2nd centuries BC. These parallel traits are not the result of a single ethnic move-ment or a single specific transmission of a cultural complex. To account for them we must rather suppose that a basic cultural continuum was established throughout the steppes among tribes having a similar pastoral economy, and that through this continuum ideas acceptable to nomads were diffused with an even greater speed than was usual among settled and more conservative peoples. A cultural tradition was thus gradually established which united the steppe dwellers of west and east. Certainly when they appear in the pages of written history the inhabitants of the eastern steppes are found sharing in a cultural community which extended west to the Transeuxine plains and north to the basin of the Yenisei around Minusinsk and the grassy highlands of the Altai region. In common with populations elsewhere in the steppe zone the eastern nomads possessed an art based on a few animal designs, in a style which pervaded the steppes, varying locally, but on the whole maintaining an extraordinary uniformity of artistic inspiration and technique. Hitherto discussion of the steppe cultures has largely turned upon this *animal art*, as it is preserved in the bronze plaques which the tribes made to adorn themselves and their horses. It has its roots in the neolithic and early bronze-age traditions of inner Asia, and in its later development furnishes an index of the degree and direction of influences reaching the nomads from the ancient settled civilizations situated at opposite ends of their range. But a preliminary problem is the rise of nomadism itself.

Recent study in China and the Soviet Union illustrates further both the broad unity and the local diversity which characterize the nomad world.[5] The earlier Karasuk culture (whose relations with Shang China were discussed in the second chapter) appears to be no less based on settled agriculture than the Shang bronze age. Evidence for the horse-riding which nomadism presupposes is not found in south Siberia or Mongolia in the period corresponding to the late Shang. When we first meet the Hsiung Nu, about 400 B C, they are already great horsemen and depend on moving herds. The archaeological problem is to determine at what date between these extremes, the 10th and the 5th centuries B C, nomadism and horse-riding were adopted in the eastern steppes. One explanation advanced is the disturbance in a primitive population caused by the northern advance of Chinese farming civilization during the Ch'un Ch'in period (722–481 B C), as the feudatories pressed their frontier towards the natural northern limit of the Ala-shan – Su-shan line.[6] This theory supposes the northerners driven from their land, and envy of the Chinese peasants' crops giving rise to vagabondage and brigandage among the steppe tribes. It is also suggested that nomadism was spread through Mongolia by neolithic peasants from the north of the territory, living by stock-raising, who advanced south-wards and imposed their economy on the crop-raising neolithic farmers of the Great Wall zone. Perhaps the climatic factor was responsible for the change. The warmer and rainier weather inferred for the Shang period (cf. p. 44 above) may have given way to a drier climate and the desiccation of the Gobi area have begun or been intensified in the centuries following Shang. Such a process would lead to a shrinking of pasturage and a gradual confinement of cattle to favoured areas.[7]

A slow movement in the wake of retreating pasturage in itself hardly accounts for the seasonal and longer-range periodic movements of nomadic tribes possessing large herds. More probably in most areas it only aggravated the effects of overgrazing occasioned by an improvement in stock-raising methods and a rapid growth of the herds. None of the theories proposed to account for the rise of nomadism adequately explains the causes of this economic advance, and even less the cultural phenomenon associated with it: that is, a remarkably uniform diffusion of art and techniques through the whole steppe zone of Asia in the 6th and 5th centuries B C. The new culture marks, moreover, a notable advance in metallurgy and war over the culture pre-existing in any area to which it spread. The tribesmen who appeared in the eastern steppes around 500 B C, who are evidently not related to their predecessors in the region, were armed with a short sword of a new kind, and tipped their arrows with a new and superbly designed bronze point.

Gryaznov adopts the theory of cultural expansion to account for the rise of nomadism in Kazakhstan, in the area defined in north and south by the Siberian taiga and the settled oases respectively, extending east to the Sayan range and west to a frontier with the Srubnaya bronze culture of south Russia. He describes the Andronovo culture of Kazakhstan, with its large proportion of heavy cattle and its small proportion of horses, as a settled mixed-farming culture. The Andronovo is supplanted by the local variety of the Karasuk culture, in about 1000 BC, and in this case the indications are of horse-raising communities. Horse-riding is specially necessary for the control of heavy cattle, which continued to be the chief stock until the end of the Kazakhstan bronze age, in the 8th or 7th century BC. But if the increase of herds necessitated the practice of transhumance, as Gryaznov believes occurred in the Karasuk period in Kazakhstan, a further increase could compel complete nomadism. These conditions for the transition to full nomadism seem to have been complete by the end of the bronze age, and were operative in the western province of Andronovo where the Scythian and Sauromatian cultures were formed in the 8th and 7th centuries BC. With iron, and a greatly improved bronze metallurgy, and the fruits, in weapons and art, of contact with the high civilizations of western Asia, the Scyths and their like combined nomadic economy and nomadic mentality. Once established, these traits formed a complex of extraordinary stability and uniformity.[8]

So it is worth considering more closely the rôle of the Andronovo bronze culture in spreading the knowledge of metallurgy through inner Asia. A cultural unity had been achieved in Kazakhstan among its neolithic inhabitants even before the introduction of metallurgy in the Andronovo period. The earliest stage of the Andronovo, called the Okunevsky, is confined to the upper Yenisei valley in south Siberia, though there its relation to another, more primitive bronze-using culture, the Afanyevskaya, is obscure. It is the second phase of the Andronovo culture, the Fyodorovski stage, which produced an explosive expansion and carried Andronovo technology and farming (with its emphasis on stock-raising) to the boundary of the Srubnaya culture on the Ural river in the west and to the middle Urals in the north.[9]

In the east, on the Yenisei, there is intensified Andronovan settlement dating from the 16th or 15th century, a fact which some scholars interpret as a movement of pastoralists into the Upper Yenisei basin from eastern Turkestan, although the by-passing of the well-grassed highlands of the Gorny Altai shows that the Andronovans were not nomads for whom the supply of grassland outweighed every other need. The Andronovan custom of trade in bronze products was inherited by its Karasuk successors, and it was on a basis of Andronovan culture as affected by Chinese influence that the Karasuk bronze age took shape. In its turn the Karasuk culture transmitted a still more advanced metallurgy westwards, but it spread less far and was subject to greater regional variation. The older culture had created a uniformity of tribal life throughout the steppes to a degree which was not to be re-established again until the rise of the nomadic cultures of the iron age. The substitution in south Siberia and the adjacent steppes of a Karasuk tradition for the preceding Andronovan tradition meant that in the steppes generally eastern bronze influences replaced western ones.

When the archaeological evidence becomes unambiguous, from about 500 B C onwards, nomadic pastoralism in the Asiatic steppes is found combined with the specific material culture, typified by knife and sword, arrowhead, and animal art in the form of plaques designed as harness ornaments. There is no reason to assume that the economy, nomadism, and the culture, reached the steppe zone of north China simultaneously. But the factors tending to produce nomadic pastoralism were probably no less operative in the eastern than in the western steppes. Nomads may have lived in Mongolia and the Chinese Northern Zone by the 8th century B C. It was in this century that the inroads of barbarians into the territories of the northern Chinese states became a serious trouble, and thereafter the coalitions of the steppe tribes were a force to be reckoned with.[10] But the Scythian-type cultures of the east (with knife and dagger, bronze socketed arrowhead and some artistic motifs of western origin) make a later appearance in the archaeological record. In most cases they can be traced back only to the 5th century B C. Thus the second stage of the Tagar culture of south Siberia, in which iron for the first time assumed some importance, began in this century, and north Chinese material of comparable type, for example in the Ordos, is of similar age. At this time the older more northerly cultural axis, represented by the link of Karasuk with the Chinese Northern Zone, was replaced by a more westerly one extending through what may be called the Scythic continuum as far as the north coast of the Black Sea.[11]

In the period after the move of the Chou king's capital to Loyang in Honan, Chinese history has more to say about invasion by the Ti and Jung barbarians on the north and north-east than along the north-west marches. In the 8th century the state of Chin undertook to drive the non-Chinese inhabitants out of the highlands of the territory now called Shansi and drove them east of the T'ai-hang range. Chin's purpose was aggrandizement, the appropriation of land and population, and not only the suppression of turbulence on its frontiers. Similarly, in the mid-7th century Chin began to eject the Ti tribes situated to the west of the Yellow river on the edge of the Ordos. The Jung joined forces with the Red Ti living in the interior of the T'ai Hang mountains, and though the Red Ti seem not themselves to have been the object of special attack by the Chinese, like the Jung, they now became the main instigators of raids into the heart of the central plain, either alone, or allied with Jung or White Ti.[12]

These minor invasions punctuate the history of the northern Chinese states in the 7th century. Wei, Lu and even the powerful state of Ch'i were attacked. It is interesting to note that just as the famous Scythian raid into Western Asia in the early 7th century was aimed at a nodal point of trade passing between powerful states, in the region of Lake Urmiya, so the Red Ti and their allies made their assaults on the region through which much of the trade of north China must have passed, for already Ch'i was distinguished by its commercial activity. But the invaders were always driven off, or returned voluntarily to their own territory. At the end of the 7th century the Ti coalition broke up, and in the early decades of the following century Chin defeated the tribes separately. But soon attacks by other coalitions of barbarians were resumed. Between 531 and 490 BC Chi sent no less than seven expeditions against the confederacy headed by the Hsien Yu, whose capital was at Lao Hsun in Hopei, but could not put them down, and was once defeated. In all these marches and counter-marches of barbarians attacking and defending themselves one territorial fact is clear: that a boundary between eastern Jung and western Ti ran north and south along the line of the T'ai-hang mountain range. The Jung and the Ti might appear in coalition, but their separate identities were maintained. The same line of division is apparent in the archaeological record: the T'ai Hang range marks also the eastern limit of the nomadic culture of Scythic type. Beyond, to the east and north, was the region of the slab-grave culture, which is discussed in the next chapter.

In spite of these hostile contacts of the Chinese with northern tribes from the 8th to the 6th centuries BC, the exchange of goods between them must have continued. The distribution of the earliest forms of Chinese currency in the northern area must indicate a measure of trade.[13] The money of the northern states of Chao, Yen and Ch'i, the earliest form of which circulated from the 6th century BC, has been found in Inner Mongolia, along the line of the walls. It is significant that Ch'i's money was cast in the shape of a knife of an archaic form, a shape more familiar to the tribes-men of the north than to the inhabitants of central China. Ch'i's departure from the spade-shaped bronze coins of the other states, some of which were of equal date, suggests either that its subjects or its prospective northern customers were familiar with the corresponding knives (cf. plate 79). From the 8th century, we must suppose, the northern tribesmen were well on the way towards the life of nomadic stock-raisers. The economic character of the Northern Zone gradually changed, but its distinctness from China proper in cultural and industrial traditions still persisted. Meanwhile the physical interpenetration of nomads and Chinese in the northern territories continued. Political and cultural cleavage had not yet resolved itself into a well-defined frontier dividing taxable peasantry from elusive nomads. This last phase dates only from the 4th century, when Chou built its wall in the north-west (*c.* 353 BC), Chao a wall along the

Yin Shan, and Yen a wall along the north-eastern frontier (*c.* 300 BC). The walls were joined into a continuous frontier by the first Emperor of Ch'in. Under the Han emperors it was to be elaborated further as a line of defence, until it in many ways resembled the Roman walls and *limes*. It was the Han policy, for example, to establish colonies of veteran-farmers near the wall. The chief difference lay in weapons: the Chinese wall was designed for defence by infantry armed with the crossbow. The nomads seem never to have mastered or favoured this arm, and replied with bow and arrow.[14]

Two archaeological questions are posed against this historical background: what can be said of the material culture of the eastern steppes before Scythic features were introduced in arms and art? After the Scythic influence made itself felt what contribution did China make to the needs of the nomads? The bronze material which bears on these questions comes mostly from the zone of the Great Walls, little of it more closely localized and still less obtained in excavations; but its import is clear: the knives and socketed axes illustrate the continued activity of the Northern Zone during the western Chou period.[15] The socketed axes include a few which closely parallel some of the earliest south Siberian types, such as those with a clear wide moulding at the mouth, or a double cordon with a single lug at the side; but others reproduce the plain, long type which represents the further development of the Shang socketed axe in China proper, and a few of which can now be dated (figure 28a, b). The axe from Shang-ts'un-ling is not later than the mid-7th century and is more probably of the 8th; and this type continued in use at least until the 5th century BC. A cordoned axe from Hsi-feng in Shansi dates before 750, and is more typical of the steppe type. The tendency to increase the length of the axe is a Chinese feature. The typical product in the north-China steppe in the pre-Scythic period was a longish socketed axe with a moulding at the mouth, straight sides and slightly splayed blade, with sharp rectangular or hexagonal section; and a shorter axe of less precise outline and having a narrow moulding or double cordon at the mouth. These stand midway between the characteristic south-Siberian and Chinese traditions.

The Scythic dagger and short-sword has a roof-shaped or heart-shaped guard: the daggers in the Northern Zone and Mongolia which most obviously fall in the pre-Scythic period are those lacking these features. In Siberia the daggers are of the Karasuk period, and are distinguished by the notches on either side of the blade near the base of the hilt (figure 45a, b, c). Such daggers are found sporadically in north China, having slits in the grip and often a pommel of an open-work sphere, features which complete their identity with the Siberian pieces. But the well-marked midrib which often appears is an individual Chinese feature (figure 46). In the Chao-wu-ta-meng region of Inner Mongolia two notched daggers

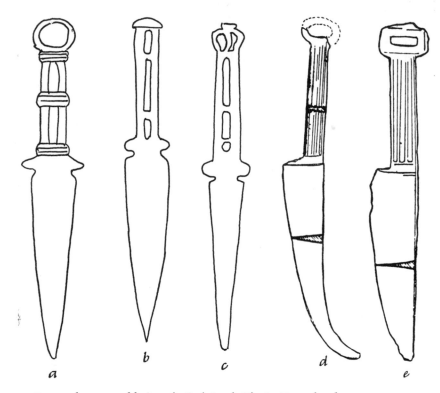

a b c d e

45. Bronze daggers and knives. (*a, b, c*) South Siberia, Karasuk culture, 11th–8th century BC. After Kiselev; (*d, e*) Chang-chia-p'o, Feng-hsi, Shensi, 10th century BC. Length all *c.* 180 mm.

were excavated with a *ko*-halberd, the latter of a form datable to the 7th century BC (plate 80). The socketed axe which accompanied them was of the second kind described above, but with an edge splayed unusually far. The group contained also a bronze dagger sheath decorated with a key-fret meander in low relief, and a bronze helmet of a design deriving from a Chinese prototype of Shang date. The Shang design was transmitted ultimately to the western steppes. A helmet found in a tomb of the early Sauromatian period at Krasnyi Yar in south Russia is dated to the 7th or the earlier 6th century. The knights of Timur's army in the 13th century AD wore helmets of the same ancient lineage (plate 77).

Bronze dagger sheaths are another eastern pre-Scythic form not found beyond north China and Inner Mongolia. While the sheaths are at home in the Northern Zone, their ornament is of a style established in the northern states of China proper, where it reflects an influence of nomad taste. The usual decoration of the sheaths is open-work of dragons, in panels or interlaced. They are made mostly for daggers with a wing-shaped guard, a

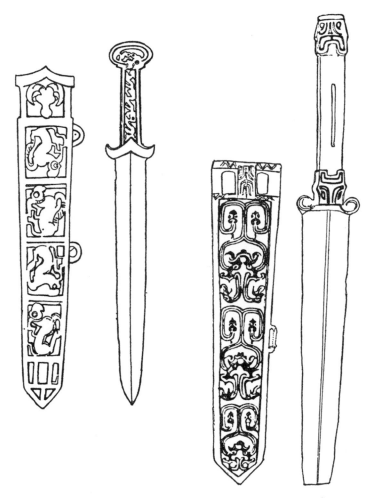

46. Bronze daggers with openwork sheaths, of the type characteristic of
the Northern Zone of China. Length *c.*250 mm. Late 8th–7th century
BC. After Okazaki.

sign that their date approaches the beginning of the Scythic period. An
example from Inner Mongolia shows that these scabbards belong there to
the late 8th or the 7th century BC. The ornament of one of the finest
specimens suggests that it cannot be earlier than the 6th century BC (figures
46).[16]

The bronze knives found in the region of the Great Wall are superior
in ornament and finish to the similar knives known from graves of the
Tagar period in south Siberia, and they are more varied in shape (plate
83). They certainly appear for these reasons to be an invention of the
Northern Zone, although not enough of them are dated to identify beyond

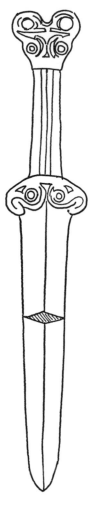

47. Bronze dagger of the Chinese Northern Zone, showing the adaptation of the paired bird-heads to the decoration of terminal and guard. Late 8th–7th century BC.

doubt the post-Shang, pre-Scythic types. Nevertheless, some features point
to this dating. Knives with handles ending in ram or horse heads, or large,
well-defined rings are a specific Chinese contribution, and are not later
than the mid-7th century BC. The earliest ring-knife with good associations
is a Shang specimen from Hou-kang near Anyang (plate 78), and one from
Feng-hsi in Shensi belongs to the 10th century BC (figure 45). Some knives
of this kind were also excavated on the western Chou habitation site at
Feng-hsi. Two of them have the strongly up-turned point, a feature confined to China and Mongolia. Though precise centres of production have
not yet been discovered there can be little doubt that the bulk of the knives
was manufactured in Sui Yüan or in north Shansi, and there are no grounds
for questioning Kiselev's conclusion that during the western Chou period,

no less than during the Shang dynasty, the north Chinese workshops developed the forms of knives which became characteristic of Siberia in the 7th and 6th centuries, that is, in the earlier Tagar period, before the arrival of Scythic influence. In short, wherever it appears, in east and west, in Scythic and pre-Scythic time, the single-edged bronze knife is an eastern-derived type.[17]

Some artistic motifs found in the early Tagar, that is, the pre-Scythic Tagar culture of south Siberia, seem also to have originated in the eastern steppes, although they make appearances also much farther west. One of these is a standing animal, with head lowered and apparently grazing. It is a horse, or a goat, or even something indeterminate between the two. As in the steppe animal art in general, the connexion with reality was soon lost and the design entered the stock of conventional motifs. At Chao-wu-ta-meng in Inner Mongolia this 'standing animal' is used to decorate the pre-Scythic dagger and the *ko*-halberd (plate 80). The latter fixes the date, which can hardly be after the 7th century B C. The animal has penannular, claw-like feet, a mannerism which was destined to pervade the later animal art of the steppes. In south Siberia the standing animal is characteristic of Tagar art (cf. plate 82c); but according to Kiselev it was first introduced there at the end of the Karasuk period, in the 10th or 9th century B C, as the terminal of a knife handle. In the early Tagar period it is used on knives and on battle-axe blades. It appears also on a dagger of the notched kind in the British Museum – another earnest of its pre-Scythic date.[18]

Another motif with similar history is the animal curved into a ring, forming a roundel generally perforated at the centre: it might serve as a cheek-piece, but it has no loops on the undersurface for attaching bridle straps.[19] In the Minusinsk basin this motif can be traced to the Tagar I stage, and it is therefore legitimate to seek comparison in China. There an eagle-head, and a snake, or serpentine dragon curved into a circle were popular designs for cheek-pieces in the 8th–7th centuries B C (figure 48). Coiled, dragon-like monsters have been found in Scythian tombs in south Russia (plates 73, 74). Hence it was formerly assumed that the animal-in-a-ring, which in the Scythic period in north China is relatively common, must have travelled there from south Russia. The dating now available in China indicates an origin rather in the east, but a two-way communication was established in the Scythic world, and it remains possible that a specific westernized version of the animal-in-a-ring was later transmitted eastwards.

The animal represented in the south-Siberian and south-Russian roundels is something between a tiger and a dragon, and the creatures which are paired in a circle on an ornamental roundel found at Shang-ts'un-ling and Hsin-ts'un are plausible ancestors (plates 73, 70). No prototype appears in the pre-Scythian west, whereas in the northern and eastern steppes the

48. Bronze harness ornaments excavated at Hsin-ts'un, Honan.
(*a*, *b*) Bird-head in a circle and the abstracted version; (*c*) paired bird-
heads. 9th–8th century BC.

motif would be a natural derivation from China, simplified and in provincial fashion brought nearer reality than the conventionalized Chinese
design. The Shang-ts'un-ling roundel is dated to the 8th or early 7th century
BC, and the subject and style of its ornament are closely related to the circular
design of dragon-heads found at Hsin-ts'un, which must belong to the 9th
century at the latest.

Thus in art no less than in armament a commerce of ideas may be traced between north China and south Siberia subsisting after the Shang-Karasuk contact, with China still the remote nourisher of the heirs to the Karasuk culture. The cultural common ground so created now facilitated the rapid transmission of the complex of weapons and artistic motifs which are intimately associated in the Scythic culture of the nomads. From the early 6th century B C the new ideas spread like wildfire through the whole steppe zone.

In the west the bearers of Scythic culture were peoples of Iranic race: Scyths of south Russia, Sauromatoi and Śākas of south-east Russia, western Kazakhstan and central Asia; but it is clear that the cultural continuum was itself independent of racial boundaries.[20] As an archaeological concept Scythic culture is composed essentially of (1) the adoption of iron metallurgy; (2) the use of the *akinakes*, a short sword, of specific design and systematic development; (3) the customary conservative use of certain artistic motifs, particularly the stag and the animal combat, all of which are combined with (4), the pastoral nomadic life and a patriarchal, little centralized social organization.

The burial rite is not included in this definition, for while common traits appear everywhere in the Scythic period the method of burial varies from place to place, preserving some features of the pre-Scythic customs of each region.

The most important advance of recent years has been in the interpretation of material from the territory of the ancient Sauromatoi – the steppe region lying north of the Caspian Sea, between the Volga and Ural rivers.[21] The kurgans and other tomb forms of the Sauromatoi are found in two groups, a western one along the Volga between Saratov and Stalingrad (Volgograd) and an eastern one south and east of Orenburg, on the Upper Ural river and its tributaries. The Ural river marks the boundary between the Srubnaya and the Andronovo bronze cultures. Here, in the 8th and 7th centuries B C, took shape a complex that was heir to both Srubnaya and Andronovo traditions. It constitutes a transitional period (a proto-Sauromatian, or proto-Scythic period) which leads to the characteristic Sauromatian culture of the 6th–4th centuries. The corresponding culture of the south-Russian Scyths was raised on a basis of the Srubnaya bronze age. Transitional periods in both the Scythian and the Sauromatian areas saw the evolution of tomb structure towards the classical kurgan form, the spread of a characteristic pottery, wide employment of the horse (as indicated by bone cheek-pieces ancestral to one of the Scythic types) and, at least by the 7th century, the adoption of iron.

Thus at last is seen an interruption of the Andronovo continuum. There is a hint of incipient nomadism; and, as between the Scythian and the

Sauromatian area, the beginning of regional variation in mobile equipment; but we are not yet in sight of a community of ideas spread through
the steppe zone of Asia and reflecting the full impact of nomadic economy
and the establishment of the Scythic continuum. The weapons and art
which hall-mark the latter do not appear in the transitional graves: no
short-swords (akinakai), no three-bladed bronze arrowheads, no animal
art. Therefore, if the accepted dating of the transitional graves be correct,
the Scythic elements cannot be dated in the western steppes earlier than the
6th century.

This dating relies heavily on the historical notices of the Scyths, but with
good reason. The change in the culture of the western steppe resulted from
contacts with the higher civilizations of Western Asia and Iran which took
place in the 7th century BC. The Scyths' raid into Western Asia and their
'period of contact' in the Urartian and Median territories culminated in
their rule over the Medes for a space of twenty-eight years.[22] But the placing
of these twenty-eight years within the 7th century remains disputed,
estimates for the end of Scythian rule varying from 652 BC to 609 BC. The
second date is that argued by Sulimirsky, whose study of the distribution
of Scythic arrowheads in Western Asia gives a particular archaeological
weight to his opinion.[23] The expulsion of the Scyths from Western Asia
and their return to the south-Russian steppes took place after the fall of
Nineveh in 613 BC and, as most authorities agree, probably not later than
about 590 BC.

To suggest that the western element which entered the Scythic steppe
cultures was transmitted precisely by the Scyths as they returned to their
homeland and their relatives in south Russia, would be to oversimplify
the problem. The Śākas, Iranian tribes related to the Sauromatians, inhabit-
ing the region from the Aral Sea to the T'ien Shan, were certainly also in
contact, though remoter contact, with centres of civilization; but among
remains in the Ili valley, attributed to the Śāka Tigrahauda, nothing can
be dated so early as the 7th century.[24]

The channel of communication between the barbarian and civilized
worlds in the west lay through the Caucasus, where Scyths must have
been known throughout the 7th century. The earliest approximately dated
instance of a characteristically Scythian artistic motif is the stag with folded
legs depicted on the gold pectoral of the Ziwiye treasure. This is reported
to have been unearthed at Sakkez, the capital of the Scyths while they were
settled to the south of Lake Urmiya. Barnett has shown that the date of
deposition of the treasure need not be much before 600 BC, and it has been
suggested that it was abandoned by the Scyths on their hurried departure.[25]
The deer motif is a quite specific emblem. It cannot anywhere in the
Scythic area be dated as early as the 7th century. In the north Caucasus, the

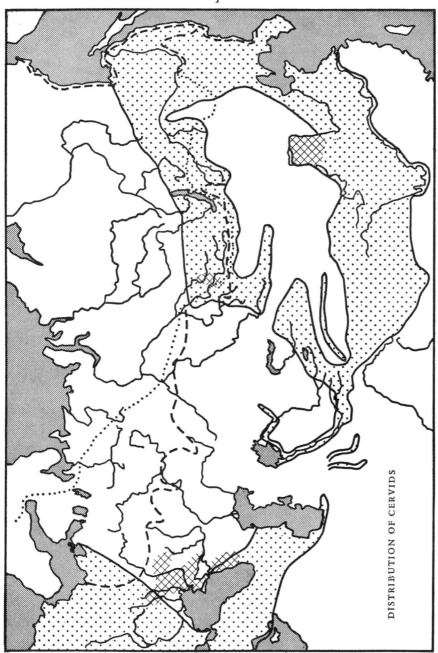

DISTRIBUTION OF CERVIDS

49. The present distribution of cervids in Asia and the find places of
Scythic representations of the deer emblem. The cross-hatching indicates
regions where the finds are concentrated. The upper boundary ....
shows the southern limit of reindeer and the lower boundary —————
the southern limit for elk. The red deer inhabits the dottted areas.
After N.L.Chlenova.

Kuban valley and south Russia it can be dated to the 6th; its far dispersal, through the steppe zone from Bulgaria to the Altai, falls in the 5th.

The conventional stag design, with folded legs, is a Scythian invention, but as an emblem the animal must have had a special meaning for other steppe tribes farther east (plate 93; figure 49).[26] If the connotation was at first one of race, the stag as an emblem of all the tribes of the Iranian connexion, it can hardly have remained such in its ultimate dispersal to China. The silver dish from Ziwiye has other motifs that were destined to be implanted in Scythian tradition – an eagle-head and a crouching monster, remotely connected with the grazing animal of pre-Scythic Siberia and the bird-head motif of western-Chou cheek-pieces in China. The crouching monster appears at Ziwiye with conventional muscle marks derived from the Caucasus and from a much earlier period,[27] and appears to be of Assyrian origin. A similar design can be dated in China to the 8th– 6th century B C (plates 84, 85).

The animal combat is another theme of Assyrian invention, adopted enthusiastically into Scythian and Persian art, which subsequently travelled eastwards through inner Asia as an important component of the Scythic complex (plates 88-92). In the table of figure 50 the oblique broken line marks the earliest appearance of the animal combat theme in each territorial division. This chronological horizon applies equally to the stag emblem of the Scythic world. In the Kuban the kurgan at Temir Gora has none of the Scythian features under discussion and belongs probably to Scyths of the period prior to their raid into western Asia. Other Kuban tombs, notably the kurgan of the Seven Brothers, contained developed versions of the combat subject (plate 88). Farther east the Maiemirsk culture has the animal-in-a-ring motif and eagle-heads, but the animal combat does not appear in the Altai until the Pazyryk period (kurgans 1 and 2, late 5th or early 4th century B C), when it accompanies griffins of Assyrian, Asiatic-Greek and a local design, and much evidence of contact with Achaemenid Persians (plate 89). It points the complexity of the movements and relations of steppe tribes that the stag emblem in its Scythian form is absent from the Altai, although the animal combat was so much appreciated there. The mannerism of twisting the haunches of an animal through half a circle, as seen in the earlier, Tuekta, stage of the Altai culture, is applied at Pazyryk to the animals of the combat scene. On the other hand the animal combat is not found in the Tagar culture of south Siberia at any stage. In the later Tagar culture, which Kiselev dates from the 5th century B C, the stag emblem, with legs folded under the animal, is fairly common in the form of bronze plaques. Some rare representations of stags are attributed to the Karasuk period, but they ceased to be made at the beginning of the Tagar period and, until the 5th century, were replaced by images of the

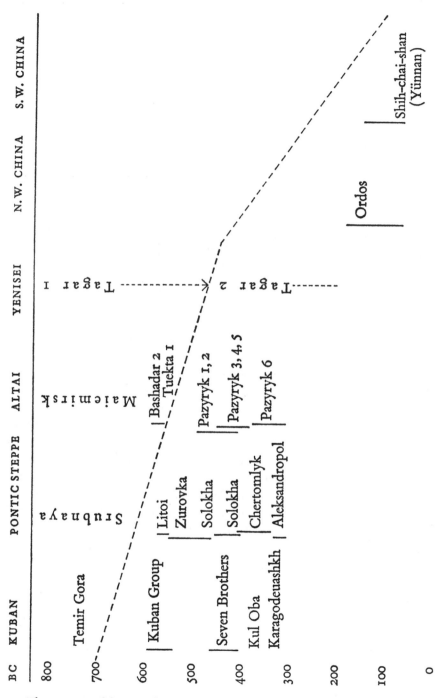

50. The progress of the animal symplegma motif through Asia from east to west, and from the 7th century BC to the 1st century AD.

I

mountain goat. The farthest travel of the stag emblem was the Ordos region of north-west China, where it arrived in the 3rd century B C accompanied by the animal-combat theme. The latter had a sequel also in southwest China (plate 92).[28]

EVEN MORE CLOSELY associated however with the Scythic diffusion than these artistic motifs is the bronze dagger or short-sword, the akinakes. Much has been written on the origin of this weapon, which maintained its popularity with the steppe nomads for six centuries. It has generally been concluded that it copied and modified a western-Asiatic type. But most writers on the subject have admitted dissatisfaction with this explanation.[29] It is reasonably certain that the spread of the akinakes did not precede that of other elements of the Scythic diffusion, but was part of it. Conversely, where this diffusion did not reach, in Manchuria and in the north-western highland zone of China, pre-Scythic forms of dagger continued in use, or were developed on independent lines.

A glance at a broad classification of the akinakai will suffice to cast doubt on the possibility of a simple origin and diffusion from the west to the east of all the types (figures 51, 52; plate 81). There is no obvious reason why the swords occurring in the Northern Zone of China and in Siberia should be virtually limited to specimens with the wing-shaped guard. It is noteworthy, too, that the type with angular guard has a distribution pattern which recalls the Minusinsk-Urals link of an earlier epoch, for it is found in south Siberia (Minusinsk and the Altai) and in the Sverdlovsk oblast' of the eastern middle Urals, that is, to the north of the Sauromatian area and not in the Sauromatian territory itself. Smirnov's dating implies that the heart-shaped and kidney-shaped guards are later variants of an original wing-shaped guard; and it shows rather more positively that the antennae terminals were subsequent to the plain transverse bar.

The single date shown in the table for the eastern region, that is, the sword with wing-shaped guard and bar terminal appearing in the Northern Zone of China in the 6th century B C, must be treated with caution. It is added in view of the daggers with sheaths, and wing-shaped guards, which are found in north China, and for which a 6th-century date was earlier suggested. The dagger type to which the wing-shaped guard is eventually added is older than the 6th century both in Siberia and the Chinese Northern Zone, but there is yet no evidence for saying this of the wing-shaped guard

The Akinakes in West and East Asia

Guard/Terminal	Horizontal Bar	Plain Antennae	Bird-head Antennae
Wing-shaped	West c7 China c6 Siberia	West c6 China Siberia	West c5 China Siberia
Heart-shaped	West c7		
Kidney-shaped	West c6	West c6	West c6
Angular (roof-shaped)	Siberia c5		

51. Table of the geographical distribution and date of features of the akinakes. Generalized from Smirnov.

itself. Should the dagger with this guard prove older than the 6th century in the Northern Zone, an important conclusion would follow: that the point of departure for the whole development of akinakai lies certainly in that area, and not in the Scythic province of the far west. The fact that the typologically earliest kind of akinakes was the only one made in the eastern steppes, and its probable early date there, point strongly to an important initial contribution from China to the Scythic tradition of the short sword; but closely dated material must be discovered in the east before an eastern origin for the akinakes can be argued with certainty.[30] Certainly some of the ornaments added to the eastern akinakai must be allowed an eastern origin, for it derives from pre-Scythic knives and daggers which are at home in Siberia and the Northern Zone. These are ring terminals, terminals in the shape of grazing animals, and terminals consisting of open-work spheres (cf. plate 82). Such forms are hardly known in the Scythian-Sauromatian world.

There is good reason also for regarding the terminal shaped as paired heads of birds of prey, which were adapted to the antennae form (or gave rise to this form), as an eastern invention. The ancestor of this design, as stereotyped as the stag itself, is to be seen on the bronze cheek-pieces of north China of the western Chou period. The Chinese bird-head appears single on a cheek-piece and paired on a horse bridle frontal, in tomb 2 at Hsin-ts'un in Honan (plates 81*b*, 83*c*; figure 48*a*, *b*). This tomb is assigned to the group representing the middle period of the site, dated approximately to the first half of the 9th century B C. The bird-head antennae terminal of swords makes a comparatively late appearance in the west, its

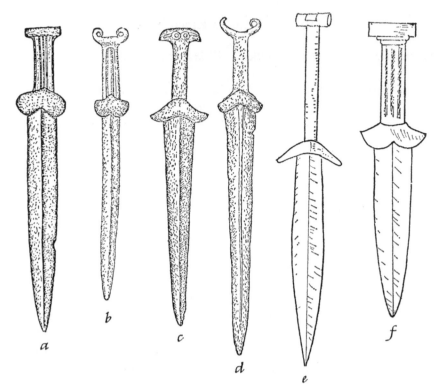

52. Akinakai. (*a–d*) Iron, from the region of the Ura lriver. After Smirnov; (*e, f*) bronze, from south Siberia, Tagar II culture. Late 6th–5th century B C. After Smirnov.

introduction being dated by Smirnov to the 5th century B C. In the Minusinsk basin the advent of daggers decorated with bird-heads is taken, among other things, to mark the beginning of the second Tagar phase, when Scythic forms are dominant. But the bird-heads may be earlier there than the date, 500 B C, at which Kiselev puts the beginning of the Tagar II phase. The stylized head of a bird of prey became as ubiquitous an emblem with the eastern nomads as did the galloping stag with the nomads of the west. Eventually the bird-heads, especially as sword terminals, passed westwards, just as the galloping stag and the animal combat went to the east. The popularity of the bird emblem ensured a welcome with the nomad artists for the various griffins whose acquaintance they made on the fringes of the Assyrian and Greek worlds.[31]

Although the Shang warrior of metropolitan China appears to have had no use for the sword, it must not be supposed that only western peoples manufactured swords in pre-Scythic times. The first hint of a sword in China is in a tomb at Chang-chia-p'o in Shensi dated to the first half of

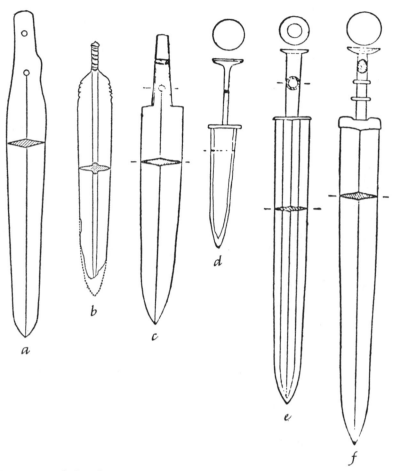

53. Bronze swords found in central China. (*a*) From Chang-chia-p'o,
10th century B C; (*b*) from Chung-chou-lu, 8th–early 7th century B C;
(*c*) from Chung-chou-lu, 6th century B C; (*d, e*) early classical type,
6th–5th century B C; (*f*) the classical type, 5th–4th century B C.
Adapted from *Lo-yang Chung-chou-lu* and Lin Shou-chin.

the western Chou period, *c.* 1000 to *c.* 950 B C (figure 53*a*). But this design
of sword did not catch on either in China or the steppes. Two other early
designs are known, both distinguished by heavy midribs. The sword without a grip terminal is of the eastern Chou I period at Chung-chou-lu
(Loyang), that is 770–650 B C (figure 53*b*), and the other, from Shang-
ts'un-ling (Honan), dates certainly before the mid-7th century, and by
some authorities is placed as early as *c.* 800 B C (plate 86*a*). The second
appears to be a later development of the first. But neither of these weapons
is closely connected with the swords that prevailed in metropolitan
China.

The metropolitan Chinese swords are of three kinds:
  I   with a narrow tang (figure 53*c*)
  II with a tubular grip terminated by a flange (figure 53*e*)
  III with a bar grip terminated by a disc, having two deep circular flanges midway (figure 53*f*; plates 86*b*, 87)

It seems that the classical sword, type III, never completely supplanted the other two. No clear territorial distinction emerges. If type III was developed from type II, as seems likely, it is probable that the latter was being made before the mid–6th century. On that assumption, type I, which approaches the short-swords of the western Chou period, must be earlier still. It would then follow that the ancestors of the classical swords were being made by the 7th century BC at least, when they were a marked advance on earlier models, which were little better than daggers.[32, 33]

But it is immediately clear that none of these types can be said in any significant degree to derive from the dagger and short-sword of Scythic tradition, or to have contributed directly to the creation of these. In the following respects the Chinese swords are distinct:
  1. The cross-section of the blade may be a plain lozenge, like that of the Scythic swords, but very often the section is faceted, giving a finer taper to the edge.
  2. Types II and III narrow slightly about two-thirds along their length from the hilt to give the carp tongue outline which is so familiar on the late bronze age swords of Europe.
  3. The guard shape peculiar to type III appears to be a local development from a straight stop ridge, possibly under the influence of the short-swords of the Northern Zone discussed above, with the wing-shaped guard, but it does not appear to have given rise to these.
  4. The handle type III, cast in a piece with the blade, is intended for binding with silk, the projecting roundels serving to anchor the cord;[34] and the terminal is regularly a circular cap dished on the upper side.

These features were not initiated in the Northern Zone or the steppes: the sword developed earlier in the former region under Chinese influence may have contributed to the akinakes tradition (as was suggested above), but the metropolitan swords were technically beyond nomad imitation, and in any case reached their classical shape after the Scythic tradition was fully formed in the steppes.

More important in Scythic arms than the short-sword was the bronze arrowhead. Its variations show a comparable mixture of eastern and western influence, and again the initial technical impulse is to be sought in China. Small, light, designed for straight flight and penetrating power, the three-bladed bronze arrowhead is the final refinement of a point suited to the powerful double-curved bow of the nomads. The latter was descended

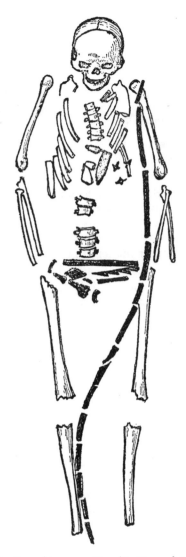

54. Neolithic burial of the *Serovskiy etap* at Bratskiy Kamen', Baikal,
showing the bone plaques of a compound bow in position. After
Okladnikov.

from the earliest type known in East Asia: that placed in graves of the
Serovskiy stage of the Baikalian neolithic in the 3rd millennium B C (figure
54). This bow was strengthened by bone plaques, which imply the principle of a compound bow, consisting of parts in different materials. From
China there is no evidence for neolithic bows; but in Shang times script
characters on bone and bronze show a bow tensed in a double curve which
can only be the effect of compound construction. Judging from the length

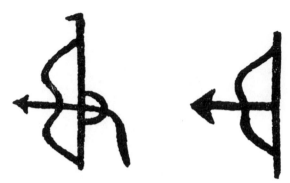

55. Ideographs of the Shang script as cast on bronze, depicting bows of double curve with arrows nocked below the centre of the string.

of the arrow shown nocked on the string, the length of the latter can hardly have exceeded 1 m, or the length of the flexed bow 1½ m. Already in these ideographs an important feature is to be detected: the arrow is nocked on the string at a point slightly below its centre (figure 55). If this is not the effect of careless drawing (and the consistent appearance of the ideographs argues that it is not) we have evidence of a design which would at first sight appear to be for the special convenience of the mounted archer, but at a period before horse-riding had been generally adopted. If the arrow is nocked below centre on the string, the grip must be sited well below the centre of the bow. When it is held, less of the bow projects below the hand to interfere with a horseman's movements. This design is preserved to the present day in the bows of the Japanese.

The earliest indubitable example of the asymmetric compound bow was recovered from tomb 406 at Ch'ang-sha and belongs to the 3rd century BC (plate 94).[34] It is made of strips of bamboo, four layers at the middle, covered with an inner wrapping of 'gummy bands' and an outer one of closely wound silk thread. The surface was finely lacquered (the lacquer and the silk having now nearly all fallen away). The bow is 1400 mm long, 50 mm thick and 45 mm wide at the centre. The two bow-tips are separate and made of horn, grooved to receive the string, which is of silk, 800 mm long and 7 mm in diameter. Enough remains of the heavier binding at the grip to show that this was situated well below the centre of the string. When strung the proportions of this bow are similar, as far as can be measured, with those of a bow represented by an openwork metal plaque decorating a Sauromatian quiver. Thus in east and west the design of the bow varied little, though no asymmetry is to be discerned in a Sauromatian plaque which represents the bow and arrow.[35]

The effectiveness of this bow both in China and throughout the Scythic world was much increased by the adoption of the carefully designed bronze points. The earliest of these are leaf-shaped, and this type persisted, becoming rarer, after the introduction of the classic three-bladed point. It was the perfected three-bladed point that spread rapidly through the steppes, becoming the very sign manual of the nomad culture. Some simpler versions of the points were made of iron, but the neat shape was better, or only, achieved by casting, and therefore called for bronze. Sulimirsky in England and Smirnov in Russia have studied the distribution of the varieties of the arrowheads made by Scyths and Sauromatians in the western steppes. The broad results of this work is summarized as follows:

    1. The earliest type appears to be the two-edged arrowhead. It is found, for example, in Phrygian layers at Boghazköy[36] and elsewhere in Anatolia, and is there referred to the Cimmerian invasion of *c.* 700–680 BC; but in the Scytho-Sauromatian region these arrowheads date from the 8th century.

    2. The earliest three-edged arrowheads seem to be those found in Transcaucasian graves (Hančar's Lelvar and Gandzha-Karabazh cultures), and are dated by Kuftin to the end of the 8th or the beginning of the 7th century BC.[37]

    3. In Western Asia the arrowheads are mostly three-edged and date *c.* 650 to the 4th century BC.

    4. No three-edged arrowheads are found north of the Caucasus before the 6th century BC.

In view of the last observation Sulimirsky argues for the invention and development of the arrowheads in Transcaucasia.[38] As he says, they were intended 'primarily to improve the arrows for the light bows of mounted archers'. But this conclusion is not stated with great conviction, and Smirnov in his great study of Sauromatian arrowheads sketches a more complex picture, accepting different places of origin for different forms of the bronze arrowheads and allowing that some have come to the Transeuxine steppes from farther east. He does not make clear his view of the single prototype which must account for the whole ramified development of the three-bladed arrowhead. He adduces no cogent reason for deriving it from Western Asia, and only in the case of the two-bladed type argues decidedly for an origin in the same Irano-Median sphere from which he believes the prototype of the akinakes to have come.[39]

    But the two-bladed bronze arrowhead on tang or socket is too uniform a shape in Western Asia and too far-spread an artefact of the late bronze age and the early iron age for any convincing genealogy to be made out for it or for its centre of invention and dispersion into the Scythic sphere to be closely defined. Even if a two-bladed form were introduced into the nomad world from the east, it might well join with and blend with other similar forms whose descent from stone ancestors is in the west.

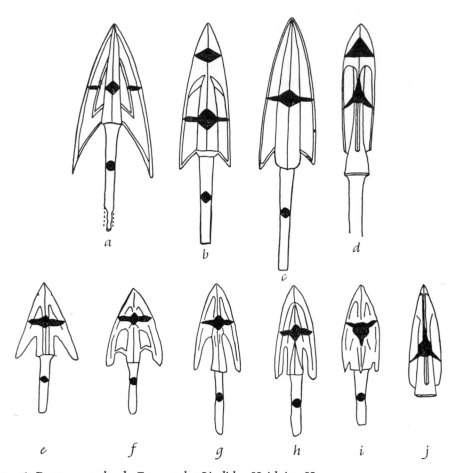

56. Bronze arrowheads. Excavated at Liu-li-ko, Hui-hsien, Honan:
(*a*, *b*, *c*) Shang dynasty, 14th–11th century BC; (*d*, *j*) late 5th–4th
century BC; excavated at Shang-ts'un-ling, Honan; (*e*, *f*, *g*, *h*, *i*) 8th or
early 7th century BC.

It is otherwise with the three-bladed form. Technically it is fully in
context in China: the kind of three-piece mould needed to cast the arrowheads resembles those to which the Chinese had been accustomed for
centuries in the manufacture of their bronze vessels. Moulds of this kind
were not used in the west apart from their adoption for the bronze points.
All Chinese bronze arrowheads, including the Scythic kind, are furnished
with pointed tangs for insertion into shafts of bamboo, the material always
used for this purpose and so easily had. With rare exceptions the nomads'
arrowheads are socketed; but the design of this type of point as a whole
would appear to have proceeded from the tanged point in the first place.
The detailed moulding, profiling of the blades and delicate execution

which characterize the best points in all the regions and varieties, are characteristics of Chinese bronze-work which go back long before the adoption of the three-bladed arrowhead in the 7th century BC (figure 56).

Already in the Shang period the principles of design of the three-bladed points are foreshadowed, as in the pieces excavated at Hui-hsien (figure 56a): the outline is ogival, the midrib carefully prolongs the shaft, being no wider; the cutaway of the trailing barbs, the lightening openwork in the blades of some, are principles which persisted. From Shang-ts'un-ling a developing series of points can be shown from about 800 BC to about 650 BC. The three-bladed arrowhead fits well at the end of the series and there are no grounds for making it earlier than the 7th century; but the three-bladed form is seen to develop smoothly from its predecessors, which are most elegant two-bladers. The most natural explanation of the diffusion of the three-bladed point would be one which attributed to China's Northern Zone the function peculiar to it already for many centuries, introducing a Chinese arrowhead into the Scythic continuum through the Northern Zone and the eastern steppes. But the archaeological evidence for this view of the problem is not yet assembled. Whereas the arrowheads of the Scythian-Sauromatian area have been studied intensively, and statistically, those found in China and, still more, those of the Northern Zone and of Mongolia, are still poorly collected and published, and lack adequate context such as only excavations can provide.

In sum, the nomad world of the steppes was buttressed at both ends of its range by regions of particular prosperity and inventiveness, the south-Russian steppes and the grasslands we have designated the Northern Zone of China. Borrowings from the centres of civilization in east and west were made through the terminal steppe regions, but the process was such that creative industry in these regions was stimulated by their civilized neighbours, rather than reduced by them into cultural thraldom. The nomads were themselves not without influence on the settled populations in Western Asia and in China, populations mixed to some extent on the frontiers, but the cleavage in material culture was ever sharply cut.

The attainment in the steppes of the full nomadic economy, the political alliances of powerful tribes and their effective contacts with civilized industry, resulted in a rather well-defined cultural horizon, a continuum of basic cultural uniformity throughout the steppe zone. A zone of contact was established by the end of the 6th century BC, and in the material culture we are justified in speaking broadly of a Scythic and a pre-Scythic period in the steppes. The Scythic diffusion was in no wise a simple cultural movement from west to east or from east to west; ideas were contributed from both ends of the nomadic range, and spread rapidly through the steppes as integral elements of the cultural continuum. In the pre-Scythic period the region lying between central China and the upper Yenisei already enjoyed the advantages of a cultural continuum of a distinct character, stretched between the Northern Zone of China and the Minusinsk basin of south Siberia, both bronze-producing centres with related traditions. The creation of the new Scythic cultures in the middle of the 1st millennium BC largely substituted east-west cultural affinities and movement for what had previously been a channel between the north and south.

Much of what has been said amounts to an historical parallel of west and east in the Scythic period. It is important therefore to note one significant respect in which the two ends of the nomadic world differed. In the west, at such un-nomadic centres as Olbia, the Scyths imitated Greek craft and art: they were Hellenized to some extent. In the east no such compromise with civilization in art and urbanism took place. In the art of metropolitan China we can distinguish styles of the 6th–5th centuries BC which constitute a northern province. They are exemplified in the bronze vessels of Shansi of the Li Yü style (plate 76), in which the prominence of the ram, modelled and included in flat design, is a token of the pastoral preoccupations of the inhabitants of these grassed uplands above the Yellow river valley. A pendant to the Li Yü style is that represented by the bronze vessels found at T'ang-shan in Hopei, where the local influences are distinct.[40] Both styles show a love of interlaced design which is a step away from the static motifs of the central Chinese tradition. Nevertheless, the art of the eastern nomads of the north-west marches of China, whom we can now identify as the Hsiung Nu, remained quite distinct from that of Shansi and Hopei. The nomad art is the animal style *par excellence*, based on flat designs of conventionalized but real beasts, in which those ancient emblems, the deer and the bird of prey, are lovingly diversified. In the Ordos, within the great northward loop of the Yellow river, on the frontier of Hsiun Nu territory, bronze harness plaques were made in numbers so immense that the tiny surviving fraction graces every major museum in the world (plate 91). Evidence for dating the beginnings of this art are meagre; but certain stag designs can be little later than 500 BC. The floruit of the art was undoubtedly in the 2nd and 1st centuries BC. Artistically the Ordos animal plaques are a crowning achievement of Scythic culture in the east, as the equivalent ornaments from Scythian and Sauromatian kurgans are in the west.

5

Provinces apart : north-east and south-west

WHAT WAS BRONZE-AGE CULTURE in regions of East Asia lying outside both the Chinese orbit and the sphere of full Scythic influence as
denoted by the triad: short-sword, bronze arrowhead, animal art? From
south Russia the Scyths, and after the 2nd century BC their heirs the
Sarmatians, made inroads in Europe to the west of the Black Sea: their
western boundary in Russia was fluid.[1] At the eastern end of the Scythic
continuum somewhat firmer boundaries can be drawn. The characteristic
culture did not penetrate eastward over the Hsing-an mountains into
Manchuria south of the Great Wall; or, in south Siberia, beyond Baikal
into the Selenga and Orkhon valleys. These lines mark the eastern limits
of nomadic life and culture. In Transbaikalia the earliest remains assigned
to nomadic culture are found in tombs built of comparatively thin slabs
of stone shaped roughly square or oblong. The tombs are of three types.
The most elaborate have walls of slabs on a rectangular plan, projecting
noticeably about the ground surface and without cairn or mound. These
are the so-called *mayaki*, or beacons (figure 57), found in the Selenga basin
along the Orkhon and Tola rivers, on the banks of Lake Kosogol and in
east Transbaikalia generally. A few occur in Mongolia. The corners of
the rectangular setting of slabs are often marked with large pointed stones,
and several such tombs may be annexed one to the other. This method of
burial is intelligible as a simplified derivative of the south-Siberian kurgans
of Karasuk date, and the mayaki are assigned by Sosnovskiy and Kiselev
to 8th–6th centuries BC. It is chiefly in tombs of this description that the
bronzes of Transbaikalia are found.[2]

The second tomb type has a lower quadrangular fence of slabs which is
surmounted by a flat cairn, and are found chiefly in south Transbaikalia.
They sometimes contain iron weapons alongside of bronze ones, and so
appear to be at least a little later than the mayaki. It is interesting to note
that iron was introduced in Transbaikalia before the arrival there of the
Hsiung Nu with their Scythic culture: the Hsiung Nu headquarters was
moved from the Ordos and the Yin-shan in the Chinese Northern Zone
across Mongolia to Noin Ula on the Tola river only in 119 BC, and there
is no reason to think that their influence was effective in the north much

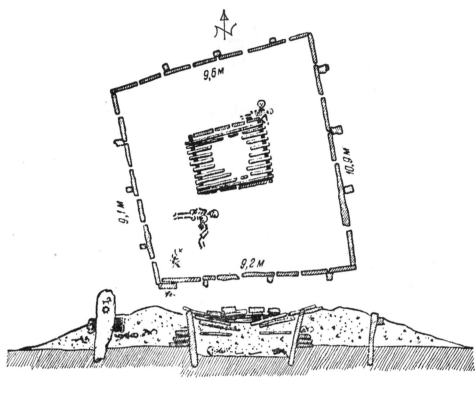

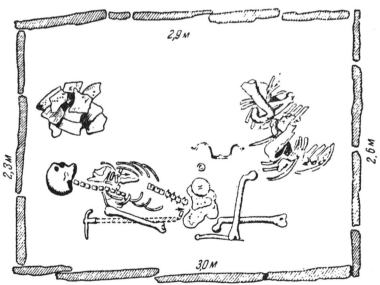

57. *Mayak* tomb of the early Tagar period near Raykov, Khakassia, south Siberia. 8th–7th century BC. After Lipskiy.

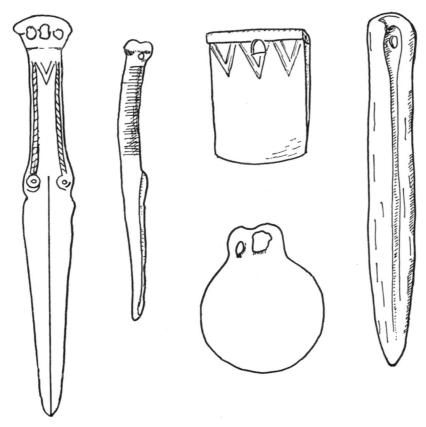

58. Bronze dagger, knife, socketed axe and mirror, and a bone knife, from *mayak* tombs of north-east Mongolia. 5th–1st century B C. After Larichev.

before that date. A third form of tomb found in Transbaikalia is approximately quadrangular, with incurving sides and tall stone pillars at the corners. The tombs are sited singly or in groups and usually separate from tombs of the other two types. Little is known of the builders of these so-called figured tombs: the only metal reported from them is one button. But we note that they betray no more trace of Scythic influence than the rest.

The bronzes, found mostly in the *mayaki*, include knives and daggers with terminals of standing animals (figure 58). The dagger is of the pre-Scythic variety without a guard, and both dagger and knife are forms which in south Siberia are assigned to the Tagar I period. The socketed axe has Karasuk ancestry but looks later than the Karasuk period. The mirror, with its projecting handle in the shape of a standing animal, indicates the third and last division of Tagar culture, the beginning of which is marked down as low as the 2nd or 1st century B C. These bronzes, coming from different tombs, are not necessarily all of similar age. The earlier-looking pieces, the knife, dagger and socketed axe – and the mayaki which contain them – may go back as far as the 7th century B C. But it is clear that the slab-tombs continued in use in Transbaikalia through the Scythic period and probably at least until the time of the northern move of the Hsiung-nu nomads at the end of the 2nd century B C. The builders of the slab-graves in Transbaikalia were heirs to the pre-Scythic culture of the eastern steppes, to which both the Chinese Northern Zone and south Siberia had contributed. Their close connexion with Tagar culture allies them to south Siberia, and one might be inclined to regard them as a retarded offshoot of the Siberian tradition but for one particular: their pottery is different from that of Karasuk or Tagar. The complexity of East-Asian cultural boundaries appears no less in this instance.

The pottery vessels of this Transbaikalian culture have handles and applied ornament which ally them to the ceramics of Manchuria. This singular fact points a connexion with the extreme north-east region of China: there we find a culture of remarkable uniformity, distinguished most obviously by its slab-built tombs, extending from the east end of the Great Wall across the Liao and Sungari rivers to the mouth of the T'u-man river on the coast of the Japan Sea. Some of the objects found in Manchurian graves of this slab-grave culture, which are without exception single burials, find parallels in Korea and Japan.[3] It is clear that the first bronze-using cultures of the latter countries derived from Manchuria and the makers of the slab-graves. They are essentially a prolongation of the pre-Scythic steppe tradition, and so arose at several removes from the direct influence of metropolitan China. But the slab-tombs themselves, at least in typical form, did not travel either into the Korean peninsula or across the sea to Kyūshū. Here no less than in the arrest of the eastward encroachment of Scythic culture the barrier to cultural movement was human rather than climatic or geographic. Only a selection of assimilable traits were diffused into regions where tribal conservatism and poverty slowed down material progress to a greater degree than in the steppes to the west.

The region of slab-grave culture to the north-east of China can be divided into three zones running south from a line drawn approximately between the middle Liao and the middle Sungari rivers: in the west, Hopei and Jehol; in the middle, the upper Sungari centring on the Chi-lin district; and on the east coast the valley of the T'u-man river (figures 1, 59). The last zone, lying beyond the Ch'ang-pai mountains, was in special isolation and culturally as retarded as regions much farther north. Not even the Han emperors could assert their authority on this seaboard. The

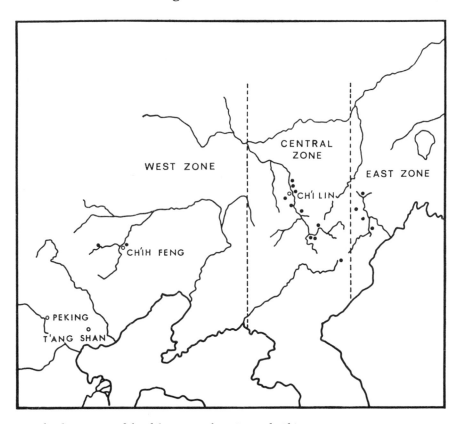

59. The three zones of the slab-grave culture in north China.

slab-grave settlements in the western and central zones, from Hopei to Chi-lin, occupy similar sites. The cemeteries are large, usually situated on hilltops or against fairly steep hill slopes. The dead are buried with their heads to the east – as they were in the preceding neolithic period and in the majority of graves of the Lungshan culture. The slab-built cists are never much larger than is required to contain a single corpse (figure 60; plates 95-97). The grave goods of pottery vessels and stone tools are placed respectively at head and waist, or sometimes in a small compartment of their own added to the grave at the foot. The dead were laid supine, with the hands on the pelvis, or occasionally on the side with the legs a little flexed. The stone axes are rougher versions of the oblong perforated type which characterize the Lungshan farther south and were bequeathed to the Shang bronze age. A few massive stone adzes of trapezoid section also occur. Bronzes are found in the western and central zones, but are quite lacking in the eastern, maritime zone. This distinction is further discussed below.

K

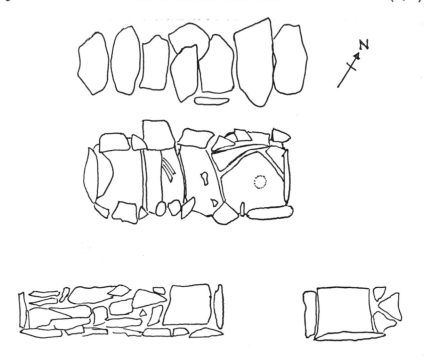

60. Plan and elevation of a slab-built single grave at Tʻu-chʻeng-tzǔ, Chi-lin, Manchuria. Length *c.*2 m. After Kʻang Chia-hsing.

A number of sites in the central zone have been excavated in the immediate vicinity of the cemeteries, and in general the habitations seem never to have been far from the graves. The settlement at Sao-ta-kou near Chi-lin occupied 52,000 sq.m. The houses at Tʻu-chʻeng-tzǔ in the same region had sunken floors, the walls were often of *pisé* built in layers in the Shang manner, and the floor spread with clean clay like the houses of Lungshan villages. Both of these building habits had disappeared from central China by the beginning of the Chou period. They point to a cultural connexion with the Lungshan neolithic, but not necessarily to an influence proceeding from central China itself. The fireplaces inside the houses are built of stone slabs, and in the neighbourhood of the dwellings are the usual storage pits. Our knowledge of the domestic animals of these people is owed mainly to their custom of placing parts of animals on the stones covering the slab chambers of the graves. Commonly this was the head or jaw of a dog or pig; but cattle and sheep also appear, and occasionally a joint of venison.[4]

Agriculture is indicated mainly by the crescentic stone knives which were sometimes placed in graves. They are an unchanged survival from the neolithic and earlier bronze age of metropolitan China. More rarely stone hoes accompany the burials, and probably the larger stone 'plough-shares' known from isolated finds in Hopei and Manchuria belong also to the slab-grave period (plate 10).[5] These signs of food production compare poorly, however, with the impression of advanced neolithic economy gained from a western-zone site such as Hung-shan in Manchuria,[6] and we may assume that food-gathering still counted for something in the economy of the slab-grave population. The crescentic stone knives re-corded from the slab-graves and others, rectangular in shape, found sporadically in the valley of the Liao river are descended from those char-acteristic of the Lungshan culture, which were inherited by the peasants of the Shang period. Their presence in the north-east is hardly evidence of ethnic immigration or even cultural influence from central China in the Scythic period. Even if dimly on our present knowledge, the slab-grave culture presents a picture of settled agriculture of long standing and stock-raising in which hunting still played a minor rôle. Two kinds of millet have been identified in excavations.[7] This settled population proved immune to the Scythic cultural influence and it did not experience the necessity or the attraction of nomadism. Horses and big-horned cattle were bred, but apparently not in large quantities and they were not the economic staple. The latter was provided rather by pigs and sheep. Numerous clay spindle-whorls found on the sites attest the unnomadic practice of weaving; and the depth of cultural deposits on the habitation sites is itself an argument against the life of itinerant pastoralists.

Compared with the complicated mosaic of fundamentally different cultures which we encounter in Manchuria during the neolithic period, the culture of the slab-graves ushered in a period of comparative uniformity in economy and material equipment – a uniformity which extended broadly along the northern edge of Mongolia into Transbaikalia. Against this background we can observe some interesting variation, as between the different zones defined above and even within a single zone. From west to east the culture is increasingly poorer.

The western zone of the slab-graves is best known from the excavations of Hung-shan-hou in Jehol, close to the Hung-shan neolithic settlement already mentioned and one of the rare sites where bronzes have been found. The latter show a certain independence from the tradition of central China and supply an approximate date. The most important are socketed axes. None was extracted from a slab-grave, but a stone bivalve mould for casting the socketed axes, found in Habitation Site no. 1 and demonstrably contemporary with the slab-graves, validates the association of this bronze type with the slab-grave culture. The axe is of a form hardly to be dated after 500 BC, is possibly as early as the 9th–8th century BC, and is of a shape at home in the Northern Zone rather than in central China.[8]

Bronzes found in tombs, disc-buttons, simple spiral bracelets and a leaf-shaped arrowhead equally distinct from the pre-Scythic Chinese type and the Scythic arrowheads themselves, have parallels in Transbaikalia. Some bronze knives obtained in the district and reported to come from the graves are of the shapes common in the Tagar I period of south Siberia; and the same is true of some small bronze ornaments. This evidence would show that the western zone contains slab-graves of approximately the 8th–6th centuries B C, a period corresponding to the *mayaki* of Transbaikalia. Such early dating encourages us to look for connexions with neolithic pottery of the same region (plate 98). The slab-grave pots, from both tombs and habitation sites, appear to be descended from earlier types made in the region. The sandy, red-slipped ware derives from the old painted ware; other coarser, grey, bucket-shaped jars probably represent the old conical beakers. A common jar of sub-spherical shape, with short, upright neck and two horizontal lugs no doubt descends from the taller neolithic urn. The most telling aspect of the slab-grave pottery at Hung-shan-hou is the presence of the *tou* tazza and a form of trilobate vase related to the Chinese *li*. This is irrefutable evidence of an influence from the Yellow river valley; and since it takes the form of pottery, we may think of an actual migration. But an ethnic movement, if it occurred, was still not on a scale capable of bringing Chinese bronze casting and all its sophistication into the north-east. Meanwhile the question of the final date of the neolithic in this region – whether it lasted until the beginning of the slab-grave culture, or whether we are to look for some intervening material as yet undiscovered – remains unanswered.

The material excavated at Hsiao-kuan-chuang, near the town of T'ang-shan in Hopei, corresponds closely to that found farther north at Hung-shan-hou.[9] The tombs and the pottery are similar, the latter including the *li* and the sub-spherical vase with handles, but the pottery has a greater degree of Chinese sophistication. More important, the stone axes are of the *walzerbeil* type of central China, and the shape of bronze axe, as revealed by one-half of a bivalve stone mould, is of the elongated form with cordons near the middle of its length; that is, an axe of old central-Chinese tradition. There were found also moulds for spearheads approximating to the Chinese design: nowhere else in the slab-grave area were bronze spear-heads made (figures 35, 61). The bronze knife represented by another mould at T'ang-shan is *sui generis*, the only approximate parallel with it belonging to the middle zone of the slab-grave culture. One emphatically extraneous object at T'ang-shan is a bronze ornament of the south-Siberian type known once as a 'Siberian fibula' (figure 61a). Considering its close-ness to the central plain of China, the situation in north Hopei reflects not unexpectedly a strong Chinese metropolitan influence, but its cultural

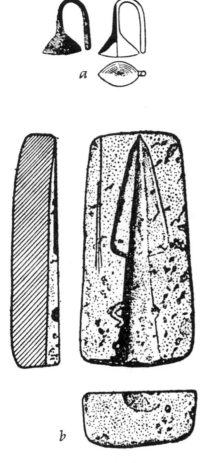

61. (*a*) Bronze ornament: 'Siberian fibula', length 22 mm; (*b*) one-
half of a stone bivalve mould for casting a bronze spearhead, length
150 mm. Both from Hsiao-kuan-chuang, T'ang-shan, Hopei. 7th–6th
century BC. After An Chih-min.

affinities lie nevertheless to the north, with links both to the north-east
and the far north-west. T'ang-shan is situated just south of the eastern
extremity of the Great Wall, yet its culture reveals nothing of nomadism,
the excavated material implying the same degree of settled life as is inferred
in the rest of the slab-grave zone.

Farther east, in the central zone of the slab-grave culture, most of the
cemeteries are in the Sungari valley south of the town of Chi-lin. The
eminences they occupy are the outermost foothills of the Ch'ang-pai range.
The most important excavations are those at T'u-ch'eng-tzǔ, where the
slab-graves had granite sides and sandstone floors.[10] The pottery is little

different from that found farther west: the *li* was made, but had degenerated still farther from the type of central China. A jar with transverse handles is the common form (plate 98, centre). At T'u-ch'eng-tzŭ and in the eastern zone at Hsia-ying-tzŭ on the Yellow river a local variation of the burial rite was observed. A small clay cup was placed inside the stone cist and was the only vessel accompanying the burial. The head end of the cists is generally a little open, and the rest of the grave pottery is buried just beyond it. The most striking vessel is still the jar with transverse handles, but it is joined by a basin with a perforated bottom; and there are tripod vessels. The last differ from those found in the western zone: in the west they are formed of three swelling lobes, while here they stand on three points, in outward appearance more or less resembling the Chinese *ting*, though the tripartite subdivision of the interior vouches for their affiliation to the *li* type. No explanation of this regional difference can be found in the development of *li* in central China, and the divergence of shapes within the slab-grave area thus appears to be a local change, unaffected by influence from the south. The cultural movement from central China which must be postulated to account for the presence of the *li* in the slab-grave sphere at all is to be dated apparently before *c.* 500 B C; and, as far as the evidence of this vessel is concerned, we need not suppose any further migration from, or cultural contact with, central China to have taken place for as long as the slab-grave culture subsisted. We may surmise further that slab-grave settlement in the central zone is generally somewhat later than that in the western zone. The bronzes found in the two areas point to this difference.

Bronze is sparse throughout the slab-grave region, but the recorded types are telling. A shape of flat sickle is not paralleled in China; some ornaments consisting of a connected row of three or four hollow hemispheres transports us at once to south Siberia, where they are common in the Karasuk period but appear not to have survived into the Tagar period.[11] Another bronze from T'u-ch'eng-tzŭ is a plain flat blade with a single perforation (figure 62). It is perhaps too primitive to support typological inference, but we may note that no specimen resembling it is reported from central China or the western zone of the slab-grave culture itself. The bronze sickles may join the stone hoes as evidence for the practice of agriculture at T'u-ch'eng-tzŭ.

Two important bronzes come from the central-zone site of Sao-ta-kou; one is a knife of a shape corresponding to the stone mould found at T'ang-shan; and the other is a socketed axe strikingly different from that represented by the T'ang-shan mould. These pieces point to an interesting divergence of the western and central zones, the axe indicating a probable later date for the latter. The axe is not to be paralleled among specimens found in

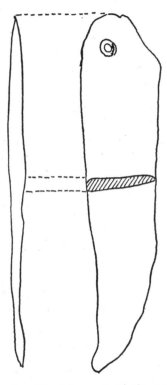

62. Bronze blade from a tomb at T'u-ch'eng-tzǔ, Chi-lin, Manchuria.
Length 73 mm. 4th–3rd century B C. After K'ang Chia-hsing.

central China, where this tool went out of fashion about the 7th century
B C, but its widely splaying blade resembles pieces known in south and
south-west China which are as late as the end of the Warring States period
and the earlier Han period (cf. plate 70). The slab-grave specimen may not
be so late, but it is not likely to be earlier than about 500 B C. In estimating
dates for the different local varieties of slab-grave culture some interpretations have given decisive importance to the presence or absence of *li*, even
divorcing the graves and the traces of habitation at a place according to
its presence or absence, and not allowing that the *li* may have lingered on
in use in the remote north after it had ceased to be made in central China.[12]
But precisely such retardation is to be expected in the slab-grave sphere.
Thus the hemispherical bronze ornaments lead back to Karasuk, the *li*
develops on lines divergent from China, and the absence of elements of
Scythic culture from the later slab-graves is a measure of isolation.

The dating of the western and central zones must remain tentative:
much influenced by a single socketed axe we might hazard a conjecture
that in the western zone the span of the culture falls mainly before, and in

the central zone mainly after, 500 BC. There is no sign of the Han influence that was eventually to make itself felt even in the remote north-east, so we may infer that the slab-grave culture lasted little after 200 BC. The slab-grave movement is from west to east, and presents itself as a gradual penetration rather than a single great migration. Signs of local diversity even within the sphere of the central zone are considerable. At T'u-ch'eng-tzǔ there are many net weights and no stone sickles, while at Sao-ta-kou crescentic stone sickles are specially numerous and arrowheads are fewer. Are we to deduce that at the latter site millet was more intensively culti-vated, and hunting mattered less? Are we to assume, with Mikami, that two populations inhabited the central zone, both building tombs of the same form? These are questions which only further excavations may answer.[13]

Two further arguments support a later date for the central as compared with the western zone. The red slip of the western-zone pottery has been abandoned, and the pottery has only a plain, sandy surface; and at a number of western sites have been found some of the comma-shaped ornaments of jade known by their Japanese name: *magatama* (plate 99).[14] The latter are typical of Korean and Japanese tombs of the last centuries BC, and in Japan they continue to be found in tombs of the proto-dynastic period as late as the 4th–5th centuries AD. In Manchuria they occur also in slab-graves of the eastern zone, and are joined there by rings and tubular beads of jade which connect clearly with Baikalia. The Manchurian maga-tama are of a type found in Japan from the 2nd century BC.

The eastern zone of the slab-graves lies in the valley of the T'u-man river.[15] Throughout the area of the culture the proportion of stone tools increases from west to east, and now it reaches a maximum. No bronze at all is found in the tombs; there are no stone hoes of the unmistakable waisted kind with an hour-glass outline, and crescentic stone knives are rare. The stone axes are flat and long, belonging to the eastern tradition, but the outlines are less regular than those included in the Lungshan tradition; they are thicker and tend to be narrowed towards the butt. The uncouth pottery conforms distantly to the trend followed in central China inasmuch as it includes a form of footed vessel of *tou* type, and no longer includes the *li*; but no comparison is close enough to support dating. The arrowheads are of obsidian and polished slate, the former appearing to belong to the earlier phase. It is in the supposed later graves, containing only slate arrowheads, that occur the daggers of polished slate and bone which are the most characteristic artefacts found in the eastern zone. Some of the bone daggers from Hsia-ying-tzǔ, the site most thoroughly in-vestigated, suggest some of a bronze prototype by the outline of the blade and the presence of a ridge – sometimes very shallow – corresponding to the guard on a Scythic dagger (figure 63).

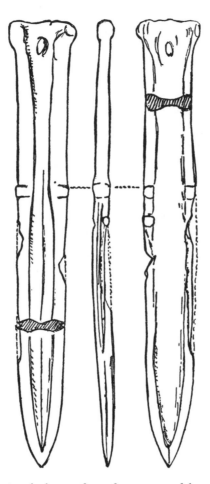

63. Bone daggers imitating the bronze form, from a stone-slab grave at Hsia-ying-tzŭ, Yen-chi-hsien, Manchuria. Length 200 mm. 4th–3rd century BC. After Mikami.

Thus the finds made in the eastern zone of the slab-grave culture carry further, and to the point of extinction, the progressive extenuation of elements of pottery and bronze, derived from higher culture, which is observable from west to east through the slab-grave area. In the eastern zone, behind the Ch'ang-pai range in the fastnesses of eastern Manchuria, life still preserved a mesolithic stamp and China was very remote. Communication with Baikalia may have been more effective. The Manchurian bone knives find close parallels there, even to the insets in the blades of some of them, the obsidian used for this purpose in Manchuria being replaced by flint in Baikalia. It is possibly in this direction also that we should look for the bronze model which is copied by the stop-ridge appearing on some of the bone daggers. If this Scythic characteristic was not conveyed through Manchuria, the Scythic influence in general having failed to cross the Hsing-an mountains, it may still have been passed eastwards from Baikalia along the Amur valley. The possibility of cultural communication along this route is indicated by the nature of finds made a short distance to the north-east of the Chinese eastern zone of slab-graves, in the maritime province of the Soviet Union.

In this region, lying between the river Ussuri and the coast and extending north to the Amur mouth, there are no slab-graves. The large shell-mounds which accompany settlements point to an even more primitive level of existence. It is natural to look for links along the Amur valley with Baikalian culture, and they are not lacking. Stone working and pottery techniques are similar, and the siting and nature of the settlements reflect similar economic preoccupations. Like the sites of the Angara Valley, those of the lower Amur are sited with an eye to fishing, along terraces at the mouths of Amur tributaries and of lesser rivers at the sea; and their existence is betrayed by the huge heaps of food refuse consisting of mollusc shells. Shell-mounds are characteristic of similar settlements of Kamchatka and the Japanese islands : they spread through a region which earlier also shared common traditions, those of the settlements of fishermen found along the lower Amur and in Japan. In the maritime province they occur in great numbers on the coast around the bay of Peter the Great – the Vladivostok region. Farther to the east and north they are hardly less frequent, but here very few have been examined. The excavated sites are located mainly in the province. Why shell-mounds should appear at a more or less discrete moment in time, and comparatively late in the history of the primitive fishing economy, is a question to which no satisfactory answer has been given. One can only guess at a decline in the catch of fish.[16]

The pottery found in a few of the shell-mounds betrays no contact with the far north, but rather with the Baikalian grooved ware of the Glazkovskii stage (figure 64). Its horizontal handles and the use of a red slip (a striking sophistication in this context) denote the influence of the slab-grave culture, as does also the presence of bowls on a high foot in the manner of the *tou*. If these connect with the Lungshan neolithic of eastern China the contact can only have been through the mediation of the slab-grave communities. There is no sign here of the migration which is adduced to account for the presence of the *li* tripods in Manchuria. Two fragments from a site at Tavrichanka are exceptional, having key-fret designs in concave line and in raised line respectively which have been thought to derive from Chinese bronze decoration. The parallel is not a cogent one : the pattern may be a variant of meander designs found on the pottery of the Amur neolithic. But this suggestion raises a question : did

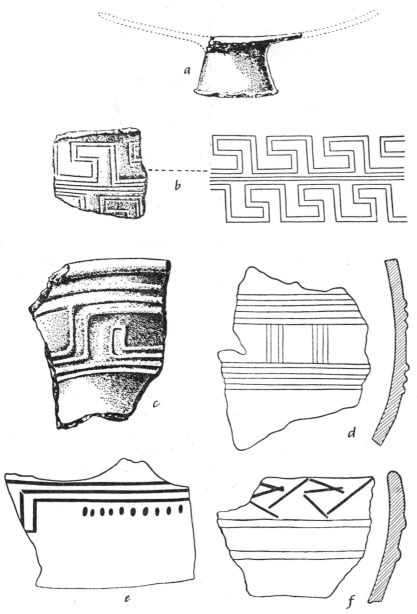

64. Pottery from the Primor'ye. (*a*) From Popov Island; (*b, c*) from
Tavrichanka; (*d*) from the Peschaniy Peninsula; (*e*) from Nayezdnik
Bay; (*f*) from Ambaboza Bay, Lake Uvambapouza. (*b*) is 65 mm wide
and the rest are to scale. 6th–1st century BC.

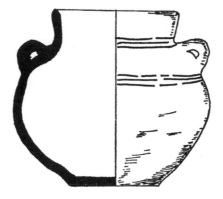

65. Pottery jar from the Peschaniy Peninsula, Primor'ye. 6th–1st century B C. After Okladnikov.

the culture of the shell-mounds follow immediately upon the Amur neo-lithic? The latter was well established on the lower Amur, as is shown by the populous habitation site on the island of Suchu in the river itself (figures 64*b*, *c*, 65).

In 1956 Okladnikov held that the succession from the neolithic to the shell-mound period was not a direct one. He believed that a phase inter-vened which in the maritime province is represented by sites with abundant obsidian flaked tools and coarse pottery with incised zigzag ornament, the origin and affinities of which have not yet been determined. It could be argued that a conflation of the Baikalian tradition of grooved pottery and this intrusion of incised design gave rise to the triangles and zigzags of double parallel grooves which predominate on the shell-mound pottery.

In the shell-mounds agriculture is indicated by the waisted stone hoe and by crescentic slate sickles with a single perforation. A small, pecked stone is found which is thought to be a quern. The crop, one must assume, was millet, but the extent of cultivation cannot have been very great. The crescentic knives are found still much farther north: examples in the British Museum come from the Kamchatka peninsula, where little agri-culture might be expected (plate 100). Beyond the limit of tillage the stone knives may have served to cut wild vegetation, as no doubt they did also on occasion even in the heart of neolithic China. The shell-mounds in the maritime province which contain pottery have tools only of polished stone, and not the scrapers, arrowheads and knives of chipped flint which elsewhere in the province are the normal neolithic equipment. Moreover, the implements of polished stone seem to be remotely influenced by contact with metallic prototypes. The outstanding pieces are daggers which have well-defined terminals, guards and midribs down the blades. One kind seems to copy an ordinary Scythic dagger, the other a dagger with a blade

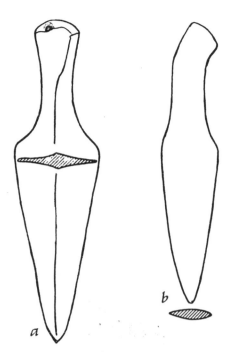

66. Slate daggers from the Primor'ye. (*a*) From Presnoye Ozero, Ol'ginskiy rayon; (*b*) in the Vladivostok Museum. Length 250 mm and 220 mm resp. 3rd–1st century BC. After Okladnikov.

of triangular outline, broad at the base. This may imitate a pre-Scythic type of bronze dagger (figure 66).

The existence of elements, however slight, of Scythic design in artefacts of the maritime province, contrasting with the virtual absence of Scythic influence in the slab-grave culture of Manchuria, points to the Amur valley as a probable channel of contact. By this route influences originating in south Siberia, conveyed through Baikalia and down the Amur, appear to have been more effective on the far north-eastern seaboard than any arriving from the south and the sphere of China proper. If the prototypes of the stone daggers and knives indeed include both Scythic and pre-Scythic forms, including some knives remotely reminiscent of Karasuk types, this is a situation only to be expected in so isolated a region. Unfortunately no trail of bronzes can yet be followed along the Amur towards Baikalia; but the area of the lower Amur is still one of the least explored by Soviet archaeologists.

The date of the shell-mound culture in the maritime province is still much disputed. Instancing the signs of remote contact with the Chinese neolithic, and the signs of closer contact with metal-using culture in Baikalia, Okladnikov suggests that the shell-mounds began to form as early as the closing centuries of the 2nd millennium BC, and he allows it to last until about the beginning of the Christian era.[17] One of his arguments is that iron nowhere appears in the shell-mound settlements. But this reasoning allows too little time by way of cultural retardation. If the polished stone daggers resemble the Scythic form, contact with the metal prototype must have occurred after 500 BC; and even if it is argued that the pre-Scythic daggers supplied the model, this only puts back the date by two or three centuries, and not into the 2nd millennium. The parallel of polished stone tools between the maritime province and the eastern zone of the slab-grave culture suggest that those shell-mounds at least which contain polished stone are approximately contemporary with the slab-graves on the Tou-man river, which also would indicate a period extending after about 500 BC. It is possible, even probable, that other shell-mounds which have only chipped obsidian tools and no pottery or polished stone, represent older settlements, and not merely impoverished ones. But the answer to this question, and to that of the relationship with the preceding neolithic, are matters for future research.

At the lower end of the time scale we can be more certain, for the slate daggers of the maritime province and of the Yayoi culture of Japan are identical. It is generally agreed that the Yayoi begins in the 2nd century BC, and it is clearly intrusive: the path of the movement which created this culture is marked by the finds on Tsushima island, lying between Kyūshū and the Korean coast, nearer to the latter, at a distance of less than fifty miles.[18]

While no bronzes have been found in the shell-mounds of the maritime province, some stray pieces are on record, notably a short sword said to have been found near Vladivostok; but the most important specimens are those which were cited earlier in another connexion. They include the Seima-type spearhead from Kazakevichevo on the Ussuri river, two chisel-heads which would be at home either in China of the western Chou period or in south Siberia, and a socketed axe.[19] The last has points of resemblance with the axes found on the upper Angara, Maksimenkov's type VIII, which of all the Siberian socketed axes comes closest to the Chinese proto-type. There is no means of relating these pieces to the shell-mounds: but it is noteworthy that pointing equally to China and Siberia they mark a trade route that can only have passed along the Amur valley.

In view of these dates and routes of influence it is of interest to consider some bronze swords which appear in the north-east in pre-Han tombs and were due to have a long history (figure 67; plate 101). Similar weapons were made in large numbers in the first bronze-age phases in Korea and Japan. The design of the blade is quite individual, the outline parallel-sided or with a double curve, rising to points about the middle of the edge.

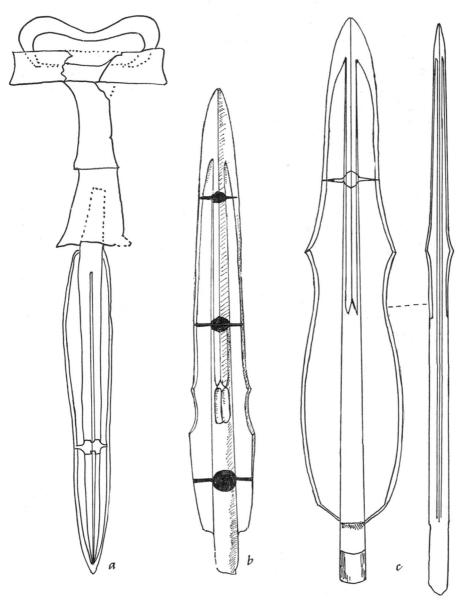

67. Bronze swords from north-east China and the Primor'ye. (*a*) From
Hou-mu-ch'eng-yi, Liaoning, with stone inlay in the handle. Length
365 mm. After Hsü Hung-kang. (*b*) From Izvestkovaya Sopka on the
Maykhe river, Primor'ye. Length *c.* 300 mm. After Okladnikov and
Shakunov. (*c*) From Shih-erh-t'ai-yung-tzŭ, Ch'ao-yang, Liaoning.
Length 330 mm. All 3rd–1st century BC. After Chu Kuei.

The lower part of the midrib is faceted, the edge bevelled over its whole length, and the point is rhomboid in section. Three of the swords have recently been excavated in China, all in Liaoning province on the Korean border, from chamber-tombs built of thin stone slabs or reinforced with walls of small boulders. The grave goods included no objects indicating Han date, which would be strange, in tombs of this kind in this part of China, if they belonged to the Han period, and the socketed axes placed in the tombs are of the type with widely splayed edge which must be later than 500 BC.[20] The Chinese excavators estimate a date in the 4th or 3rd centuries BC. The originality of the sword design suggests a local weapon of wood or stone which was cast in bronze on the advent of the metal. The handles, separate castings and intended to have a decorative stone inlay, depart from all Chinese precedent. This sword has a sequel in the first, or Kyūshū, phase of the Yayoi culture of Japan. But the elaborate hilts of the Japanese swords are cast of a piece with the blade, with a terminal forming rings in a manner recalling the bird-head antennae swords of the steppes, though a connexion with these cannot be established by the existence of intermediate designs. The adaptation of this blade as a spearhead was the work of Korean bronze-smiths and they were imitated in Tsushima and Japan.

A DETAILED ACCOUNT of the sequel to the neolithic in south China and South-east Asia, beyond the great cultural barrier formed by the Yangtze and its lakes, lies outside the theme of this book; but certain aspects of the process are of interest for the contrast they make with situations that have been described for regions farther north. The most effective expansion of Chinese civilization from its 'nuclear area'[21] on the middle Huang-ho was southwards down the broad corridor determined by the outlying mountains of the Tibetan massif in the west and in the east by the inner edge of the Fukien highlands. The advance had begun in the Shang period, and characteristic Shang bronze vessels have been found near Ch'ang-sha in Hunan[22]; but bronze-using culture was not fully established on the middle Yangtze until later, probably not much before 500 BC. The territory lying between the east and west limits described above, and extending from the Yangtze lakes south to the line of the Nan-ling range, formed the Ch'u state, whose political history begins in the 11th century BC with the admission of a Ch'u prince into the Chou confederacy. Apart

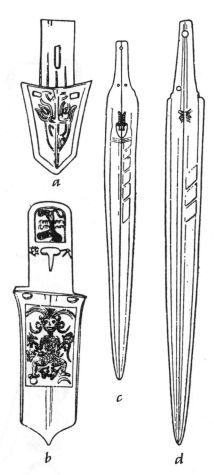

68. Bronze halberds and swords of southern type. (*a, c*) From a tomb
at Tung-sun-pa, Szechwan; (*b, d*) from a tomb at Ching-men, Hupei.
After Yü Wei-chao, Feng Han-chi, *et al.*

from the Shang vessels, which are not in any case local products, the history
of Ch'u bronze-working before the 6th century is quite obscure. A *ko-*
halberd from Hunan inscribed with the name of the fourteenth Ch'u king,
Jo Ao, belongs to the 8th century B C: it is descended from the Shang model
and its shape looks older in comparison with contemporary halberds from
the territory of the central Chinese states.[23] From the late 6th century
onwards, however, the Ch'u area produced weapons and other bronzes
which do not differ significantly from those of metropolitan central China.
It was particularly after the Ch'u expansion to the left bank of the Huai
river in the mid-5th century that Ch'u metallurgy developed on a grand
scale. The basin of the Huai river in Anhui became a focus of influences

L

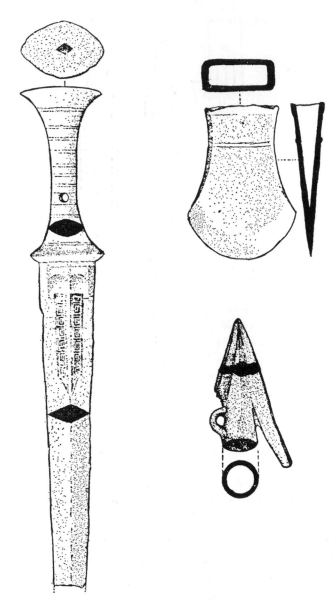

69. Bronze sword, socketed axe and arrowhead from Kuangtung province. Height of the socketed axe 100 mm, the rest to scale. 4th–3rd
century B C. After Yang Hao.

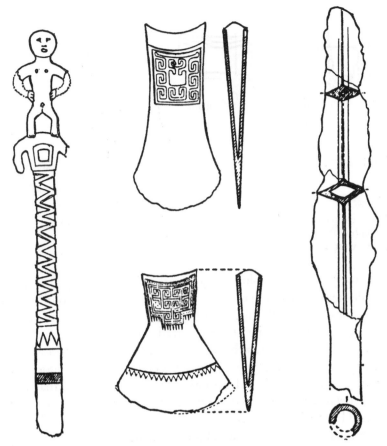

70. Bronze dagger, socketed axes and spearhead excavated from a tomb
in Ch'ing-yüan-hsien, Kuangtung. Length of the spearhead 260 mm,
the rest to scale. 4th–3rd century BC.

from north and south, the former contributing the technique and a traditional bronze art, the latter fostering the development of the artistic themes
which constitute the Huai style.[24] After about 500 BC the relationship of
Ch'u to the Scythic sphere, as expressed in weapons and elements of the
animal style in art, is not different from that of central China itself. Judged
by its bronzes, the state of Ch'u did not fill the rôle of intermediary between
central China and neighbouring barbarian cultures which was assigned
to the Northern Zone.

Bronze weapons related to but still distinct from those of the main
Chinese tradition, and decorated in a local style, are known at present
from the coastal region south of the Nan-ling mountains, from the upper
Yangtze and Szechwan, and especially from Yünnan at the necropolis of
the Tien kings near the lake of the same name (figures 68-71; plates 64,

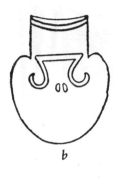

a   *b*   *c*

71. Bronze socketed axes of the southern type (*a, b*) From the Szechwan boat-coffin burials; (*c*) excavated at the Nguang Chang cave, near Fang, northwest Thailand. 3rd–1st century B C.

92, 102, 103).[25] The Nan-ling range marks the boundary between the Ch'u–Chinese sphere and that of the Dong-son culture of South-east Asia and the Indonesian peninsula. The bronze drums, which are the most characteristic product of the Dong-son tradition, hardly encroach on the territory of Ch'u. The few which have been found in Hunan are not of the early type. The latter, type I in Heger's classification, include Yünnan as the northern sector of their distribution.[26] Heger suggested that Yünnan may have been the centre from which the technical and artistic traditions represented by the drums diffused to south and east. The finds made recently at the Tien necropolis add force to his argument.

In view of the relative isolation of the Ch'u region from the south as the Dong-son tradition was forming in the last few centuries B C, it is suggested that the southern metallurgical tradition was initiated by influences passing along the Chinese coast.[27] In the south-east coastal region the appearance of bronze is associated with the later phase of the pottery with impressed decoration which continues the ancient tradition of corded ware characteristic of the 'south-east neolithic' culture (figure 72). The new ware is hard baked, covered with ornament consisting of small geometric diapers, and suggests that a superior pottery kiln was adopted about the same time as knowledge of bronze manufacture was acquired. This influence, originating in central China, extended to the Tonkin province of Vietnam, and there the high-firing kiln was used for simple pots covered with the cord and basketry impressions of the immemorial tradition. In the south-east zone of China sporadic small bronzes are found, such as knives descended from the Shang ring-handled type, and their imitations in stone, but there is no evidence that metal was used in any quantity before

72. Diaper designs stamped on hard-fired pottery characteristic of the south-east and southern coastal regions of China in the 5th–1st centuries B C.

Han times. The bronzes mark also a cultural cleavage inside the area of distribution of the geometric pottery, being found only north of the Ch'un-t'ang river, that is, in the area where stone axes and sickles of Lungshan type were made. The bronze drums and socketed axes with wide lunate blade which belong to the Dong-son sphere are found only in Kuangtung and westwards to the northern provinces of Vietnam, and have no connexions farther along the coast to the north-east.[28] South of the Min river of Fukien, around the coastal provinces as far as the Vietnam border the geometric pottery is accompanied by stone axes of the shouldered and segmented varieties. This is the cultural realm of South-east Asia. The spread of geometric pottery had disregarded an old neolithic division, but this division subsisted in other artefacts. While it is conceivable that practical knowledge of metallurgy reached the south by this coastal route, there is yet no satisfactory evidence for this theory. It remains possible that the earliest bronze weapons made in the south-Chinese coastal provinces imitated metropolitan types which were current in Ch'u, or the impulse may have come from Yünnan.

Around the Tien lake in Yünnan, in the vicinity of the modern town of Kunming, a prosperous community of farmers and stock raisers were known to the Chinese from the end of the Chou period.[29] According to the account given to Chinese emissaries who reached Tien as recorded by Ssŭ-ma Ch'ien, the king of the country was descended from Chuang Ch'iao, a general and kin to the Ch'u royal house. The story went that King Wei of Ch'u who reigned from 338 to 329 B C sent the general to Tien in an armed expedition. Before Chuang Ch'iao could return, his homeward route was cut by an advance of the troops of Ch'u's enemy Ch'in. So the Chinese expeditionaries were cut off in Yünnan; they settled there, took wives, their descendants being the comparatively civilized inhabitants of Tien, and Chuang Ch'iao's descendants providing the kings. But Ssŭ-ma Ch'ien puts the Ch'in advance in 277 B C, fifty-two years after the Ch'u raid into Yünnan. For literal acceptance the Tien story smacks too much of a dynastic fiction adopted to legitimize the Tien kingship in Chinese eyes, which for private reasons was countenanced by Ssŭ-ma Ch'ien. The legend also explained an ancient debt to Chinese culture. More reliable historical notices refer to the 2nd century B C. One party at the Chinese court was convinced that through Tien lay a route to the desirable land of Shen-tu, which must have been part of India or of south-east Asia. Another, more realistic, view saw an independent Tien state as supporting the rebellion of the southern Yüeh tribes against the extension of Chinese rule and trade to the south-Chinese coast. A punitive expedition against Tien was planned for the year 109 B C. Just before it set out the Tien king Ch'ang Chiang made his submission to the Son of Heaven. So instead of certain defeat, he received the Chinese emperor's gold seal with its purple ribbon, and was confirmed as King of Tien.[30]

The Tien necropolis on the low hill of Shih-chai-shan near the east shore of the lake was excavated in 1956 and 1957. Tomb no. 6 contained a gold seal inscribed 'Seal of the king of Tien'. It is not clear how long the Tien royal title was suffered to survive – possibly not more than thirty or forty years after the submission. If tomb no. 6 is not that of Ch'ang Chiang himself it probably belongs to one of his more immediate successors. The chief graves were found richly furnished with bronze weapons, ornaments and drums, the largest and most instructive collection of bronzes belonging to the southern tradition. If tomb 6 is to be dated after 109 B C the remaining larger graves cannot be far removed in time from it, since the contents are very similar. The excavators divide the graves into three chronological groups according to coins occurring in three graves, and to the neatness and wealth or roughness and poverty of the burials. This theory takes the age of the earlier graves back to the time of the alleged expedition of Chuang Ch'iao, but the grave goods in no case warrant so early a date. The coins give no more than a *terminus post quem*: the grave, with three mintings of the early 2nd century B C, also contained a bronze mirror of a common Chinese type which was not made before the middle decades of the 1st century B C.[31]

The Tien bronzes are easily separable into pieces imported from China and pieces of local manufacture. Apart from mirrors, the former are mainly vessels, of banal types, and all, like the fragments of jade *pi*-rings, belong to the 1st century B C. Weapons of contemporary Chinese types, particularly the bronze crossbow locks common in Chinese graves of the period, are conspicuously lacking. Either such things were too greatly prized by the

Tienians to be abandoned in graves, or the Chinese resident saw that none was allowed to reach them.

Among the local bronzes the drums are the most ambitious works. While conforming to Heger's early type I, they are sufficiently varied in shape to suggest that Tien was either the inventive centre of drum making when the tradition of drum manufacture (and no doubt their trading) was founded, or was near to the centre. The idea of covering the tops of drums with lively scenes of people, houses and animals modelled in the round – and obviously cast by the lost wax technique – appears to be the Tienians' own. One composition shows a battle scene dominated by a mounted warrior wearing armour and including another firing a crossbow: perhaps a skirmish with Chinese troops is depicted. Another elaborate drum-top has a house on piles, itself sheltering a row of drums, while below people crowd around a human victim tied to a stake. This sculptural skill cannot be matched in contemporary China; it reappears in some clay tomb figures of Han date made in the south-west, and it may not be fanciful to connect it with the originality of Thai Buddhist sculpture in later times; for part of the Thai migration which later descended through Siam to the sea began from Yünnan. The Tien bronze weapons include *ko*-halberds unlike those in contemporary use in metropolitan China or made in the later centuries of the Chou period, comparing in shape more closely with *ko* of the western Chou period. The long-bladed axe with shaft tube, often decorated with superbly modelled figures of animals, recall the long-bladed axes made in the Shang period (and perhaps the western Chou period) in the Chinese Northern Zone.

If these weapons connect Tien with the centre and north-west of China in pre-Scythic times, one theme of Tien's dynamic art links it with the north-west of the period of Scythic culture: two centuries after it had been introduced into the Hsiung Nu territory of north-west China as part of the Scythic complex the animal combat theme penetrated farther south. It is represented in Tien by bronze plaques in high relief, interpreted with a keenly sympathic eye and a gift for realism unsurpassed in any province of the animal style. The geometricizing mannerisms favoured in the steppes do not appear here, but the local emblem of a snake, forming the ground line, is added to the designs in most cases. This surprising recurrence of the combat theme in Tien art marks the latest and farthest extension of the tradition which began in Western Asia, but the route and means by which it reached Yünnan remain mysterious. The plaques, like those of the north, are intended as harness ornaments, and the Tienites, unlike the population of central and south China, were noted horsemen. Ssǔ-ma Ch'ien attributes to them a nomadic economy, saying that they followed their herds from place to place; but their nomadism was of another kind than that of the steppes, and the culture so fully recorded at Shih-chai-shan shows the advantages of settled life.

The drums, lunate axes and daggers which link the Tien with the Dong-son sphere appear there in richer variety and a wider context than has yet been discovered at any other site attributed to Dong-son tradition. Judged on the still limited information available from South-east Asia and the southern islands, Shih-chai-shan bids fair to be regarded as the type site of Dong-son culture, the centre from which its traditions of material culture were launched. The connexion of Tien with the north, in weapons and art, promises to be more difficult to elucidate. It is characteristic of the eclectic traditions of Tien that they made long iron swords like those which had long been used in China, but added to them bronze grips, and put them in sheaths of sheet gold, decorated with *repoussé* ornament, which recall sheaths made in the western steppes. The cultural frontiers which lie between Tien and the Scythic world have still to be determined.

Notes and References

KKHP : Kʻao-ku hsüeh-pao. KK : Kʻao-ku. WW : Wên-wu

INTRODUCTION

1. Wu Chu-kan and N. N. Cheboksarov *op. cit.* in n. 5, p. 154; for a short account of *Sinanthropus pekinensis* and the site of the find see Marcellin Boule *Les Hommes Fossiles* (3rd ed. by Henri V. Vallois) pp. 109-28.

2. J. Maringer *Contribution to the prehistory of Mongolia*, Reports of the Sven Hedin Expeditions, Publication 34, VII, Archaeology 7 (Stockholm 1950).

3. Wang Kuo-wei *Ku-pen Chu-shu chi-nien chi-chiao* and *Chin-pen Chu-shu chi-nien su-cheng* (Collected Works, series III). The translation of the modern text of the Bamboo Books appears in *Journal Asiatique* 3e serie XII (1841) 537-78, XIII (1942) 381-431.

CHAPTER ONE
Neolithic frontiers in East Asia

1. Radiocarbon dating accepted by Japanese archaeologists takes pottery back to the 11th millennium BC in Japan. E.g. level 9 at Uwaguroiwa: 10215 ± 500 BC; Natsushima: 7290 ± 500 BC. Both of these sites are in the Kantō. The pottery of Natsushima is reconstructed as pointed-base vessels (cf. our fig. 4b, c). The radiocarbon dating of the Jōmon culture is discussed by Kigoe Kunihiko in *Nihon no kōkogaku* (Kawade, Tokyo 1965) vol. II, p. 448 ff; and by Esaki Teruhiko in *Kōkogaku kōza* (Kōzankaku, Tokyo 1969) vol. 3, p. 48 ff.

2. The term 'horizon' denotes here a widespread cultural phenomenon, relatively uniform, which cannot for the present be further analysed by defining movement or difference of date within its geographical limits. The use of this term need not imply acceptance of the neo-diffusionist interpretation applied to it by some writers: cf. K. C. Chang *The Archaeology of ancient China*, p. 246: 'a highly homogeneous style of artefact brought into a large area by a rapid, or even explosive, expansion out of a centre'. It is however the lack of a definable centre which justifies the term. Cf. *ejusd.* 'Prehistoric ceramic horizons in S. eastern China and their extensions into Formosa' *Asian Perspectives* VII (1963) 243-50.

3. The *locus classicus* for the Hoabinhian culture remains the monograph of its discoverer: Madeleine Colani 'L'âge de pierre dans la province de Hoa-Binh' *Mémoires du Service Géologique de l'Indochine* XIV, fasc. I (Hanoi 1927). See also J. M. Matthews 'A review of the "Hoabinhian" in Indo-China' *Asian Perspectives* IX (1966) 86-95; *ejusd.* 'The Hoabinhian affinities of some Australian Assemblages' *Archaeology and Physical Anthropology in Oceania* I (April 1966). Cf. also J. Golson 'Both sides of the Wallace line', in ed. N. Barnard *Early Chinese Art and its possible influence in the Pacific Basin: proceedings of a symposium held at Columbia University* (in preparation). The south Indo-China province of the culture has part-polished stone axes but lacks pottery. The same appears to be true of the Hoabinhian found in north Thailand (see W. Watson and H. H. E. Loofs 'The Thai-British Archaeological Expedition' *Journal of the Siam Society* LV (1967) 237-62). The shouldered stone axes which accompany the earliest pottery in Indo-China, in the late phase of the Bacsonian, can be shown in south China and Thailand to belong to a comparatively late stage of pottery-using, pre-metallic culture, later than the fully developed neolithic of central Thailand as found at the site

of Kok Charoen (cf. Watson and Loofs *loc. cit.*)

4. There is yet no proof that the tradition of smooth pottery on the Chinese central plain is later in origin than the impressed pottery, however probable this may seem on general grounds. The deep deposits at the sites of Pan-p'o and Miao-ti-kou show a degree of development in the Yangshao pottery, and some scholars define earlier and later typological stages for it. But the distinction is certainly not clear enough to be generalized over the central Yangshao area as a whole. The painted pottery was found in graves which could not be related to the stratigraphical sequence. No site resembling those of the primitive neolithic of the Yangtze valley, with impressed pottery only, has been excavated in the Yangshao domain. Chêng Tê-k'un (*Archaeology in China: Prehistoric China*, p. 74 f.) postulates an early Yangshao stage (naming *inter alia* the small proportion of corded pottery as a sign of early date) contrasting with a middle stage exemplified almost wholly from Pan-p'o, and a late stage comprising the Kansu Yangshao. The argument for the early stage is unconvincing, but there is some stratigraphical proof for the later date of the Kansu development: see note 7 to this chapter.

5. I.e. the site of Chuan-lung-ts'ang in the region of Pao-t'ou in Inner Mongolia (*Wen-wu ts'an-k'ao tzŭ-liao* 1954.8, 162-4). The remaining Gobi material, though not inconsiderable, has all been collected from the surface (references in Cheng T.K. *op. cit.* p. 54). The repeated blend of microliths, polished stone and occasional pottery appears, however, to be more than accidental. So far positive evidence is lacking for separating these elements chronologically and geographically. There is implied an overlap of cultural frontiers of the kind revealed in China proper by the discordant distribution of neolithic traits. Wu Chu-kan and N.N. Cheboksarov ('O nepreryvnosti razvitiya fizicheskogo tipa, khozyaystvennoy deyatel'nosti i kul'tury lyudey kamennogo veka na territorii Kitaya' *Sovetskaya Arkheologia* 4 (1959) 3 ff.) summarize as follows: At the end of the palaeolithic and in the mesolithic period the main racial groupings affecting China are already differentiated: i.e. northern, eastern and southern mongoloids and australoids. The late palaeolithic of north China and Siberia forms a single Sino-siberian cultural province. The Upper Cave stone industry of Chou-kou-tien parallels that of Siberia of like age, especially in heavy scrapers and points. In the Ho-t'ao (the region within the northward loop of the Yellow river) tools of this kind are found together with microliths, and may be as early as the beginning of the upper palaeolithic. The Upper Cave and Ho-t'ao material is particularly close to that of Transbaikalia. In contrast to the rest of forested Siberia and to temperate Europe, microliths are not characteristic of the Selenga or the Yellow river basins. Their early presence in the Ho-t'ao is exceptional. Later the microliths become dominant throughout the Gobi region, this indicating the manufacture of armed missiles, and eventually the bow. The latter possibly came into use as early as the end of the east Asian Pleistocene. The recovery of forest in north China and Manchuria from the beginning of the holocene must have then created an ecological division which had not previously existed in such discrete terms. In Mongolia communities of oasis-dwellers formed, while the inhabitants of the woodlands of Manchuria and north China, still related by material equipment to their contemporaries in south Siberia, were set on the path towards neolithic culture. Apart from the Ho-t'ao, where life remained on a very primitive level even when the neolithic was fully developed on the middle course of the Yellow river, the microlithic element is prominent in the comparatively advanced neolithic of Hopei: cf. Ch'en Hui *et al.* 'Hopei T'ang-shan-shih Ta-ch'eng-shan yi-chih fa-chüeh pao-kao' *KKHP* 1959.3, 17-34; Fei Chao-tsung 'Yu kuan Hopei Ch'ang-ch'eng ch'ü-yü yüan-shih wen-hua lei-hsing ti t'ao-lun' *KK* 12 (1962) 658 ff. The best summary of the Chinese material is Kuo Mo-jo, Fei Wen-chung *et al.* 'Chung-kuo jen-lei hua-shih ti fa-hsien yü yen-chiu' (Peking 1955) Institute of Vertebrate Palaeontology of the Academy of Sciences.

6. A.P. Okladnikov *Neolit i bronzovyy vek Pribaykal'ya* (Moscow 1950) pp. 51-97. The earliest, Khonskiy, stage, though lacking pottery, is included in the succession since the adoption of the bow is for Soviet

archaeologists the diagnostic of the Siberian neolithic.

7. The distribution of impressed ware in Chinese neolithic cultures was first discussed by Yin Ta (*Chung-kuo hsin-shih-ch'i shih-tai*, Peking 1955) in his analysis of Lungshan traits. Chikamori Tadashi (Donson seidōki-bunka no kigen ni kansuru isshiron' *Shigaku* 35 (1963) 65-96) summarizes the evidence from excavation, distinguishing the primitive low-fired pottery from the succeeding high-fired ware. From the area of advanced Lungshan development in Shantung and the adjoining coastal region to the south the proportion of impressed pottery found on excavated sites increases westwards into the central plain, i.e. into the Yangshao domain, and southwards, i.e. into the mountainous zone of cultural retardation. The tradition of impressed pottery flourished still in the Shang period in central China, using various diaper stamps as well as cording, and ceased there soon after the end of Shang rule. In the south-east the tradition survived until the Han period, continuing in the high-fired pottery which followed on the introduction of a superior type of kiln from central China about 500 B C. For the broad chronological division of the south-east neolithic see specially Liang Chao-t'ao 'Wo kuo tung-nan yen-hai hsin-shih-ch'i shih-tai wen-hua ti fên-pu hô nien-day t'an-t'ao' *KK* 1959.9, 491 ff.

8. Acad. of Sci. Institute of Archaeology *Hsi-an Pan-p'o* (The neolithic village at Pan-p'o) Peking 1963.

9. M. Bylin-Althin 'Ch'i Chia P'ing and Lo Han T'ang' *Bulletin of the Museum of Far Eastern Antiquities* (Stockholm) 18 (1946) 383-498; Hsia Nai 'Ch'i-chia-ch'i mu-tsang ti hsin-fa-hsien chi ch'i nien-tai ti kai-ting' *KKHP* 3 (1948) 101-17. Before the appearance of Hsia Nai's article J. G. Andersson's view that the Ch'i-chia culture was earlier than any of the painted potteries in Kansu was still generally accepted. Hsia Nai showed that it is in fact later than the Kansu-Yangshao series. Since the latter must be regarded in some sense as an expansion from central China, although incorporating new elements, the Ch'i-chai culture is intelligible as a later diffusion from the Lungshan domain, similarly selective and differentiated.

10. The tradition of impressed pottery in central and north Thailand is found at an early stage already combined with smooth-faced wares. Its cording and stamping is analogous to but still distinct from the Chinese equivalent. The earliest excavated specimens belong to the second or the beginning of the first millennium B C. The pottery is technically advanced, and it is not yet clear whether it marks a cultural intrusion with initial differentiation or emerges from a local tradition whose more primitive manifestations still await discovery. Cf. Watson and Loofs *loc. cit.*, note 3 above; W. Watson 'The Thai-British Archaeological Expedition' *Antiquity* XLII (1968) 302-6. At Kok Charoen in north-central Thailand impressed pottery outweighed the smooth ware, which consisted mainly of the superior burial pieces, but at Ban Kao some 400 km to the south-west its proportion is much reduced, the burial pottery being almost entirely smooth; cf. P. Sørensen *Archaeological excavations in Thailand* vol. II (Ban Kao, Copenhagen 1967).

11. T. de Chardin and Fei Wen-chung *Le néolithique de la Chine* (Peking 1944) pp. 23-32; Liang Ssǔ-yung 'Je-ho Ch'a-pu-kan Lin-hsi Shuang-ching Ch'ih-fêng têng ch'u so ts'ai-chi chih hsin-shih-ch'i shih-tai shih-ch'i yü t'ao-p'ien' *KKHP* 1 (1936) 1-68; V. Ye. Larichev 'Drevnie kul'tury severnogo Kitaya' *Ak. Na. SSSR Sibirskoye otdelenie, Trudy seriya istoricheskaya* 1 (Saransk 1959).

12. Japan provides the classic instance of the divorce of food production from the arts of pottery and advanced stone-working which accompany it generally in Europe. After many millennia in which pottery was made (cf. note 1 above) agriculture with wet-growing rice was introduced in the late 2nd or the 1st century B C, when the Jōmon culture was supplanted by the bronze-using Yayoi culture of strong continental affinities. Only at the very end of the Jōmon period, on some sites in western Honshu, is there the hint that agriculture may have been adopted into the ancient insular culture, undoubtedly under Yayoi influence. Cf. Suaki Hidechika 'Chūkoku Shikoku no banki nōkō to sono hyōka' *Kōkogaku kōza* (Kōzankaku, Tokyo 1969) 378 ff.

13. The clear separation of Yangshao and Lungshan culture in Honan was demonstrated by stratified sites excavated a generation ago and summarized in Wu Gin-ding's pioneering analysis *Prehistoric pottery in China* (London 1938). The interpretation now adopted in China, arguing a gradual change of Yangshao into Lungshan as a primary process in Honan, does not dispose of the problem presented by a good number of sites in that province where the fully evolved Lungshan supervenes on the Yangshao without a transitional phase. See note 33 below.

14. Migration has often been invoked to account for technological analogies between east and west, e.g. F. A. Kuttner 'Acoustical-mathematical knowledge: migration from West Asia to East China before 1000 BC, in ed. Pope and Ackerman *A survey of Persian art*, pp. 3220ff. The author concludes '. . . that some time around, or soon after 1400 BC, a whole clan or guild of bronze-casting artisans migrated, for reasons as yet unknown, from northern Iran to Honan'. None of this or similar theories can be supported by archaeological analysis. V. M. Masson, excavator of the bronze-age sites with painted pottery in south Turkmenia which might come most into question here, opposes the idea that the rise of neolithic culture in China was in any way stimulated by contacts with more advanced centres farther west. The adoption of farming in the Yellow river valley was according to Masson as independent a phenomenon in China as the transition to food-producing economy was in Peru in the third millennium BC.

15. The most extensive and revelatory excavations, on which the interpretation and classification now adopted in China almost wholly depend, are those at Pan-p'o (see note 8 above) and at Miao-ti-kou (*Miao-ti-kou yü San-li-ch'iao*, Peking 1959). The findings of the first are summarised by Cheng T. K. and of both by Chang K. C. in their books cited above.

16. Andersson reported a find of rice from the eponymous Yangshao site in Honan, but the stratigraphy there has since been shown to be complex and possibly disturbed ('remains of four periods'; cf. Fang Hsi-shêng 'Honan Shêng-ch'ih Lu-ssŭ Shang-tai yi-chih shih-chüeh chien-pao',

KK 9 (1964) 431ff. In Yangshao context at Liu-tzŭ-chen in Shensi rice was tentatively identified from husks. Neither instance warrants attribution of rice to Yangshao farmers. Rice is first identified with certainty in the eastern part of the Yangtze, in each case in the context of a local variety of Lungshan culture. Cf. W. Watson 'Early cereal cultivation in China', in ed. P. J. Ucko and G. W. Dimbleby *The domestication and exploitation of plants and animals* (London 1969).

17. A theory of the eastward growth of the fluviatile plain of the Yellow river is propounded by I. A. Smalley 'The loess deposits and neolithic culture of northern China' *Man* 3 (June 1968) 224-41. Chronology makes a difficulty for the argument from geology that the Lungshan was wholly subsequent to the Yangshao. But even had the eastern fluviatile plain been already formed by the Yangshao period the condition of soil and vegetation may still have prevented neolithic farmers from occupying it.

18. Other modes of burial with ascertainable geographical and chronological limits are inhumations in boat-shaped wooden coffins in Szechwan (cf. Szechwan Provincial Museum *Ssŭ-ch'uan ch'uan-kuan-tsang fa-chüeh pao-kao*, Peking 1960) and collective burial such as that encountered at the Yangshao site of Yüan-chün-miao in Shensi (Acad. of Sci. Institute of Archaeology *Hsin-chung-kuo ti k'ao-ku shou-huo* (Peking 1962) pl. III, no. 1). The prone burials can be traced to the Yangshao/Lungshan transition in Honan; cf. the lower level at T'ai-chang-ts'un, Chien-ju-hsien, where however the burials of the upper, Lungshan level, are supine (see *K'ao-ku t'ung-hsün* 1958.8, 1ff).

19. R. Heine-Geldern's theory connecting the distribution of stone axe forms with major migrations from the Chinese mainland to the south, then east and west, is well known: i.e. shouldered axes correlating with the distribution of peoples of Austro-Asian language from Indo-China to Assam and India, the rounded axes (*walzenbeile*) with a Melanesian migration, being characteristic in eastern Indonesia; and the squared axes (*vierkantbeile*) with an Indonesian migration, spreading also through Burma to India and becoming characteristic

in western Indonesia, a 'roof-shaped' form developing in Java (R.Heine-Geldern 'Urheimat und früheste Wanderungen der Austronesier' *Anthropos* XXVII (1932)). Apart from the shouldered axes, which show a coherent distribution in China, Heine-Geldern's theory does not gain from the now greatly increased knowledge of axe forms in central China and their cultural affinities. His derivation of the *vierkantbeil* from the Yangshao proves incorrect, and it does not connect closely with typical Lungshan material. The *vierkantbeil* may have developed at a relatively late period within the sphere of the shouldered axes, but its distribution does not reflect the kind of cultural cohesion which might support the inference of migration by discrete ethnic groups in a delimited space of time. In Thailand, in the 1st millennium BC, *vierkantbeile* reduced to the size of small adze or chisel blades appear to antedate the shouldered axes. Heine-Geldern's theory is critically commented by Matsumoto Nobuhiro *Indo-shina no min-zoku to bunka* (Tokyo 1942) p.69ff. On the Chinese segmented axe see Lin Hui-hsiang 'Chung-kuo tung-nan-ch'ü hsin-shih-ch'i wên-hua t'ê-chêng chih yi: yu-tuan shih-pên' *KKHP* 1958.3, 1-16.

20. An Chih-min 'Chung-kuo ku-tai ti shih-tau', *KKHP* 10 (1955) 27-51.

21. Described here as 'advanced' because of the presence of big-horned cattle.

22. Hamada K. and Mizuno S. *Ch'ih-fêng: Hung-shan-hou* Archaeologia Orientalis series A no. 6 (Tokyo 1938).

23. Liang Ssŭ-yung 'A prehistoric site at Ang-ang-hsi' *Bulletin of the National Research Institute of History and Philology, Academia Sinica* 4 (1932) 1-44; A.S.Louk-ashkin 'New data on neolithic culture in northern Manchuria' *Bulletin of the Geological Society of China* 9 (1931) 171-81; Yin Ta *Chung-kuo hsin-shih-ch'i shih-tai* (Peking 1955) p.12ff; Chang T.K. *op. cit.* p.137ff.

24. Cf. Li Wên-hsin 'Yi-lan-wo-k'ên-ha-ta ti tung-hsüeh' *KKHP* 7 (1954) 61-75.

25. Settlements with shell-mounds in the Soviet maritime province are found in a comparatively limited area along the shores of the Amur estuary. Cf. A.P.Okladnikov 'Primor'ye v I tysyacheletii do nashey ery' *Sovetskaya arkheologia* XXVI (1956) 54-96;

ejusd. *Dalekoye proshloye Primor'ya* (Vladi-vostok 1959) p.86ff.

26. It is tempting but possibly unfounded to connect the appearance of the fish motif in neolithic art, notably on the Pan-p'o painted bowls, with the fish pendants of jade and bronze placed in tombs of the Chou period. In later traditional ornament in China the fish is a banal invocation of human fertility.

27. One of the oldest groups of neolithic dwellings, built partly underground, was discovered in 1934 on the island of Sucha in the Amur river: wooden pillars rising from the floor of the pit supported a roof which was covered with earth. Stone tools and richly decorated pottery were preserved in the houses. On the same island a village of slightly later date consisted of hundreds of similar houses conglomerated to form a honeycomb of pits. Cf. A.P.Okladnikov 'U istokov kul'tury narodov dal'nego vostoka' in *Po sledam drevnikh kul'tur ot Volgi do Tikhogo Okeana* (Moscow 1954).

28. *Hou Han Shu chüan* 115: *Tung-yi chüan*: 'They habitually live in pits, and the deeper these are, the nobler. The great families go down successively to nine steps.'

29. J.G.Andersson 'Prehistory of the Chinese' *Bulletin of the Museum of Far-eastern Antiquities* (Stockholm) 15 (1943) 291-6. Andersson does not dogmatize on the relation of Yangshao in Honan to that in Kansu, but his belief that the culture began about the same time in both regions seems to presume an initial Western-Asiatic influence and adumbrates the priority of Kansu in the development of Chinese painted-pottery neolithic. Andersson was first to point out the resemblance of some Yangshao decorative motifs to motifs used much farther west. He says 'In Ma Ch'ang time [i.e. in the post-Yangshao period in Kansu] when the decorative style was already on the decline, there developed strong parallels on the one hand to Anau and on the other to Tripolye. With our present limited knowledge it is premature to discuss where these cultural impulses first arose and how they migrated across Asia.'

30. Chang Hsüeh-cheng 'Kan-su ku-tai wên-hua yi-ts'un' *KKHP* 1960.2, 11-52. The situation in Hsinchiang is little known, and resemblances of its painted pottery to potteries found farther west are not yet

sufficiently investigated. Around Lopnor occurs a pottery of pink or cream fabric with painting in dark colours reminiscent of that on pottery from Anau (cf. Huang Wên-pi *The exploration around Lopnor*, Peiping 1948). Near Kucha and Tihua similar ancient-looking pottery more closely resembles that of south Turkmenia, according to V.M. Masson (*Yuzhno-turkmenistanskaya arkheologicheskaya kompleksnaya ekspeditsia*), S.V. Kiselev (*Sovetskaya arkheologia* 4 (1960) 244 ff.) reports Huang Wên-pi as dating the Tihua pottery to the beginning of the first millennium BC, and he goes on to cite parallels with settlements in Ferghana, also dated to the 11th or 10th century BC. It is therefore possible that all the Hsinchiang painted pottery reported so far is later than the earliest Chinese painted pottery, and therefore offers no evidence to link this with western regions.

31. The Asia-wide distribution of the pottery tripod is discussed, and used as a basis for dating, by F.A. Schaeffer *Stratigraphie comparée et chronologie de l'Asie occidentale* (London 1948) pp. 598-604. It is further discussed by Masuda Seiichi 'Ulam material and the *li* tripod', in ed. Pope and Ackerman *A survey of Persian art*, 2nd edition (1968) pp. 3213-19, where it is concluded that *li* tripods 'were not peculiar to prehistoric Chinese culture, but were distributed over a wide area ranging from Mongolia and China to northern Iran . . . developed from a type of leather bag which had been used by pastoral people ranging over Siberia and China'.

32. The implications of the theory that Lungshan culture developed spontaneously from the Yangshao are taken by K.C. Chang as the basis of his diffusionist presentation of the neolithic: a creative 'nuclear area' on the middle Yellow river near its confluence with the Wei-ho, and a progressive travel of Lungshan culture through central China to north-east and east, carrying advanced farming and other techniques, and in its further extensions developing local idiosyncrasies, which require the term 'Lungshanoid'. This process is identified with the spread of the power and civilization of the Han race. Cf. K.C. Chang *The archaeology of ancient China*, p. 77 ff. and p. 299 ff.

33. The 'transitional' sites are listed by K.C. Chang *op. cit.* p. 89. Their individual character was in most cases previously recognized and attributed to 'culture contact' between Yangshao and Lungshan in the area of overlap. The sites in Honan where a 'classical' Lungshan overlies Yangshao material at least equal those for which clear transitional character is claimed.

CHAPTER TWO
Isolation and contact in the high bronze age

1. See Introduction, p. 7.

2. Tsou Hêng 'Shih lun Chêng-chou hsin-fa-hsian ti Yin-Shang wên-hua yi-chih' *KKHP* 1956.3, 77 ff. The succession from the earlier Shang settlement at Chengchou to the later at Anyang is argued chiefly on ceramic typology and more generally from the style of bronzes. At Chengchou the three earliest levels are present at People's Park (Jen-min kung-yüan) area no. 7 and at Erh-li-kang area no. 1. These are placed prior to the earliest material excavated at Hsiao-t'un (Anyang). Then follow in order a fourth (upper) at Erh-li-kang and the two later divisions of Hsiao-t'un material. The site at Hsiao-t'un could not be divided stratigraphically in the ordinary sense, though positions prior to, coincident with and posterior to the major building foundations are held to correspond to three successive phases of the occupation. These distinctions could not be generalized over the site, and Tsou Hêng's presentation of three Hsiao-t'un periods is deduced typologically. Cf. Shih Chang-ju 'Yin-hsü tsui-chin ti chung-yao fa-hsien, fu lun Hsiao-t'un ti-ts'êng' *KKHP* 3 (1947) 1 ff; Acad. of Sci. Institute of Archaeology *Chêng-chou Erh-li-kang* (Peking 1959).

3. J.G. Andersson ('Prehistory of the Chinese' *Bulletin of the Museum of Far-eastern Antiquities* (Stockholm) 15 (1943) 177) attributed bronze 'buttons' and other small fragments of bronze to the graves of the late painted-pottery culture of Hsien-tien in Kansu. In a context of Ch'i-chia culture (coeval with or possibly earlier than Hsin-tien) small copper awls and disparate fragments were found at the site of Huang-niang-niang-t'ai in Kansu (Kuo Tê-yung 'Kansu Wu-wei Huang-niang-niang-t'ai

yi-chih fa-chüeh pao-kao' *KKHP* 1960.2, 53ff). None of this material indicates any connexion with the central Chinese tradition in forms or techniques. The specimens from Huang-niang-niang-t'ai are of hammered natural copper, or of bronze cast in open moulds, neither of these processes of manufacture being known in metropolitan China, but characteristic of the early bronze phase in south Turkmenia. The amount of metal in Ch'i-chia and Hsin-tien graves is evidently very small, for wider investigations in 1956 produced none from burials of either culture (cf. Hsieh Tuan-chü: Kansu Yung-ching-hsien Chang-chia-chü yi-chih-hou fa-chüeh chien-pao, *KK* 1959.4, 181-4.

4. V. I. Saraniadi: K stratigrafii vostochnoy gruppy kul'tury Anau, *Sovetskaya Arkheologia* 3 (1960) 141ff; V. M. Masson 'The first farmers in Turkmenia' *Antiquity* XXXV (1961) 203-13.

5. The tradition of bronze technology found in the Andronovo culture is distinct from both south Turkmenia and China, evidently making use of the method *à cire perdue* from the beginning. Cf. S. S. Chernikov 'Rol' andronovskoy kul'tury v istorii Sredney Azii i Kazakhstana' *Kratkie soobshcheniya instituta Etnografii* 26 (1957) 28-33.

6. M. F. Kosarev 'Bronzovoi vek lesnogo Ob'-Irtysh'ya' *Sovetskaya Arkheologia* 3 (1964) 37ff; 'Sredneobskiy tsentr Turbino-Seiminskoy bronzovoy metallurgii' *ibid.* 4 (1963) 20-6.

7. V. I. Matyushchenko 'K voprosu o bronzovom veke v nizovykh reki Tom' *Sovetskaya Arkheologia* IV (1959) 154-65.

8. While the problem of the origin of the Andronovo culture remains unsolved it seems that the manner of the diffusion of its bronze tradition, like that of the corresponding Karasuk culture with which it is broadly contemporary, was determined by the pattern of the preceding ethnic and cultural community established in the neolithic period. The core of the west Siberian bronze age is Andronovan, although according to N. L. Chlenova (O kul'turakh bronzovoy epokhi lesostepnoy zony zapadnoy Sibiri, *Sovetskaya Arkheologia* XXIII (1955) 35ff) there is a remote Karasuk influence present there. In the zone of wooded steppe 'pre-Scythian' elements

are discernible in bronze-using culture from the start, and this shows its separation from the Karasuk tradition where such traits are lacking. An eastern boundary between the Andronovan and Karasuk traditions is difficult to draw. In the west the Andronovo separates from the Srubnaya on the north-south line of the river Ural. See note 28 below.

9. The debate on the climate of the Shang period in central China is summarized by Chêng T. K. (*Archaeology in China* vol. II, Shang China, p. 83ff). De Chardin and Young argued for warmer climate from the animal remains; from a statistical study of rain-sentences inscribed on the oracle bones Wittfogel also concluded for a 'slightly warmer climate'. Tung Tso-pin urges the pitfalls of deducing *frequency* of rain from the oracle sentences. None of these authorities cites the Siberian archaeological evidence for climatic improvement in an early part of the local bronze age.

10. Much of the background to the study of the oracle bones, as to much else relating to the early dynastic period, is given in H. G. Creel *Studies in early Chinese culture* (London 1938). There has been no comprehensive account in an occidental language of the content of the oracle sentences. Tung Tso-pin and Ch'ên Mêng-chia have continued the pioneering work of Lo Chên-yü and Wang Kuo-wei with historically interpretative studies, the first in a series of works dividing the sentences chronologically according to occurrences of the diviners' names, the latter attempting the first synthetic appraisal of grammar and content in his magistral *Yin-hsü pu-tz'ŭ tsung-shu* (a comprehensive account of the oracle sentences from the Wastes of Yin) Peking 1956. It is worth noting that scapulimancy, or the method applied to other bones, whereby cracks produced by heat are interpreted, is not confined to China. It is known sporadically in east Asia, and has been recorded in use by Mongols in recent times. The practice ceases in China with the end of the Shang dynasty. Bones used in scapulimancy were found on a 'Chou site' at K'ê-shêng-chuang in Shensi (*KK* 1959.10, 516ff) but this is to be presumed 'predynastic Chou' and of date corresponding to the Shang period.

11. See note 2 above. The archaeological literature for the Shang period is summarized by Chêng T.K. *op. cit.*, note 9 above, and W. Watson *China before the Han dynasty* (London 1960). The reports of the excavations of 1930-6 are in course of publication by the Academia Sinica of Taiwan.

12. See Introduction, p. 6.

13. Thus far no city wall has been found at Anyang, but the Shang city at Chengchou was surrounded by a rectangular wall with lengths of 2,000 and 1,725 metres on east and west respectively. Evidently a square perimeter was intended. The relation of the wall to the stratigraphy of the Shang occupation sites at Chengchou suggests that the wall was in existence at an early stage of the city's history. It was raised on a foundation of rammed earth 19-20 metres wide; no doubt the remaining fabric of the wall was similar, built in the manner of foundations of the 'middle' period at Anyang. The orientation of the wall was that favoured in the square-walled cities of later times, the sides facing the four cardinal directions.

14. From its centre in northern Honan the most natural path taken by the later cultural expansion from Shang was towards the south-east. Due south of the Shang territory was the region which later entered the boundaries of the Ch'u state, and where Shang influence is hardly to be demonstrated from cultural remains. Some Shang bronze vessels, bells and arrowheads are reported from an area about 25 miles north of Ch'angsha in Hunan, but the archaeological context was not established. Cf. Kao Chih-hsi 'Hunan Ning-hsiang Heng-ts'ai fa-hsien Shang-tai t'ung-ch'i ho yi-chih', *KK* 1963.12, 646-58; and W. Watson 'Traditions of material culture in the territory of Ch'u' in ed. N. Barnard *Early Chinese Art and its possible influence in the Pacific Basin: proceedings of a symposium held at Columbia University* (in preparation).

15. See note 2 above. The results of the stratigraphical observations at Hsiao-t'un cannot be applied satisfactorily beyond the precincts of the two capital cities. Many 'Shang sites' are so classified on the evidence of the grey, wheel-turned pottery which is characteristic at Anyang and Chengchou. The particular origin of this ceramic is obscure: although it must derive from a local neolithic tradition it is not closely allied to any Lungshan ware. Chêng T.K., adopting an earlier view of Chinese archaeologists, speaks of a 'grey pottery culture', but this addition to the cultural sequence is no longer accepted in China.

16. The Chinese shaft-tombs with annex seem to represent a tradition introduced from the north-west from about the middle of the 5th century BC, which in the main had ceased by 300 BC. Characteristically the burial is in the annex, and crouched, thus connecting with the tradition of crouched burials which extended from the north-west along the Yellow river in the middle Chou period (cf. Kao Ch'ü-hsün 'Huang-hê hsia-yu ti ch'ü-chih-tsang wên-t'i' *KKHP* 2 (1947) 121-66). Typical annex tombs are seen at Pan-p'o in south Shensi (Chin Hsüeh-shan 'Hsi-an-p'o ti chan-kuo mu-tsang' *KKHP* 1957.3, 63-92); while farther east the annex becomes vestigial, containing only grave-goods and being added to rectangular pits of the normal central-Chinese type (cf. Acad. of Sci. Institute of Archaeology *Hui-hsien fa-chüeh pao-kao* (Peking 1956) p. 33, fig. 46; p. 55, fig. 64).

17. Shang cremation is reported from a single occurrence at Chengchou at the Ming-kung-lu site (*Wên-wu ts'an-k'ao tzǔ-liao* 1956.10, 50ff). It was not found at Anyang. The evidence hardly warrants the inference that cremation was a regular practice in the early Shang period.

18. Fifteen Shang tombs were excavated at sites in the eastern suburbs of Loyang (*KKHP* 9 (1955) 92-104). They are smaller than the great cruciform tombs at Hsi-pei-kang near Anyang (see the following note) but reproduce all the main features of these in the construction of the wooden burial chamber, having a dog as sacrificial victim in a pit beneath it and a wide step in the pit side at the roof level of the chamber for the placing of grave-gifts and human victims.

19. For example, the floor of the cruciform burial chamber of tomb no. 1001 at Hsi-pei-kang was 12 metres from the surface. Ramps led from each side to the surface, the southern one sloping smoothly to the lowest level of the pit and the others descending in steps only to the level of the shelf at the top

of the burial chamber. In the basal pit were the skeletons of a man and a dog, and at each side of the eight outer angles of the burial chamber was buried a kneeling servitor.

20. In artistic style also the Anyang phase is a logical step beyond Chengchou. The development is not merely from simple to complex in the design of the principal motif – the *t'ao-t'ieh* monster mask – for this is already elaborated at its first appearance in bronze. But the Anyang bronze vessels multiply and diversify detailed and secondary ornament to a further degree, introducing two or three levels of relief, boldly projecting handles, etc. Cf. M. Loehr *Ritual vessels of Bronze Age China* (New York 1968) p. 13, where the evolution is divided into five stages on stylistic criteria, the first two stages being dated to the Chengchou period.

21. No parallels outside China, that is, in the Shang and Chou periods. In the metropolitan armies iron replaced bronze on a large scale from the 3rd century BC. But archaic forms of bronze weapons surviving in Szechwan seem to have been transmitted to Yünnan, appearing there in large numbers and idiosyncratic shapes at the necropolis of Shih-chai-shan. Thence too appear to derive some rare examples of bronze *ko*-halberds found in Thailand, which are again of individual shape and larger than the Chinese models.

22. Chao Chin-ku *et al.* 'Chêngchou Shang-tai yi-chih ti fa-chüeh' *KKHP* 1957.1, 53 ff; socketed axe fig. 3, no. 6, halberd pl. 5, no. 9: all from Erh-li-kang, the axe in stratum and the *ko* from a grave.

23. S. V. Kiselev 'Neolit i bronzovyy vek Kitaya' *Sovetskaya Arkheologia* IV (1960) 244 ff. In this article, written shortly before his death, Kiselev records the conclusions he reached after a visit to China and discussions with Chinese archaeologists. The theory he first advanced in his *Drevnyaya Istoriya Yuzhnoy Sibiri* (1951 ed., p. 178 ff) of the dependence of the south Siberian bronze age on Shang China is further elaborated. Cf. also K. Jettmar 'The Karasuk culture and its south-eastern affinities' *Bulletin of the Museum of Far-eastern Antiquities (Stockholm)* 22 (1950), and 'The Altai before the Turks' *ibid.* 23 (1951).

24. V. Gordon Childe 'The socketed celt

M

in upper Eurasia' *The Institute of Archaeology Annual Reports* X (1953) 11 ff.

25. O. N. Bader *Drevneyshie metallurgi Priural'ya* (Moscow 1964). This book describes material from the two Turbino cemeteries, of which the first has been studied and periodically excavated since 1889. Both sites were investigated by Bader in 1958-60. Cf. also *ejusd.* 'Borodino, Seima and their contemporaries: key sites for the bronze age chronology of eastern Europe' *Proc. of the Prehistoric Society* XXII (1956) 143-72; *ejusd.* 'Poselenie Turbinskogo tipa v srednem Prikam'ye' *Materialy i issledovaniya po arkheologii SSSR* 99 (Moscow 1961); L. Ya. Krizhevskaya, N. A. Prokashev 'Turbinskiy mogil'nik na reke Kame' *ibid.*; M. F. Kosarev 'Sredneobskiy tsentr Turbino-Semeyskoy bronzovoy metallurgii' *Sovetskaya Arkheologia* IV (1963) 20 ff.

26. The Seima and Turbino material is discussed in M. Gimbutas *Bronze Age Cultures in Central and Eastern Europe* (The Hague 1965). The author notes the evidence in bronzes for commercial relations between the Urals and China, with Tomsk and the Yenisei basin as intermediate stations. She equates the period of exchange particularly with the Seima phase of the Turbino culture, in this following Bader. Cf. also N. Ya. Merpert 'Iz drevneyshey Istorii srednego Povolzh'ya' *Materialy i issledovaniya no arkheologii SSSR* 61 (1958) 45-157; Max Loehr *Chinese Bronze Age Weapons* (Ann Arbor 1956) *passim*; S. Piggott *Ancient Europe* (Edinburgh 1965) pp. 130-1.

27. O. N. Bader *Drevneyshie metallurgi Priural'ya* p. 143. Chernikov (*ut sup.* note 5) champions the view that the socketed axe was invented in the Andronovan tradition. Against this theory stands the difficult fact that there is nothing Andronovan in the ornament cast on the axes. Chernikov's analysis and periodization of the Andronovo culture is of fundamental importance for the regional relations of the Siberian bronze age.

28. G. F. Debets 'Rasovye tipy naseleniya Minusinskogo kraya v epokhu rodovogo stroya: k voprosu o migratsiakh v doklassovom obshchestve' *Antropologicheskiy Zhurnal* 2 (1932) 30 ff. The proportion of Europaeoid skulls in south Siberia increases

in the following Tagar period. Debets' theory is that 'Andronovan tribes' (apparently of uncertain origin and cultural character) moved into the Yenisei basin and there assimilated the previous occupants of Afanasyev cultural tradition. The resulting culture is then defined as the earliest (Okunevskiy) phase of the Andronovo culture. The appearance of mongoloids in south Siberia cannot be connected with the political upheaval occasioned in China by the Chou conquest of the Shang in the 11th century B C. Between the publication of his *Ancient History of South Siberia* in 1951 and his death in 1964 Kiselev reconsidered the date of the beginning of the Karasuk culture. He had originally placed it in the 12th century B C, arguing *inter alia* from the fact that the northern penetration of Karasuk influence could not antedate the first, Glazkovo, stage of the Baikalian bronze age. This date he later changed to the 13th century B C. In either case it is implied that the connexion between Shang and the Seima-Turbino centre was prior to the rise of the Karasuk tradition. Similarly Kiselev's original lower date for the Karasuk of south Siberia, the 10th century B C, was revised to 9th or 8th century in view of analogies with western Chou. Kiselev's view of the Karasuk as a comparatively well integrated cultural tradition has not gone unchallenged: cf. N.L.Chlenova 'O kul'turakh bronzovoy epokhi lesostepnoy zony zapadnoy Sibiri' *Sovetskaya Arkheologia* XXIII (1955) 35ff. The same author ('Pamyatniki karasuk-tagarskogo vremeni v minusinskoy kotlovine' *Sovetskaya Arkheologia* 3 (1963) 48ff) divides the Karasuk culture of the Yenisei basin into four stages, the first (Lukavskiy) dating from the late 14th century B C and the fourth (Korolevskiy) descending to the beginning of the 7th century B C. See note 8 above.

29. O.N.Bader *Drevneyshie metallurgi Priural'ya*, figs.33-9. M.Gimbutas *op cit.* p.631, fig.442, no.8; p.632, fig.443, no.1. The Borodino treasure is illustrated by M. Gimbutas *ibid.* pl.12.

30. As argued by Kiselev, who regarded the Karasuk material from the cemetery at Old Tomsk as equivalent to the latest phase of the culture in its Minusinsk development. The coincidence at Tomsk of bronzes and round-bottomed pots characteristic of the Karasuk suggests migration and not only trade. As in the case of the Minusinsk basin itself, the establishment of full bronze age culture in the Tomsk region is thus placed later than the passage of axe and spear types between the Urals and Shang China.

31. A.P.Okladnikov 'Primor'ye v I tysyacheletii do nashey ery' *Sovetskaya Arkheologia* XXVI (1956) 54ff; cf.p.93 and fig.19.

32. This belief is not recorded in literature or evidenced in archaeology before the Han period, when the orifices of the corpse might all be stopped with jade in accordance with codified ritual. See S.Jenyns *Chinese archaic jades in the British Museum* (1951) pp.xix-xx and pl.XXIX.

33. See S.Jenyns *op.cit.* pp.v-cii; A. Schüller ('Shichangit, ein Epi- Metaleukophyr-pyroxenit als Randfazies ehemaliger leukophyrischer Gänge in Sepertin und Gabbro' *Bulletin of the Geological Institute of the University of Uppsala* XL (1961) 429-53) finds evidence to suppose that nephrite may have been mined anciently in Honan, in Shang territory, but this possibility is by no means proved. See also S.H.Hansford *Chinese Carved Jades* (London 1968) pp.32-3.

34. N.Egami and S.Mizuno *Nai-Mōkō Chōjō chitai*, in Archaeologia Orientalis series B, vol.I (Tokyo 1935) pp.24-47; M.Loehr *Chinese bronze age weapons* (Ann Arbor 1956) p.65ff; Okazaki Takashi 'Hoppō keito dōken to Chugoku-shiki dōken' in *Kodai hoppō bijutsu* (Osaka Municipal Museum 1954) pp.12-29.

35. M.Loehr *op.cit.* p.2ff.

36. Magdalene von Dewall *Pferd und Wagen im frühen China* (Bonn 1964).

37. Fêng Tê-chih *et al.* '1953 nien Anyang Ta-ssŭ-k'ung-ts'un fa-chüeh pao-kao' *KKHP* 9 (1955) 25-90; Kuo Pao-chün *Chün-hsien Hsin-ts'un* (Peking 1964) p.28 ff, p.47ff.

38. J.Needham and Lu Gwei-djen 'Efficient equine harness' *Physis* (Firenze) vol. II, fasc.2 (1960) pp.121-62; Lefebvre des Noëttes *L'attelage et le cheval à selle à travers les âges: contribution a l'histoire de l'esclavage* (Paris 1931).

39. G.D.Lu, R.A.Salaman and J.Needham 'The wheelwright's art in ancient China' *Physis* (Firenze) vol.I fasc.2,3 (1959).

40. S.I.Rudenko *Kul'tura naseleniya Gornoaltaya v skifskoye vremya* (Moscow 1953) p.232ff; *Kul'tura naseleniya tsentral'nogo Altaya v skifskoye vremya* (Moscow 1960) p.223ff; Wang Po-hung *et al.* '1955-57 nien Shensi Ch'ang-an Fêng-hsi fa-chüeh chien-pao' *KK* 1959.10, 516-30, esp. pp. 528-30; Chang-chia-p'o ti hsi-Chou chê-ma-k'êng.

41. Kuo Pao-chün *Chün-hsien Hsin-ts'un* (Peking 1964) p.XL. The Shang type of rectangular cheek-piece survived into the 9th century B C.

42. In general the aspects of change and continuity in bronze art and technique in the transition from the Shang to the Chou period are intelligible by making two assumptions: that the Chou conquerors had been familiar in their north-western territories with a bronze metallurgy hardly less advanced than that of the Shang bronze-casters; and that the motifs used in Chou art were broadly similar to those of Shang, but distinct in parts of the iconography and in stylistic treatment. At least one bronze vessel has been proposed on the evidence of its inscription as a Chou product of pre-conquest date. Cf. W.Watson *Ancient Chinese Bronzes* (London 1962) p.48f; and M.Loehr *Ritual Vessels of Bronze Age China* (New York 1968) p. 50.

CHAPTER THREE
Technology

1. For neolithic kilns cf. Acad. of Sci. Institute of Archaeology *Hsi-an Pan-p'o* (*The neolithic village at Pan-p'o*) (Peking 1963) p.156ff; *ejusd. Miao-ti-kou yü San-li-ch'iao* (Peking 1959); for Shang dynasty kilns cf. Ma Ch'üan, Mao Pao-liang 'Chêng-chou fa-hsien ti chi-ko shih-ch'i ti ku-tai yao-chih' *Wên-wu* 1957.10, 58ff; Yün P'êng *et al.* 'Hsing-t'ai Shang-tai yi-chih-chung ti t'ao-yao' *ibid.* 1956.12, 53ff. A Chou period kiln is described in Mêng Hao 'Honan Wu-an-hsien Wu-chi ku-ch'êng-chung ti yao-chih', *KK* 1959.7, 338ff, and a Han brick-built kiln in Ning Tu-hsüeh 'Chiu-ch'üan Hsia-ho-ch'ing Han-tai chuan-yao yao-chih shih-chüeh chien-pao' *Wên-wu* 1958.12, 36-7.

2. Lin-shan-chai kiln at Chêng-chou, see Ma Ch'üan, etc., *ut sup.*

3. R.Ghirshman *Fouilles de Sialk* (Musée du Louvre 1938) vol.I, p.37ff.

4. In the Shang period the prevailing pottery is grey and evidently was fired in a reducing kiln atmosphere. Even earlier, in the Yangshao period, both oxidizing and reducing atmospheres have been deduced experimentally for red pottery; and in the case of the thin, black, burnished ware of Lungshan and some fine grey ware of the early Shang period, it has been shown that the kiln atmosphere may have been at first oxidizing and later reducing. The white pottery of Shang is made of almost pure kaolin and even in an oxidizing flame would not necessarily turn red, but the success in maintaining its whiteness nevertheless points to a reducing atmosphere.

5. A full account of the Shang pottery excavated at Anyang is given in the first part of the third volume of the Hsiao T'un report published by the Academia Sinica, Taiwan (*Yin-hsü ch'i-wu: chia-pien: t'ao-ch'i shang-chi*). An analysis of the high-fired pottery is given on page 19:

SiO	71·66
Al₂O₃	18·6
Fe₂O₃	3·12
FeO	0·49
CaO	0·68
MgO	0·83
Na₂O	1·06
K₂O	2·25
TiO₂	0·85
MnO	0·02

It apparently was not possible to make an independent analysis of the very thin layer of glaze, but the composition of glaze and fabric together demonstrates the felspathic character of the former. The post-Shang history of hard glazing is obscure. At T'un-hsi in Anhui (Yin Ti-fei 'Anhui T'un-hsi hsi-Chou mu-tsang fa-chüeh pao-kao' *KKHP* 1959.4, 59-87) a large quantity of hard-glazed pottery of the 9th century B C was found. Thereafter the tradition seems not to be documented before the 4th century B C (cf. a vessel copying a bronze form in the Seattle Museum of Art). The type of hard-glazed pottery known as 'proto-porcelain' seems to have been first made in the mid-Han period, and not for long. The use of lead-fluxed glaze in China dates from the 3rd century B C. The adoption of lead-glaze at about the same time in the Near East poses the question of a contact with China, but as concerns ceramics no proof of contact can be brought.

6. Only one foundry floor is clearly described as such in the reports of the Anyang excavations. Well-reinforced narrow channels, mostly interpreted as drains, are a ubiquitous feature of the site. It is possible that more of these than has been supposed were connected with bronze smelting and founding. See references under notes 10 and 11 below.

7. Liao Yung-min 'Chêng-chou-shih fa-hsien ti yi-ch'u Shang-tai chü-chu yü tsao-t'ung-ch'i yi-chih chien-chieh' *Wên-wu* 1957.6, 73-4.

8. W.P.Yetts *The Eumorfopoulos Collection* (London 1929) vol. 1, pp.36-7: 'Among many ancient Chinese vessels which I have examined there is not one which appears to be cast in moulds by the direct method. . . . The familiar tradition that the more elaborate bronzes were always cast *à cire perdue* is amply verified by scrutiny of specimens . . .'.

9. O.Karlbeck 'Anyang moulds' *Bulletin of the Museum of Far-eastern Antiquities (Stockholm)* 7 (1935) 39-60.

10. Shih Chang-ju 'Bronze casting of the Yin Dynasty' *Bulletin of the Institute of History and Philology of Academia Sinica* 26 (1955) 95-129.

11. N.Barnard *Bronze casting and bronze alloys in ancient China* Monumenta Serica Monograph XIV (1961).

12. Shih Chang-ju 'Yin-hsü tsui-chin chih chung-yao fa-hsien' *KKHP* 2 (1947) 1-81; the positive model for the mould is described on page 40 and illustrated in figure 10.

13. Cf. an ivory goblet and a pottery *tou* found at Chengchou: W.Watson *Archaeology in China* pl.38; Chêng T.K. *Archaeology in China* vol.II, Shang China, pls.XXII upper and XXIX upper.

14. This could not be said if we accepted an explanation of the scored lines suggested by O.Karlbeck. He speculated that the lines were marked on the soft clay of the footrim mould-core by a network of silk threads which held the core in place in the assembled mould, thus ensuring the proper spacing for the casting of the bottom of the vessel. Apart from the implausibility of

such a contrivance, the use of a cat's cradle of threads appears to be ruled out by the fact that the lines appear sometimes on convex bases, which imply a concave surface on the core.

15. N.Barnard *op.cit.* pp.108-9. The author's denial of the employment of wax casting in China before the Han dynasty is unnecessary to the main argument on the unusual elaboration of piece-mould work. In fact, bronze and gold with intricate *ajouré* ornament requiring a wax technique were manufactured, at the latest, from about 400 BC. The possibility of an earlier employment of wax is discussed in this chapter. Yang Ken and Liu Ssǔ-chu ('Chan-kuo liang-Han t'ieh-ch'i ti chin-hsiang-hsüeh k'ao-ch'a ch'u-pu pao-kao' *KKHP* 1960.1, 73-103), speaking of the period of the Warring States, allow that 'the wax model method may also have existed'.

16. For the *Ssǔ mu wu ting* see Ch'ên Mêng-chia 'Yin-tai t'ung-ch'i san pien' *KKHP* 1954.7, 29f and pls.40-3.

17. Satō Taketoshi *Chūgoku kodai kōgyōshi no kenkyū* p.320ff. The use of bellows, singly and in gangs, is reflected in literature from the 5th century BC. The bellows in this period seem to have been used for smelting and casting iron rather than bronze. Cf. Yang K'uan *Chan-kuo shih* pp.11-12.

18. Ch'ang Wên-chai 'Hou-ma tung-Chou hsün-jên-mu' *Wên-wu* 1960.8/9, 15-18; Chang Wan-chung 'Hou-ma tung-Chou t'ao-fan ti tsao-hsing kung-yi' *Wên-wu* 1962.4/5, 37-42; Yeh Hsüeh-ming 'Hou-ma Niu-ts'un ku-ch'êng-nan tung-Chou yi-chih ch'u-t'u ti t'u-t'ao-ch'i ti fên-ch'i' *ibid.* pp.43-54.

19. Chikashige Sadakiyo was the first, in his *Oriental Alchemy* (Tokyo 1936), to draw attention to the wider implications of the composition of ancient Chinese bronze. The characteristic high proportion of lead is seldom below 5 per cent, and often accounts for as much as 20 per cent. 10-15 per cent of lead is an average in Shang bronze, as much in weapons placed in the tombs as in the ornate vessels. No rationale is discernible in the varying composition: for example, the lead content is not even roughly in inverse proportion to the tin, so that the two metals do not seem to have been treated as equivalent. Bronze with

10 per cent of lead is not uncommon through the Chou period and even in Han times. For examples of bronze analyses (with further bibliographical references) see Ch'ên Mêng-chia 'Yin-tai t'ung-ch'i san pien' *KKHP* 1954.7, 15-59, esp. pp. 31-56. A notable divergence is found in the Yünnan kingdom of Tien in the 1st century BC, where the proportion of lead in bronze is much below the Chinese average even of the contemporary Han period: cf. Yünnan-shêng po-wu-kuan *Yünnan Chin-ning Shih-chai-shan ku-mu-ch'ün fa-chüeh pao-kao* (Peking 1959) p.135. Lead found as follows: a bracelet 3·8 per cent, an axe 1·74 per cent, swords and drums less than 1 per cent.

20. R.J.Gettens 'Some observations concerning the lustrous surface on certain eastern bronze mirrors' *Technical studies* III (July 1934) 29-37; 'The oxide patina on ancient high-tin bronze' *Bulletin of the Fogg Art Museum* XI (1949) 16-28; H.J.Plenderleith 'Technical notes on Chinese bronzes with special reference to patina and incrustation' *Transactions of the Oriental Ceramic Society* XVI (1938) 33-55.

21. Chêng Shao-tsung 'Jê-ho Hsing-lung fa-hsien ti Chan-huo shêng-ch'an kung-chü t'ieh' *K'ao-ku t'ung-hsün* 1956.1, 29-35; W.Watson *Archaeology in China* pls.78a, b. For a general account of iron in the archaeological record with a map of find-places see Huang Chan-yüeh 'Chin-nien ch'u-t'u ti Chan-kuo liang-Han t'ieh-ch'i' *KKHP* 1957.3, 93-108; and with fuller reference to literary sources see J.Needham 'The development of iron and steel technology in China', Newcomen Society (London 1958).

22. K.F.Smirnov *Savromaty* (Moscow 1964) esp. ch.5, p.174ff. Anthropometric evidence shows the survival of the Andronovan and Srubnaya ethnic types into the Sauromatian period. Smirnov surmises that the western Andronovo people and culture contributed largely to the expansion of population in the region between the Urals and the Volga, which, after the general adoption of iron in the 7th century BC, was the home of the Sauromatian people and culture. Some Srubnaya traits were also contributed, and an eastern ethnic component, deemed to originate from the steppes of central Asia, is indicated by the presence of brachycephalics in Sarmatian tombs, particularly in the Prokhorov region.

23. *Tso Chuan* 29th year of Chao Kung; cf. Yang K'uan *Chan-kuo shih* pp.11-12. At its introduction iron was produced mainly in Honan, in the territory of the Han and Ch'u states, and in Hopei, at the capital of the Chao state (Han-tan) and in the territory of the state of Yen.

24. Cf. Kanaseki Jo 'Ryūtsū keizai no hattatsu' in *Sekai kōkogakutaikei* (Heibonsha) (Tokyo 1968) vol.6, Asia, pp.149-61.

25. T'ang Lan 'Chung-kuo ku-tai shê-hui shih-yong ch'ing-t'ung nung-ch'i wên-t'i ti ch'u-pu yen-chiu' *Ku-kung Po-wu-yüan yüan-k'an* 2 (1960) 10-34.

26. Satō Taketoshi *op.cit.* p.364.

27. In the territory of Yen; the moulds are designed for casting hoes, axes and tubular objects possibly intended for the frames of carriage hoods. Cf. W.Watson *Archaeology in China* (London 1960) p.26, pl.78.

28. Sun T'ing-lieh 'Hui-hsien ch'u-t'u ti chi-chien t'ieh-ch'i ti chin-hsiang hsüeh k'ao-ch'a' *KKHP* 1956.2, 125ff.

29. Or can it be that the literate Chinese did not well distinguish between casting and forging? *Ye*, to work iron, is comparatively rare in early texts in the literal sense.

30. Sekino Takeshi *Chūgoku kōkogaku kenkyū*, pp.159-77: Chūgoku shoki tekki bunka no ikkōsatsu.

31. In the Eastern Han period subterranean tombs of dry-stone walling were often roofed by barrel vaulting over extended galleries or by corbelling over smaller chambers of rectangular plan. The principle of the arch inherent in some of these structures seems to have been little exploited in buildings above the ground beyond the framing of windows such as those of the mile-forts along the Great Wall. The brick and stone houses represented by the tomb models of Han date founded a tradition in which the design and ornament of buildings in these materials were borrowed from wooden trabeate structures. Since the roof remained the chief major ornamental feature of all buildings it is natural that ornament proper to timber framed roofs and eaves should be imitated to some extent in brick and stone. In later times stone might be used in faithful imitation of a very

ornate wooden building, but this seems to have been rare and such edifices were of modest size. Cf. J. Prip-Møller *Chinese Buddhist Monasteries* pls. 283-6. In general see A. Boyd *Chinese architecture and town planning 1500–1911* (London 1962); and A. Soper in L. Sickman and A. Soper *The art and architecture of China*, 2nd ed. (London 1968) pp. 216-35.

32. Acad. of Sci. Institute of Archaeology *Hsi-an Pan-p'o* (*The neolithic village at Pan-p'o*) p. 9 ff. Little is known of building habits in the Lungshan period. It is possible that rectangular ground-plans then became general even for small houses. Evidence for a rectangular building of Lungshan date is reported from Honan: Liu Hu-lan 'Honan Yen-shih Hui-tsui yi-chih fa-chüeh chien-pao' *Wên-wu* 1959.2, 41-2.

33. The first volume of Hsiao T'un report published by the Academia Sinica, Taiwan, deals with the excavations and describes the building foundations in detail: *Yi-chih ti fa-hsien yü fa-chüeh: yi pien: Yin-hsü chien-chu yi-ts'un*. The facts are summarized by Chêng T.K. *Archaeology in China* vol. II, Shang China pp. 39-59; and by Shih Chang-ju 'Yin-hsü chien-chu yi-ts'un' *Academia Sinica Institute of History and Philology: Archaeologia Sinica: Hsiao T'un* vol. I fasc. 2.

34. Acad. of Sci. Institute of Archaeology *Hui-hsien fa-chüeh pao-kao* (Peking 1956) p. 116, fig. 138.

35. T'ang Chin-yü 'Hsi-an hsi-chiao Han-tai chien-chu yi-chih fa-chüeh pao-kao' *KKHP* 1959.2, 45-54; Wang Shih-jen 'Han Ch'ang-an-ch'êng nan-chiao li-chih chien-chu' *KK* 9 (1963) 501-15.

36. An Chih-min 'Gan-lan-shih chien-chu ti k'ao-ku yen-chiu' *KKHP* 1963.2, 65-83.

CHAPTER FOUR
China and the nomad heritage

1. *Shih chi* ch. 100. Chinese tradition explained the Hsiung-nu as a mixture of Chinese and nomadic people. For Herodotus' change in the plan of his history, which gave more prominence to the account of the Scyths, see J. E. Powell *The History of Herodotus*, London 1939, where it is argued that the plan of the work matured in three stages, in the third of which the 'Persian history' was remodelled as an introduction to the account of the Persian wars with Greece, with consequent enhancement of the fateful rôle of the Scyths.

2. Cf. W. Samolin 'Hsiung-nu, Hun, Turk' *Central Asian Journal* vol. 3, no. 2, 143-50. Philology has not established a certain connexion between the ethnic names Hsiung-nu and Hun, but most scholars would agree with Pelliot: 'Les noms de Hiung-Nou, de Huns et de Hûna seraient-ils trois appellations absolument indépendantes l'une de l'autre? Ce n'est pas *a priori* très vraisemblable'. P. Pelliot 'A propos de Comans' *Journal Asiatique* (1920) 141.

3. Cf. S. I. Rudenko *Kul'tura Gunnov i Noinulinskie kurgany* (Moscow 1962); G. K. Sosnovskiy 'O poselenii gunnskoy epokhi v doline reki Chikoya (Zabay-kal'ye)' *Kratkie soobshchenia Instituta Istorii Material'noy kul'tury* XIV (1947) 35-9. A. B. Davydova, V. T. Shilov 'K voprosu o zemledelii y Gunnov' *Vestnik Drevney Istorii* 2 (1953) 193-201. According to Chinese sources stockraising was the main occupation of the Hsiung-nu, but the *Shih chi* notes that in 89 BC snow killed off their herds and that grain did not ripen in their fields. The Hsiung-nu were fully aware that their practice of agriculture gave them a military advantage over their neighbours. In 66 BC men and horses were despatched to establish agriculture in the west of the Hsiung-nu territory as a step towards extending their power westwards, particularly over their neighbours the Wu-sun.

4. It is possible that a Hsiung-nu word for sword, i.e. the akinakes, is denoted by the term *ching-lu* which appears in the *Han shu: ti li chih* as the name for shrines existing at Yün-yang, not far from the capital, under the emperor Wu Ti. Kao Chü-hsün of the Academia Sinica, Taipei, in a circulated paper (University of California, Berkeley, Department of Chinese), has argued strongly that *ching-lu*, anciently *kieng-glâg*, stands for some such word as *kingrak*, the term used in modern Turkic dialects for a double-bladed knife worn at the waist; and that the *ching-lu* was the symbol of a sword cult, a practice broadly akin to Scythic

institutions. The view of *ching-lu* as an actual transcription of akinakes, as argued by F.Hirth in his *Ahnentafel Attilas*, is hardly admissible. See also Egami Namio *Yūrashiya kodai hokuhō bunka* (Yokyo 1948) pp.225-9.

5. Cf. especially A.Gryazov 'Etapy razvitiya khozyaystva skotovodcheskikh plemën Kazakhstana i yuzhnoy Sibiri v epokhu bronzy' *Kratkie soobshchenia Instituta Etnografii* 26 (1957) 21 ff.

6. O.Lattimore *Inner Asian Frontiers of China* (New York 1940).

7. A.Gryaznov *op.cit.*; S.S.Chernikov ('Rol' andronovskoy kul-tury v istorii Sredney Azii i Kazakhstana' *Kratkie soobshchenia Instituta Etnografii* 26 (1957) 28-33) stresses the rôle of stockraising in the Andronovo culture more than Kiselev does, but both would put the transition from settled to nomadic stockraising in the period 8th–7th century BC, whether it was at the end of the Andronovan tradition or the beginning of the Karasuk-Tagar tradition as this penetrated to Kazakhstan. The connexion of this process with the spread of iron metallurgy is discussed in G.P. Sosnovskiy 'Rannie kochevniki Zabay-kal'ya' *Kratkie soobshchenia Instituta Istorii Material'noy Kul'tury* VIII (1940) 36 ff.

8. *Sauromatian* is the term applied by K.F.Smirnov (*Savromaty*, Moscow 1964) to the nomadic culture in the region of the Ural river to the north of the Caspian. This river had formerly been the boundary separating the domain of Andronovan culture from the Srubnaya tradition of the western steppes. From the Sauromatian period onwards the line of cultural separation is less distinct.

9. See chapter 2 note 28.

10. The disturbances on the north-west frontier of the Chou state in the 9th and 8th centuries BC are interpreted by R.Heine-Geldern as evidence for a far-travelling migration from the west which he believes to have reached China at about this time: 'Das Tocharerproblem und die Pontische Wanderung' *Saeculum* 2 (1951) 225-55.

11. N.L.Chlenova 'Pamyatniki karaksuk-tagarskogo vremeni v minusinskoy kotlo-vine' *Sovetskaya arkheologia* 3 (1963) 48 ff. Her periodization of the Karasuk culture brings its latest (Korolevskiy) stage down to the beginning of the 7th century BC and

Early Tagar is put at 7th–6th centuries BC. This chronology agrees with the view expressed here that the crucial initial date of the establishment of the Scythic continuum in the eastern steppes falls about 500 BC and marks the beginning of the Late Tagar. Material from the Ordos region of China assignable to the earlier part of the Scythic period is rare; it is possible that some of the animal plaques conventionally referred to the 2nd–1st centuries BC should be dated earlier. See note 26 below and cf. also S.V.Kiselev 'Mongolia v drevnosti' *Izves-tiya Akad. Nauk SSSR seriya istorii i filosofii* 4 (1947) 355-72: fig.2 material of Karasuk-Western Chou date, fig.3 material of the Scythic period.

12. Ma Ch'ang-shou *Pei-ti yü Hsiung-nu* (Peking 1962) p.92 ff.

13. *Re* currency see Kanaseki Jo as cited in chapter 3 note 24 above.

14. Wall building and its rôle in defence is described in Yang K'uan *Chan-kuo shih* pp.139-42. The earliest continuous defences along state boundaries are recorded for Ch'u in the Ch'un-ch'iu period. These and the similar walls completed by the states of Ch'i, Wei and Han in the late 5th and the first half of the 4th centuries BC were a de-velopment of the earth dikes which were multiplied in this period for flood control and irrigation. Warfare was no longer a series of contests between city states staged in flat country where boundaries were not clearly drawn or regularly defended. In the Chan-kuo period (453–232 BC) state boundaries were increasingly manned and defensive works in the form of dikes with fortresses, etc., at intervals were more or less constantly maintained. The construction of these walls as a feature of the internecine wars of the states seems to have been well under way before the pressure of nomadic peoples on the north-west frontier in the 4th century BC induced a similar policy of defence against intrusions from Mongolia into the state territories. The north-facing walls which were then built by the states of Chao, Yen and Ch'in, though not planned in concert, provided much of the length of the continuous national bulwark, the Great Wall, which was completed by Shih Huang Ti of Ch'in after he unified China in 232 BC. Only small parts of earlier walls had been faced with stone. Ch'in now revetted with

stone and set forts at close intervals upon a wall stretching unbroken from the sea to Kansu. The advantage conferred on the defenders by the possession of the cross-bow made the wall particularly effective against nomads who lacked this weapon. The cost of walled defences was now more acceptable than it can have been during the warfare of the states.

15. N. Egami and S. Mizuno *Nai-Mōko Chōjō chitai* Archaeologia Orientalis, series B, vol. I (Tokyo 1935). There is no evidence for the location of bronze casting centres in the Northern Zone. Komai and Kiselev (cf. *Drevnyaya Istoria Yuzhnoy Sibiri* 1st ed. p. 178) favoured the Suiyüan as the likely area. At a number of investigated sites droplets of bronze have been found which suggest that bronze manufacture was of a temporary kind and modest in scale. For the small objects cast in the Northern Zone no large installation need have existed. The operations possibly consisted largely of melting down cast bronze, obtained from the Chinese, for recasting. The largest objects produced by the nomad bronze founders were cauldrons, which are singularly uniform in design wherever they are encountered from the Northern Zone of China to south Russia. But the cauldrons are relatively rare and there is nothing to indicate their geographical origin beyond a general resemblance to some Chinese bronze vessels, which leads Egami to suggest that they were first made in the Northern Zone. While the composition of Northern Zone bronze appears to be normal, i.e. lacking the generous ingredient of lead present in pre-Han Chinese bronze, possibly a virtually unalloyed copper was sometimes used, as in a barbaric version of a *hsien* preserved in the British Museum which is likely to be a product of the Northern Zone.

16. Interesting variants of the scabbard-dagger are: a scabbard formed of interlaced scrolled snakes, emblems more characteristic of the south of China than the north at this period (Myron S. Falk collection); a dagger with the handle formed of close-set cells for inlay now missing; this technique is foreign to the metropolitan tradition of the late Chou period (J. W. Alsdorf collection); a dagger and open-work scabbard of silver (Frederick M. Mayer

collection). The first two are illustrated in *Arts of the Chou Dynasty* (Stanford University Museum 1958), nos. 158 and 159.

17. Cf. S. V. Kiselev 'Neolit i bronzovyy vek Kitaya' *Sovetskaya Arkheologia* IV (1960) 244 ff. The knives with ring terminals (sometimes an open rectangle) and slightly upturned point are the most characteristic. Kiselev speaks also of 'knives with hollow handles' into which a spike ('awl') is inserted, the latter decorated with a ring or the figure of a goat. This is the so-called *vkladyshevyy nozh* (knife-with-insert) of south Siberia, which according to Kiselev occurs in Chou China, having been identified by him during his visit to China in 1958, although no example of it seems to have been published.

18. Kiselev places the entry of the 'standing animal' into south Siberia at the end of the Karasuk period, but it remained characteristic of the Early Tagar. Cf. A. Salmony 'The origin and age of the "grazing" animal' *Silver Jubilee Volume of the Jimbunkagaku Kenkyūjō* (1954) pp. 336-8, where the question of origin is resolved in favour of China by a scholar with an unrivalled knowledge of the animal art of Central Asia.

19. Cf. Acad. of Sci. Institute of Archaeology *Shang-ts'un-ling* (Peking 1959): dragon in jade, pl. XXIX, no. 7; on a bronze *p'an*, pl. XIX, no. 1; double tigers on a circular domed object of bronze, pl. XXXVIII, no. 13; ouroboros dragon of bronze, pl. LII, no. 4; in stone, pl. LVII, no. 2; double ouroboroi of bronze, pl. XXIII, no. 9; interlaced scrolled dragons on bronze vessel, pl. XXXIII, no. 2. *Ejusd. Chün-hsien Hsin-ts'un* (Peking 1964): bird of prey in circle, pl. XCIV, nos. 2, 3; interlaced snakes, pl. LXXXVIII, no. 1; snake-dragons in circle, pl. LXXXII, nos. 1, 2.

20. Russian scholars argue that the inhabitants of the Altai in the Pazyryk period are to be regarded as Iranians. Cf. S. I. Rudenko 'Skifskaya problema u Altayskie nakhodki' *Izvestia Ak. Nauk SSSR Seria Istorii i filosofii* 6 (1944). It has already been noted (chapter 2 note 28 *q.v.*) that in the Tagar period of south Siberia the proportion of Europaeoid to Mongoloid skulls increases still further as compared with the Karasuk period.

21. Cf. esp. K. F. Smirnov cited in note 8

above, and *ejusd. Vooruzhenie Savromatov* (*Materialy i Issledovania po arkheologii SSSR no.* 101) Moscow 1961.

22. Herodotus, I: 106; IV: 1.

23. T. Sulimirski 'Scythian antiquities in Western Asia', *Artibus Asiae* XVII (1954) 282 ff.

24. K. A. Akishev and G. A. Kushaev *Drevnyaya kul'tura Sakov i Usuney doliny reki Ili*, Ak. Nauk Kazakhskoy SSR (Alma-Ata 1963).

25. R. D. Barnett 'The Treasure of Ziwiye' *Iraq* XVIII (1956) 111-16.

26. According to N. L. Chlenova (*Skifskiy olen'* (*Materialy i issledovania po arkheologii SSSR no.* 115) Moscow 1962), some deer plaques of characteristic Ordos form may be as early as the 6th century BC, and certainly not later than the 5th century BC. The deer with legs folded under it is said to date in south Siberia from the 5th century BC. It is an intrusive theme in the late Tagar culture, and not related to Shang as M. Loehr maintains ('The stag image in Scythia and the Far East' *Archives of the Chinese Art Society of America* ix (1955) 63-7). It is indicative of the nature of the Scythic continuum that (as Chlenova argues) the deer emblem should appear in the Ordos sooner than in the Minusinsk basin, and that in the 5th century BC the Black Sea area should appear to be independently in contact with a third area of deer tradition in a manner no longer perceptible in the 4th century BC. In the Scythic period seminal contacts between far east and far west no longer depended on the mediation of south Siberia.

27. Muscle-marks generally similar but more completely assimilated to Scythic design appear on animals carved on wooden coffins found in the Second Bashadar kurgan. See S. I. Rudenko: *Kul'tura naselenia Tsentral'nogo Altaya v skifskoye vremya*, Moscow 1960, p. 46, fig. 21.

28. I.e. in the Tien culture of Yünnan in the 2nd–1st century BC. See chapter 5, p. 149 ff.

29. K. F. Smirnov *Vooruzhenie Savromatov*, p. 29: 'The prototype [of the akinakes] has not been discovered. It appears that this form was very rapidly evolved among Iranian-speaking warriors during their campaigns into Western Asia. . . .' But according to A. I. Melyukova ('Vooruzhenie, voysko i voennoye iskusstvo Skifov'

Arkhiv I.A. 1011: Kandidatskaya dissertatsia, Moscow 1950, as cited by Bader) only *one* type of akinakes can be found an origin in the Iranian east – the territory of Iran and Media. She casts doubts on the theory of a Persian or Median origin of all types of akinakai, and especially of the form with kidney-shaped guard, since no representations of akinakai in Persia are earlier than the 6th century BC, whereas they appear in Scythian territory already in the 7th century BC. Minns and Komai have expressed similar doubts regarding a simple derivation of the akinakes from the Persian sphere.

30. An akinakes with a blade closely resembling that of a Chinese sword of 'classical' type is reported from the Minusinsk basin: N. L. Chlenova 'Bronzovyy mech iz Minusinskoy kotloviny' *Kratkie soobshchenia Instituta Istorii Material'noy Kul'tury* 60 (1955) 135 ff. The decoration of the handle rules out any question of Chinese manufacture.

31. For the bird-head see reference under note 19 above.

32. The swords are published as follows: Acad. of Sci. Institute of Archaeology *Loyang Chung-chou-lu* (Peking 1959) pl. 46; *ejusd. Shang-ts'un-ling* (Peking 1959) pl. LIV, no. 4; Wang Po-hung 'K'o-shêng-chuang ho Chang-chia-p'o ti liang-Chou mu-tsang' *KK* 1959.10, 525-8.

33. Cf. Lin Shou-chin 'Tung-Chou-shih t'ung-chien ch'u-lun' *KKHP* 1962.2, 75-84.

34. The Ch'ang-sha bow: Acad. of Sci. Institute of Archaeology *Ch'ang-sha fachüeh pao-kao* (Peking 1957) p. 59 f and pl. XXVII. For a sword with intact hilt binding said to have come from Ch'ang-sha, see W. Watson: *Handbook to the Collections of Early Chinese Antiquities* (British Museum 1963) p. 60, fig. 17.

35. K. F. Smirnov *Vooruzhenie Savromatov* pl. 9, no. 5.

36. T. Sulimirski *op. cit.* p. 308.

37. B. A. Kuftin *Arkheologicheskie raskopki v Trialeti* p. 43.

38. T. Sulimirski *op. cit.* p. 310.

39. K. F. Smirnov *Vooruzhenie Savromatov* p. 51 f.

40. An Chih-min 'T'ang-shan shih-huan-mu chi ch'i hsiang-kuan ti yi-wu' *KKHP* 1954.7, 77-86; on the date of the Li-yü

style see M.Loehr *Ritual Bronze Vessels of China* (New York 1968) p.142; and W. Watson *Ancient Chinese Bronzes*, p.58ff.

CHAPTER FIVE
Provinces apart: north-east and south-west

1. Herodotus (IV:116) locates the Sauromatoi around the mouth of the Don. The Sarmatians moved from the region north of the Aral sea into south Russia, crossing the Volga, in the second half of the 3rd century B C. Smirnov associates the Sauromatoi with the adoption of iron in the region between the Urals and the Caspian and the Don mouth (see above, chapter 3, note 22, and chapter 4, note 8). Rostovtseff (*Iranians and Greeks* p.113) connects the Sarmatians with tombs at Prokhorovka near Orenburg which contain a characteristic spearhead, a weapon notably lacking from the Scythic armament. While the chronological and archaeological distinction between Sauromatians and Sarmatians is tolerably clear the ethnic and political distinction is not. Both were peoples of Iranian stock.

2. G.P.Sosnovskiy 'Rannie kochevniki Zabaykal'ya' *Kratkie soobshchenia Instituta Istorii Material'noy Kul'tory* VIII (1940) 36ff; *ejusd*. 'Plitochnye mogily Zabaykal'-ya' *Trudy Otdela Istorii Pervobytnoy Kul'-tury* vol.1.

3. The only comprehensive account of the slab-grave culture of Manchuria and other parts of north-east China is Mikami Tsugio *Man sen genshi funbo no kenkyū* ('The dolmen and stone-cist in Manchuria and Korea') Tokyo 1961. Sites on Aniva bay at the end of the Sakhalin peninsula are described in R.V.Chubarova 'Raboty Sakhakinskogo otryada Dal'nevostochnoy Ekspeditsii v 1952 godu' *Kratkie soobshche-nia Instituta material'noy kul'tury* 71 (1958) 119ff. The material found on them was coarse, flat-bottomed pots with impressions of wrapped cord, whipped cord and comb-teeth; fine flint tools accompanied polished stone axes; the dwellings were *zemlyanki* with sunken floors. See also T.I.Andreev 'Tsai Ta-pi-tê-wan yen-hai chi ch'i tao-yü shang fa-hsien ti kung-yüan ti-erh chih ti-yi ch'ien-nien ti yi-chih' *KKHP* 1958.4, 27-41; V.E.Larichev 'Drevnie kul'tury

severnogo Kitaya' *Ak. Nauk SSSR Sibirskoye otdelenie, Trudy Seria Istoriches-kaya* tom I (Saransk 1959); Torii R. 'Populations préhistoriques de la Mand-chourie méridionale' *Journal of the College of Science, Tokyo Imperial University,* XXXVI (1915) art.8.

4. The Chi-lin region of Manchuria is the best explored: cf. T'ung Chu-ch'ên 'Chi-lin hsin-shih-ch'i wên-hua ti san-chung lei-hsing' *KKHP* 1957.3, 31-8; *ejusd*. 'Chi-lin Hsi-t'uan-shan shih-kuan-mu fa-chüeh pao-kao' *KKHP* 1964.1, 29-48; *ejusd*. 'Chi-lin ti hsin-shih-ch'i shih-tai wên-hua' *K'ao-ku t'ung-hsün* 1955.2, 5-10; Chia Lan-p'o 'Chi-lin Hsi-t'uan-shan ku-mu chih fa-chüeh' *K'o-hsüeh t'ung-pao* 1950.1/8, 573-5; K'ang Chia-hsing 'Chi-lin-shih wai-chiao fa-hsien hsin-shih-ch'i shih-tai ti yi-chih' *Wên-wu ts'an-k'ao tzŭ-liao* 1954.3.

5. *Nei-mêng-ku ch'u-t'u wên-wu hsüan-chi* (Peking 1963) pl.14 shows a finished stone 'ploughshare', but the rougher pieces on pls.15, 16 no doubt served the same purpose. Larichev in the article cited in note 3 above suggests that bronze ploughshares 'in all probability' were also used in the north-west, but no example of such a tool is reported from the region. The only bronze ploughshares recorded in East Asia come from south-west China, an area of comparatively primitive agriculture in the pre-Han period. Those excavated at Shih-chai-shan in Yünnan (excavation report *ut. sup.* chapter 3 note 19) belong to the 2nd or the early 1st century B C. They were placed in noble tombs and probably denote an agricultural rite performed by Tien kings and chiefs or are symbols of wealth in land. In the north-east, after bronze came into use, the stone ploughshares were polished and more carefully shaped. For an example of a primitive specimen found in the Soviet maritime province cf. A.P.Okladnikov *Dalëkoye proshloye Primor'ya* (Vladivostok 1959) p.130, fig.52.

6. Hamada Kōsaku *Sekihō Kōsan-go, Archaeologia Orientalis* Series A, vol.IV, (Tokyo 1938).

7. I.e. *Erichloa villosa* Kunt and *Setaria lutescens*. The possibility of rice cultivation in the slab-grave culture rests on nothing more than the finding at T'u-ch'êng-tzŭ of a pottery vessel with a pierced base, resemb-

ling the upper part of the Chinese steamer called *hsien*. This evidence is not more conclusive here than in the case of the central Yangshao culture, where Andersson pointed out the presence of similar vessels.

8. Hamada Kōsaku *op.cit.* pl.xxvi, nos. 14, 15.

9. An Chih-min 'T'ang-shan shih-kuan-mu chi ch'i hsiang-kuan ti yi-wu' *KKHP* 1954.7, 77-86.

10. For T'u-ch'êng-tzŭ see K'ang Chia-hsing 'Chi-lin-chiang-pei T'u-ch'êng-tzŭ ku-wên-hua yi-chih chi shih-kuan-mu' *KKHP* 1957.1, 43-52; anon 'Chi-lin ti-ssŭ ch'ü T'u-ch'êng-tzŭfa-hsien chung-yao ti hsin-shih-ch'i shih-tai yi-chih' *Wên-wu ts'an-k'ao tzŭ-liao* 1954.9, 158ff.

11. The bronze sickle and ornaments found at T'u-ch'êng-tzŭ are illustrated at *KKHP* 1957.1, 43-52, pl.2, no.6 and pl.4, nos.5, 7. At pl.4, no.6 are illustrated some tubular beads of white stone which are of a type known in east Siberia.

12. For example, An Chih-min argues that the dwellings at Hsi-t'uan-shan and Sao-ta-kou, where *li* were found, are pre-Warring States in date (i.e. earlier than the mid 5th century BC) while the graves near by, which lack the *li*, are later.

13. Mikami Tsugio *op.cit.* p.309.

14. Stone magatama in the neolithic of the maritime province: A.P. Okladnikov *Dalëkoye proshloye Primor'ya* p.54, fig.19, no.1. In Japan the shape is known in bone and stone in the time of the Jōmon neolithic, but in jade only from the early Kofun-jidai, i.e. after the 2nd century AD.

15. Mikami Tsugio *op.cit.* p.349ff.

16. The commonest shells are: *Ostrea edulis, Pecten Lamarc., Area Linn., Mactia Linn., Pectunculus Lamarc., Callista Poll., Mytilus Linn., Mya Linn., Rapana bezoar.* One species, reported only as *rozhok volnistyy*, is said to live at a depth of 30-70 m, and could only have been collected from a boat. The fish are salt-water species, including shark, flounder, bullhead, sea ruff, Japanese sea pike, mackerel and herring, which were probably taken by nets of various weights, and cod and tunny which suggest line fishing.

17. A.P. Okladnikov *Dalëkoye proshloye Primor'ye* p.144. The author connects the spread of shell-mounds along the coasts of the maritime province with the political

events which took place in China at the end of the 2nd and the beginning of the 1st millennium BC!

18. Cf. Mizuno S., Higuchi T., Okazaki T. *Tsushima: an archaeological survey of Tsushima Island in the Korea strait carried out in 1948. Archaeologia orientalis* Series B, vol. vi (Tokyo 1953). On the Japanese derivatives of these weapons see Mori Teijirō 'Buki' in ed. Wajima Seiichi *Nichon no kōkogaku* (Kawade Shobō) (Tokyo 1966) vol.iii *Yayoi-jidai* pp.291-6.

19. *Re* Kazakevichevo bronzes see chapter 2 note 31.

20. Chu Kuei 'Liao-ning Ch'ao-yang shih-erh-t'ai-ying-tzŭ ch'ing-t'ung tuan-chien mu' *KKHP* 1 (1960) 63-70. The identification of this weapon as a sword/dagger rather than a spearhead is borne out by the dimensions of some specimens which are clearly too heavy for hafting. Cf. also A.P. Okladnikov and E.V. Shavkunov 'Pogrebenie s bronzovymi kinzhalami na reke Maykhe (Primor'ye)' *Sovetskaya Arkheologia* 3 (1960) 282-8. Here the daggers are of the type known on Tsushima, and an isolated stumpy spearhead of pre-Han derivation has its blade treated in a manner similar to the daggers. The bronzes include also a degenerate mirror with eccentric double-loop and an over-all ornament of triangles filled with hachuring.

21. See chapter 1, note 32. The concept of a 'nuclear area' applied to technology is peculiarly appropriate to the bronze age.

22. Kao Chih-hsi 'Hunan Ning-hsiang-huang-ts'un fa-hsien Shang-tai t'ung-ch'i ho yi-chih' *KK* 1963.12, 646-58.

23. *Ejusd.* Ch'u Kung Wei ko' *Wên-wu* 1959.12, 60.

24. W. Watson 'A Chinese bell of the fifth century BC' *British Museum Quarterly* xxx (1965/6) 50-6; *ejusd.* 'Traditions of material culture in the territory of Ch'u' in ed. N. Barnard *Early Chinese art and its possible influence in the Pacific Basin: Proceedings of a symposium held at Columbia University in 1967* (in preparation).

25. Cf. Yünnan-shêng Po-wu-kuan *Yünnan Chin-ning Shih-chai-shan ku-mu-ch'ün fa-chüeh pao-kao* (Peking 1957). In the boat-coffin culture of Szechwan spearheads, tanged swords (with 'snake and hand' emblem), socketed axes with semi-circular blade, etc., occur alongside swords

and halberds of classical metropolitan types. Cf. Ssŭ-ch'uan-shêng Po-wu-kuan *Ssŭ-ch'uan-kuan-tsang fa-chüeh pao-kao* (Peking 1960). In the Tien culture of Yünnan the swords (here of iron), daggers and axes are still more distinctive, while halberds of the local tradition recall metropolitan types in use some five or six centuries earlier.

26. F. Heger *Alte Metalltrommeln aus Südostasien* (Leipzig 1902); recent important contributions to the problem of the drums are: J. Loewenstein 'The origins of the Malayan Metal Age' *Journal of the Malay Branch of the Royal Asiatic Society* 29(2) (1965) 5-78; B. A. V. Peacock 'The drums of Kampong Sungai Lang' *Malaya in History* X (1965) 3-15; H. R. van Heekeren *The Bronze-Iron Age of Indonesia* (The Hague 1958); Umehara Sueji 'Nampō Ajia no doko', *Tōhō gakuhō* (July 1962) 1-14.

27. Chikamori Tadashi 'Donson seidōki bunka no kigen ni kansuru isshiron' *Shigaku* 35 (1963) 65-96.

28. The minor geometric ornament appearing on the Dong-son bronzes, resembling the 'filler' ornament of the Huai style of the late Chou period, is found chiefly on the drums, but it had a still wider currency. It seems to represent a diffuse artistic tradition independent in origin from the bronze drums and weapons and probably already in use before the rise of the Dong-son bronze tradition. B. Karlgren ('The date of the Early Dong So'n culture' *Bulletin of the Museum of Far Eastern Antiquities* (Stockholm) 14 (1942) 28 ff) uses this type of ornament in an argument attributing the beginnings of the Dong-son tradition to the 5th-4th century B C. But such reliance on secondary elements in the ornament misconceives the nature of the

rapid adoption of bronze metallurgy in the southern area which gave rise to the first bronze-using culture hardly if at all before the Han period. Karlgren's chronology, particularly in the light of the evidence from Shih-chai-shan, puts the leading Dong-son types – drums and weapons – too early by three or four centuries.

29. The Shih-chai-shan excavation report (see note 25 above) is to be supplemented by: Sun T'ai-ch'u 'Yünnan Chin-ning Shih-chai-shan ku-yi-chih chi mu-tsang' *KKHP* I (1956) 43-63; B. Gray 'China or Dongson' *Oriental Art* O S II p. 99 ff. On the weapons see Chikamori Tadashi 'Unnan ni okeru Donson-bunka no mondai' *Shigaku* 32 (1959) 67-93.

30. *Shih chi* chap. 116: Hsi-nan-yi lieh-chuan. On the historical and literary references to the origin of the Tien kingdom and on the wider implications of its bronze culture cf. W. Watson 'The Kingdom of Tien and the Dongson culture' in *Readings in Asian Topics: papers read at the inaugural symposium of the Scandinavian Institute of Asian Studies* (Copenhagen 1968).

31. There was no funeral tablet in tomb no. 6 to identify its occupant. In tomb no. 13 was found an ideographic text on bronze which anticipates the manner of writing used much later for mnemonic liturgical records by the inhabitants of the Na-khi kingdom (cf. J. F. Rock *The ancient Na-khi kingdom of Southwest China* (Cambridge, Mass. 1947) vol. I, pls. 10, 11). While the Tien ideographs hardly prove literacy they testify to conscious independence from the Han tradition, the adoption of whose system of writing set a seal upon cultural capitulation.

Index

References to text figures are shown in italics

Cultural Frontiers
in Ancient East Asia

PLATES

*

1. Neolithic pottery fragments with cord-impressed surface, excavated at Ta-yüan-hsien cave, Kiangsu.

2. Impressions on modelling clay taken from neolithic potsherds excavated at Pan-p'o, Shensi, showing in positive form the basketwork and carved wood used for stamping the surface of the pottery during manufacture. After *Hsi-an Pan-p'o*.

3. Bowl of reddish pottery decorated with fishes in black, excavated at Pan-p'o, Shensi. Yangshao neolithic culture. Height 167 mm. After *Hsi-an Pan-p'o*.

4. Bowl of reddish pottery with ornament in black, excavated at Miao-ti-kou, Honan. Yangshao neolithic culture. Height 172 mm.

5. Red pottery amphora excavated at Pan-p'o, Shensi. Yangshao
neolithic culture. Height 310 mm. British Museum.

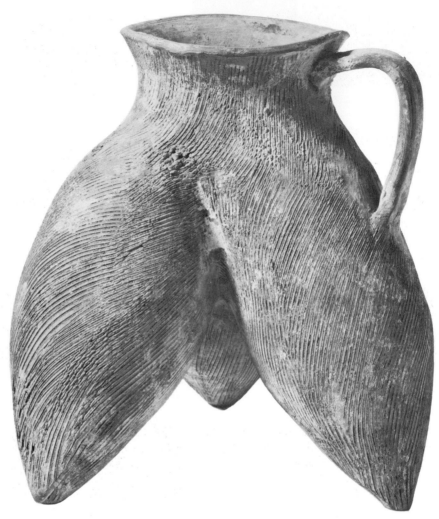

6. *Li* of grey pottery with cord-impressed surface. Lungshan neolithic culture. Height 230 mm. Avery Brundage collection, M. H. de Young Memorial Museum.

7. Stone knives of the neolithic tradition and their copies in iron.
(*a, e*) Honan; (*b, h*) Liaoning; (*c*) Kansu; (*d*) Shensi (Pan-p'o);
(*f*) Kiangsu; (*g*) Korea. After An Chih-min and *Hsi-an Pan-p'o*. Length
of knife (*a*) 160 mm, the rest to scale.

8. Stone axes. Upper row: Yangshao tradition, excavated at Pan-p'o, Shensi; lower row: Lungshan tradition, excavated at Hsi-hsia-hou, Shantung. Axe at top left length 104 mm, the rest to scale.

9. Neolithic stone axes. (*a*) Stone axe excavated near Ch'ing-ch'iang, Kiangsi; (*b*) shouldered axe, found on the surface of the site of Kok Charoen, Lopburi, Thailand. Length 170 mm and 65 mm resp.

10. Stone hoe blade, found at Alukerchen, Inner Mongolia. Length 338 mm. 10th–5th century BC.

11. Neolithic burial at Hsi-hsia-hou, Shantung. The head points to the east. After *K'ao-ku hsüeh-pao*.

12. Prone burial of the Shang period at Ta-ssŭ-kʻung, Anyang, Honan.

13. Neolithic crouched burial at Pai-tao-kou-p'ing, Kansu. The head points to the east.

14. Burial of a child at the neolithic village of Pan-p'o, Shensi. The head points to the west. After *Hsi-an Pan-p'o*.

15. Beaker of burnished black pottery excavated at Jih-chao, Shantung. Lungshan neolithic culture. Height 135 mm. After *K'ao-ku hsüeh-pao*.

16. Pottery *k'uei* excavated at Ching-chih-chen, Shantung. Lungshan neolithic culture. Height 279 mm. After *K'ao-ku hsüeh-pao*.

17. Nephrite rings. (*a*) Excavated at Turbino, Perm. Diameter 76 mm.
After O. N. Bader. (*b, c*) excavated at Glazkovo, Baikal. After Okladnikov. All 14th–10th century BC.

18. Pottery amphora of the Kansu Yangshao culture (Hsin-tien stage),
with black painted decoration. Height 310 mm. British Museum.

19. Pottery urn with black painted decoration. Kansu Yangshao culture (Ma-ch'ang stage). Height 145 mm. British Museum.

20. Pottery urn with decoration painted in black and dark red. Kansu Yangshao culture (Ma-ch'ang stage). Height 215 mm. British Museum.

21. Pottery urn with decoration painted in black and red. Kansu
Yangshao culture (Ma–ch'ang stage). Height 300 mm. British Museum.

22. Pottery beaker of northern neolithic type, found at Fu-hsün-yung,
K'o-shih-k'o-t'eng-ch'i, Inner Mongolia. Height 390 mm. After *Nei-
meng-ku ch'u-t'u wen-wu hsüan-chi*.

23. Long-bladed bronze axes. Length 95 and 110 mm, resp.
11th–10th century BC. British Museum.

24. Long-bladed bronze axes. (a) From the chariot tomb
at Ta-ssŭk'ung-ts'un, Anyang. Length 167 mm;
(b) found at Chao-tao-kou, Hopei. Length 125 mm.
11th–10th century BC. After K'ao-ku hsüeh-pao.

a

b

25. Bronze socketed axes found in the Minusinsk region of south Siberia. 13th–8th century B C. Tovostine collection. After Tallgren.

26. Bronze socketed axes. (*a*) Excavated in Cemetery 1 at Turbino, Perm, length 135 mm, after Bader; (*b*) excavated at Nan-shan-ken, Ning-ch'eng-hsien, Inner Mongolia, length 85 mm; (*c*) axe of the type found in south-west China, length 65 mm, British Museum; (*d*) from a tomb at Shih-chai-shan, Kunming, Yünnan, length 130 mm, British Museum. Respectively, 15th, 11th–8th, 3rd–2nd, 1st centuries B C.

a

b

c

d

a   b   c

27. Bronze socketed axes. (*a*) Shang type, from central China, length
95 mm, 13th–11th century B C, British Museum; (*b, c*) excavated at
Hsin-ts'un, Honan, length 120 mm, 10th–9th century B C. After Kuo Pao-chün.

28. Bronze halberd blades, *ko*. (*a*) Excavated at Hou-kang, Anyang, with the cap of the shaft end still in place; (*b*) of the commoner Shang type, with recessed ornament on the butt which may have held inlay of turquoise. Two script characters of the emblematic (clan-name) class are cast on the blade. Malcolm collection. Both 200 m long, 12th–11th century B C.

29. Bronze halberd blades, *ko*. (*a*) with separate tubular shaft mount and cap, length 240 mm, 5th–4th century BC; (*b*) with the shaft tube cast on the blade, from Shih-chai-shan, Kunming, Yünnan, length 230 mm, 1st century BC. British Museum.

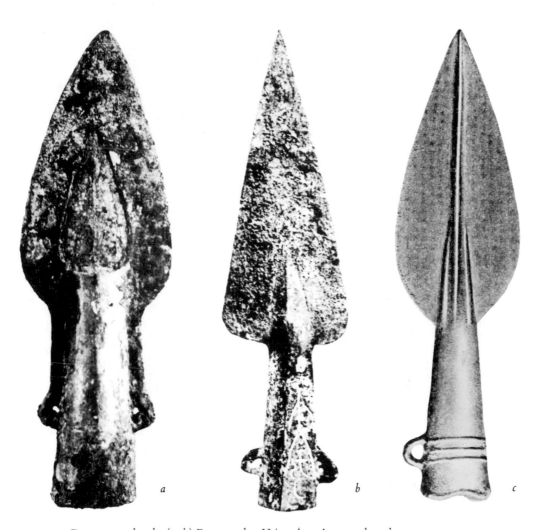

a   *b*   *c*

30. Bronze spearheads. (*a*, *b*) Excavated at Hsiao-t'un, Anyang, length 180 mm, 14th–11th century BC. After Umehara. (*c*) Excavated at Cemetery 1, Turbino, Perm, 15th–14th century BC. After Bader.

31. A Shang 'oracle bone' from Hsiao-t'un, Honan. A fragment of an animal scapula showing the oval pits carved before the oracle was taken. A heated bronze point was applied to the edge of the pits and the oracular answers divined from the cracks which resulted on the other side of the bone. British Museum.

32. Decoration on the handle of the *Ssŭ-wu-mu ting*. Height 385 mm,
Shang dynasty, 12th–11th century B C. After *K'ao-ku hsüeh-pao*.

33. Bronze *chia*. Height 250 mm, Shang dynasty, 15th–13th century BC.
British Museum.

34. Bronze *ting*. Height 240 mm, Shang dynasty, 15th–12th century B C.
Barlow Collection.

35. Bronze *ting* excavated at Hui-hsien, Honan. Height 200 mm, Shang dynasty, 15th–13th century BC.

36. Pottery vessel excavated at Erh-li-kang, Chengchou, Honan. Height
170 mm, Shang dynasty, 15th–14th century B C.

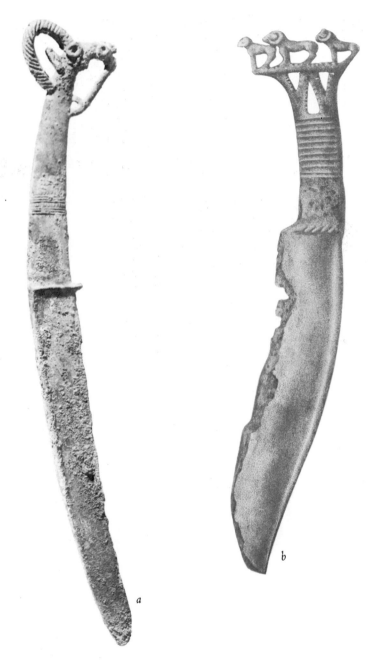

37. Bronze knives. (*a*) With ibex-head terminal. Length 318 mm, Shang dynasty, 12th–11th century BC. Malcolm collection. (*b*) With terminal ornament of rams, from the Turbino cemetery, Perm. Length 340 mm. After Bader.

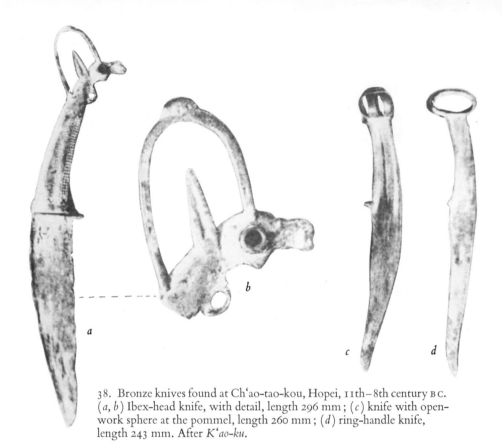

38. Bronze knives found at Ch'ao-tao-kou, Hopei, 11th–8th century B C.
(*a*, *b*) Ibex-head knife, with detail, length 296 mm; (*c*) knife with open-
work sphere at the pommel, length 260 mm; (*d*) ring-handle knife,
length 243 mm. After *K'ao-ku*.

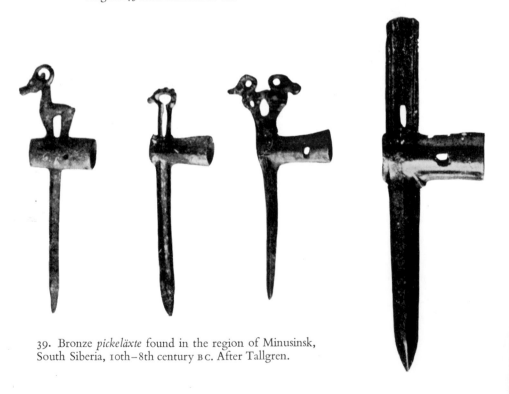

39. Bronze *pickeläxte* found in the region of Minusinsk,
South Siberia, 10th–8th century B C. After Tallgren.

40. Chariot burial at Shang-ts'un-ling, Honan. 8th–7th century B C.
After *Hsin-Chung-kuo ti k'ao-ku shou-huo*.

41. Reconstruction of a chariot found in a tomb at Liu-li-ko, Hui-hsien, Honan, 5th–4th century BC. After *Hui-hsien fa-chüeh pao-kao*.

42. Shang chariot burial at Ta-ssŭ-k'ung-ts'un, Anyang, Honan, showing the bronze mounts of the harness yokes and traces. 12th–11th century BC. After *K'ao-ku*.

43. Bronze hub-mount of a chariot wheel, with a serrated blade projecting. Length 300 mm, 6th–4th century BC. British Museum.

44. Bronze parts of bridle-bits. (*a*, *b*) Matched tiger-head cheek-pieces, formerly in the E. K. Burnett collection; (*c*, *d*) cheek-pieces shaped like heads of birds of prey curved in a ring, British Museum. Average width 80 mm, 10th–8th century BC.

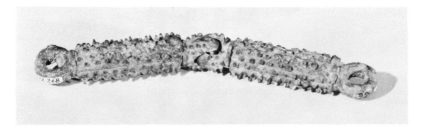

45. Linked bronze bridle-bit. 8th–6th century BC. University Museum of Archaeology and Ethnology, Cambridge.

46. Detail of the ornament on a bronze quiver inscribed with the name
of Argishti I of Urartu. Early 7th century BC. After Piotrovskiy.

47. Firing chamber of a pottery kiln excavated at Lo-ta-miao, Chengchou, Honan. The floor of the chamber, about one metre in width, is
mostly broken away. After *K'ao-ku hsüeh-pao*.

48. Detail of the side of a bronze *li*, showing the line down the centre of the mask corresponding to a division of the mould parts. Shang dynasty, 14th–12th century BC. British Museum.

49. Fragments of multipart ceramic moulds used in the casting of bronze vessels. All *c.*60 mm long, Shang dynasty, 13th–11th century. British Museum.

50. Fragment of a model used in the manufacture of piece-moulds for casting bronze, excavated at Hou-ma, Shensi. Early 5th century B C. After K'ao-ku.

51. Bronze spade found in the chariot tomb at Ta-ssŭ-k'ung-ts'un, Anyang. Length 223 mm, Shang dynasty, 13th–11th century B C. After T'ang Lan.

52. Base of a bronze *kuei* showing a chequer pattern formed by narrow raised lines covering the convex base. Shang dynasty, 12th–11th century BC. Victoria and Albert Museum.

53. Raised lines on the base of a bronze *p'an*, forming part of a dragon design. Shang dynasty, 12th–11th century BC (magnified 2½ times). Formerly Sedgwick Collection.

54. Bronze chaplet used to separate mould sides and core during the casting of a *p'an*. Shang dynasty, 12th–11th century B C. British Museum. (Magnified 6 times)

55. Bronze *kuei* excavated at T'un–hsi, Anhui. Height 160 mm, 9th–8th century B C. After *K'ao-ku hsüeh-pao*.

56. Strap mount with open-work ornament, excavated at Hsin-ts'un,
Honan. 9th century B C. After Kuo Pao-chün.

a

b

57. Open-work bronzes cast by the *cire-perdue* method. (*a*) Handle with rectangular socket in the base, height 56 mm, Malcolm Collection; (*b*) one of a pair of handles, height 57 mm, British Museum. Both 5th–4th century B C.

58. Bronze *fang-yi*, ceremonial wine vessel. Height 190 mm, 13th–11th century BC. Avery Brundage collection, M. H. de Young Memorial Museum.

59. Bronze *hu*. Height 445 mm, early 5th century B C.
Freer Gallery of Art, Washington D.C.

60. Pottery bowl with thin, yellow, felspathic glaze. Height 155 mm,
Shang dynasty, 13th–11th century B C. Nelson Gallery, Kansas City.

61. Pottery jar, hard-fired with greenish felspathic glaze on the upper part, excavated at T'un-hsi, Anhui. Height 185 mm, 9th–8th century B C. After Yin Ti-fei.

62. Stoneware vase with greenish felspathic glaze on the upper part.
Height 338 mm, early 1st century AD. Seligman collection, Victoria and
Albert Museum.

63. Earth podium of a high palace of the city of Han-tan in Hopei, capital of the state of Chao. 5th–4th century BC. After Harada Yoshito.

64. Bronze model of a house raised on pillars, excavated at Shih-chai-shan, Kunming, Yünnan. Height 100 mm, 1st century BC. After *Yünnan Chin-ning Shih-chai-shan ku-mu-ch'ün ch'u-t'u pao-kao*.

65. Pottery model of a watch-tower, excavated from a tomb at San-men-hsia, Honan. Height 980 mm, 1st–2nd century AD. After *Hsin-Chung-kuo ti k'ao-ku shou-huo*.

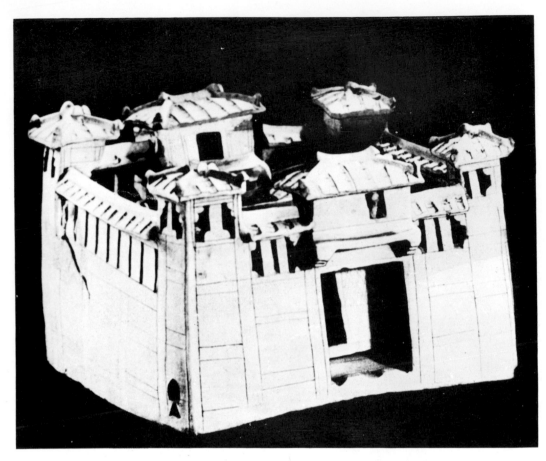

66. Pottery model of a house, from a tomb dated to AD 76, near Canton.
Height 296 mm. After *Hsin–Chung-kuo ti k'ao-ku shou-huo*.

67. Pottery model of a house excavated from a tomb at Ulatachen, Inner Mongolia. Height 360 mm, 1st–2nd century A D. After *Nei-Meng-ku ch'u-t'u wen-wu hsüan-chi.*

68. Iron belt-hook overlaid with engraved gold leaf. Length 175 mm, 4th century BC. Collection of Dr Paul Singer.

69. Bronze finial head with coiled tiger–dragon. Diameter *c.* 80 mm,
Chinese, 9th–8th century BC. Formerly in the possession of Messrs
C.T.Loo.

70. Ink-impression of the design on the head of a bronze shaft-finial,
from a tomb at Hsin-ts'un, Honan. Diameter 155 mm, 9th century B C.
After Kuo Pao-chün.

71. Bronze plaque of a dragon bent into a circle. Minusinsk Museum.

72. Tiger-dragon in a circle. Design cast on a bronze *p'an* excavated at Chia-ko-chuang, T'ang-shan, Hopei, about 500 B C.

73. Tiger dragon in a circle. Bronze plaque found in the Crimea.
Diameter 102 mm, 5th–4th century B C. The State Hermitage.

75. Fragment of the bronze ornament of a chest, from the treasure
found at Ziwiye, near Sakkez, Azerbaijan. Late 7th century B C.

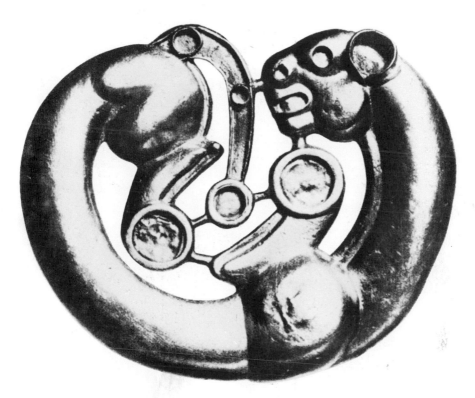

74. Gold plaque of a leopard curved in a circle. West Siberia, 6th–5th century BC. The State Hermitage.

76. Bronze *ting* decorated in Li Yü style. Height 150 mm, late 6th century B C. Wannieck collection.

77. Bronze helmet excavated at Mei-li-ho, Ch'ih-feng-shih, Inner Mongolia. Height 230 mm, 5th century BC. After *Nei-Meng-ku ch'u-t'u wen-wu hsüan-chi*.

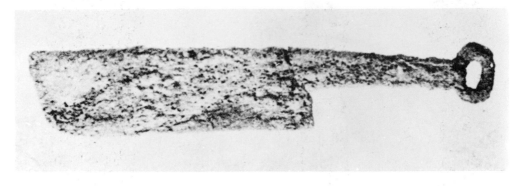

78. Bronze knife excavated at Hou-kang, Anyang, Honan. Shang dynasty, 13th–11th century B C. After *K'ao-ku hsüeh-pao*.

79. Bronze knife money, inscribed *Ch'i ch'ü hua*, 'currency of the state of Ch'i'. Length 130 mm, 6th–5th century B C. British Museum.

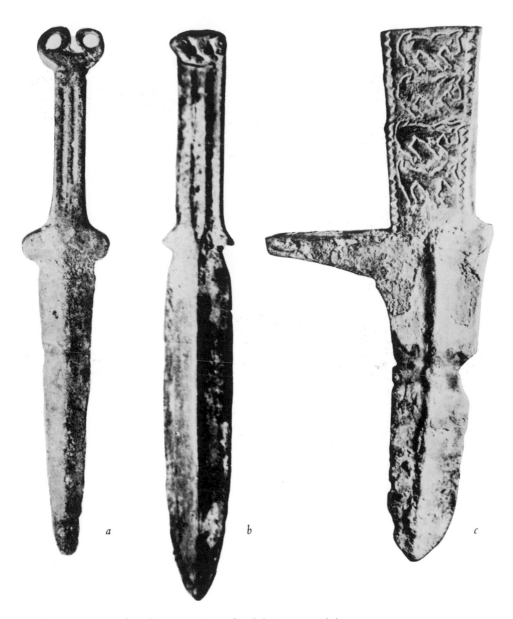

80. Bronze weapons found in Inner Mongolia. (*a*) Dagger with 'antennae' terminal; (*b*) dagger with terminal of a 'standing animal': both
260 mm long, found in a tomb at Ho-lin-ko-erh-hsien; (*c*) halberd, *ko*,
with the 'standing animal' decorating the butt: 240 mm long, found in
a tomb at Ning-ch'eng-hsien. All 8th–6th century B C. After *Nei-Meng-
ku ch'u-t'u wen-wu hsüan-chi*.

81. Akinakes-type daggers. (*a*) Bronze from the Chinese Northern Zone, length 234 mm. (*b*) Iron, with antennae terminal, from the Yeniseisk, south Siberia, length 275 mm. Both 5th century B C. British Museum.

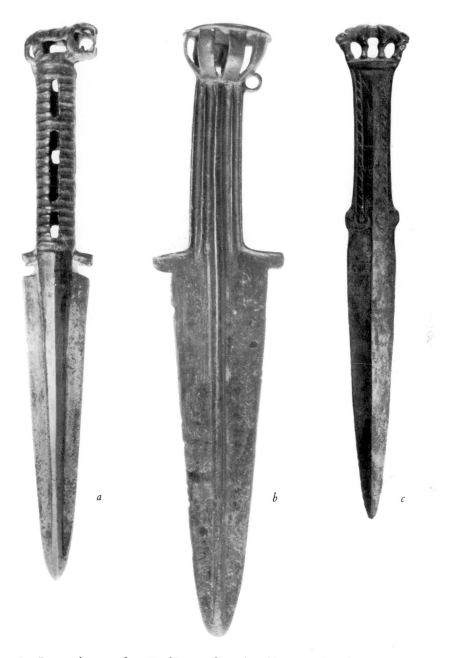

82. Bronze daggers of pre-Scythic type from the Chinese Northern
Zone. (*a*) From Shansi, with notched guard and standing animal, length
262 mm; (*b*) with *ajouré* terminal enclosing a pebble, obtained in Peking,
length 285 mm; (*c*) with vestigial notch at guard and a two–headed
standing animal, from Karymskaya, near Krasnoyarsk, south Siberia.
Length 230 mm. Both 8th–6th century B C. British Museum.

83. Bronze knives of the Chinese Northern Zone and south Siberia.
(*a*) Shang type with ibex head from the Northern Zone and (*b*) a
degenerate derivative from the Lugavskoye, south Siberia; (*c, d*) with
terminals of paired birds' heads and animal-in-a-ring. Greatest length
220 mm, 7th–5th century B C. British Museum.

84. Bronze figurine of a tiger with claw-like paws. Length 100 mm,
Chinese, 8th–6th century BC. British Museum.

85. Fragment of a gold pectoral, from the treasure found at Ziwiye, near
Sakkez, Azerbaijan. Late 7th century BC.

86. Bronze swords. (*a*) Excavated at Shang-ts'un-ling, Honan. Length
340 mm, 8th–7th century B C. (*b*) The classical Chinese sword. Length
468 mm, 5th–4th century B C. British Museum.

87. Hilt of a Chinese sword of the classical type, the guard and the grip
ribs plated with engraved gold leaf, and the grip preserving some of the
original binding of whipped silk cord. 5th–4th century BC. British Museum.

88. Gold plaque with *repoussé* design of a deer attacked by an eagle, from the kurgan of the Seven Brothers, Kuban, north Caucasus. 6th century BC. The State Hermitage.

89. Decoration of a felt saddle cover, from the First Pazyryk kurgan, Altai, south Siberia. Length 470 mm, 5th century BC. After Rudenko.

90. Gold plaque with design of a tiger attacked by griffin and wolf, from south Russia or western Siberia. Length 200 mm, 6th–5th century BC. The State Hermitage.

91. Bronze plaques from the Ordos, China. Width 120 mm, 2nd–1st century BC. British Museum.

92. Bronze plaque depicting felines attacking a wild boar, with a snake included, excavated at Shih-chai-shan, Kunming, Yünnan. Width 180 mm, 1st century BC. After *Yünnan Chin-ning Shih-chai-shan ku-mu-ch'un fa-chüeh pao-kao.*

93. Bronze deer plaque found near Hu-ho-hao-te-shih, Inner Mongolia. 4th–2nd century BC. After *Nei-Meng-ku ch'u-t'u wen-wu hsüan-chi.*

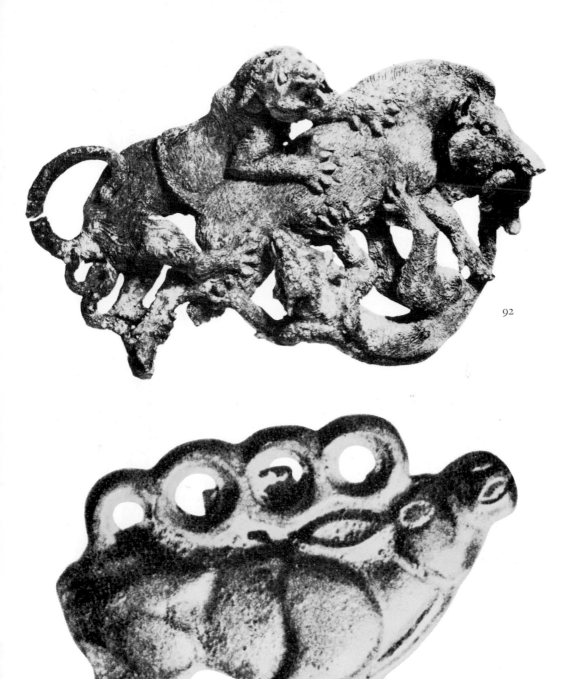

92

93

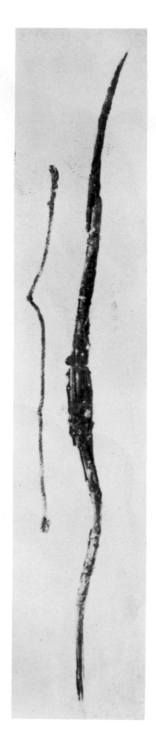

94. Bow and bow-string excavated at Ch'ang-sha, Hunan. Length *c.* 700 mm, 4th–3rd century B C. After *Ch'ang-sha fa-chüeh pao-kdo*.

95. Stone-slab grave at Hsi-t'uan-shan, Chi-lin, Manchuria, before opening, showing the side and top. After *K'ao-ku hsüeh-pao*.

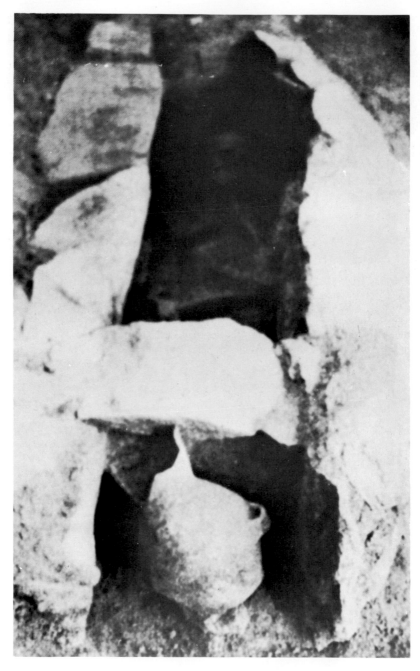

96. The same grave as shown in plate 95, seen after opening, with a separate compartment at the foot containing a pottery amphora. After *K'ao-ku hsüeh-pao*.

97. Stone-slab grave at Hsiao-kuan-tzǔ, T'ang-shan, Hopei.
After *K'ao-ku hsüeh-pao*.

98. Northern pottery. Top row: Hsiao-kuan-tzǔ, T'ang-shan, Honan; centre pot: Hsi-t'uan-shan, Chi-lin, Manchuria; the remainder: T'u–ch'eng-tzǔ, Chi-lin, Manchuria. Respectively *c.*6th, 5th and 4th centuries B C.

99. Fragments of a stone ring, stone beads and magatama, a stone axe
and bone points excavated at the Hung-chi-sung-p'ing cave, Ch'ing-
hsing-chün, Hsien-ching-pei-tao, Korea. 3rd–2nd century B C.
After Mikami Tsugio.

100. Stone axe and knife and pottery fragments from Kamchatka.
5th–1st century BC. British Museum.

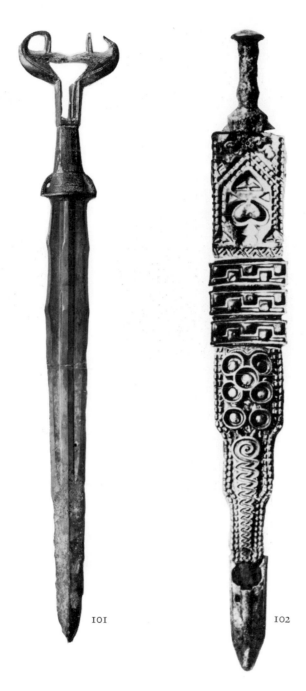

101

102

101. Bronze sword of north-eastern type, with openwork terminal intended to hold inlay. 2nd–1st century BC. British Museum.

102. Iron sword with bronze handle, in a sheath decorated with *repoussé* gold, excavated at Shih-chai-shan, Yünnan. Length *c.* 700 mm, late 2nd or early 1st century BC. After *Yünnan Chin-ning Shih-chai-shan . . . fa-chüeh pao-kao*.

103. Bronze spearhead shaped like a frog, from Shih-chai-shan, Yünnan.
Length 178 mm, late 2nd or early 1st century BC. British Museum.